SAN MIN CHU I

THE THREE PRINCIPLES OF
THE PEOPLE

A DA CAPO PRESS REPRINT SERIES

China

in the 20th century

SAN MIN CHU I

THE THREE PRINCIPLES OF
THE PEOPLE

By Dr. SUN YAT-SEN

TRANSLATED INTO ENGLISH BY
FRANK W. PRICE

EDITED BY
L. T. CHEN

DA CAPO PRESS • NEW YORK • 1975

Library of Congress Cataloging in Publication Data

Sun, Yat-sen, 1866-1925.
 San min chu i = The three principles of the people.

 (China in the 20th century)
 Reprint of the 1927 ed. which was published by Com-
mercial Press, Shanghai, in series: International
understanding series.
  I. Price, Francis William, 1895-   tr. II. Title.
III. Title: The three principles of the people.
IV. Series: International understanding series.
DS777.A55 1975   320.5'092'4   75-1033
ISBN 0-306-70698-9

This Da Capo Press edition of *San Min Chu I* is an unabridged republication
of the first edition published in Shanghai in 1927.

Published by Da Capo Press, Inc.
A Subsidiary of Plenum Publishing Corporation
227 West 17th Street, New York, N.Y. 10011

Manufactured in the United States of America

SAN MIN CHU I

THE THREE PRINCIPLES OF THE PEOPLE

DR. SUN YAT-SEN

INTERNATIONAL UNDERSTANDING SERIES

SAN MIN CHU I
THE THREE PRINCIPLES OF THE PEOPLE

By Dr. SUN YAT-SEN

TRANSLATED INTO ENGLISH BY
FRANK W. PRICE (畢範宇)

EDITED BY
L. T. CHEN (陳立廷)

UNDER THE AUSPICES OE CHINA COMMITTEE,
INSTITUTE OF PACIFIC RELATIONS

THE COMMERCIAL PRESS, LIMITED
SHANGHAI CHINA
1928

FIRST PRINTED IN 1927
SECOND IMPRESSION, NOVEMBER, 1927
THIRD IMPRESSION, DECEMBER, 1927
FOURTH IMPRESSION, JULY, 1928
BY THE COMMERCIAL PRESS, LIMITED

RIGHTS RESERVED

PRINTED IN CHINA

DR. SUN YAT-SEN'S WILL

孫中山先生遺囑

For forty years I have devoted myself to the cause of the people's revolution with but one end in view, the elevation of China to a position of freedom and equality among the nations. My experiences during these forty years have firmly convinced me that to attain this goal we must bring about a thorough awakening of our own people and ally ourselves in a common struggle with those peoples of the world who treat us on the basis of equality.

The work of the Revolution is not yet done. Let all our comrades follow my "Plans for National Reconstruction," "Fundamentals of National Reconstruction," "Three Principles of the People," and the "Manifesto" issued by the First National Convention of our Party, and strive on earnestly for their consummation. Above all, our recent declarations in favor of the convocation of a National Convention and the abolition of unequal treaties should be carried into effect with the least possible delay. This is my heartfelt charge to you.

(Signed)   SUN WEN.

March 11, 1925

Written on February 20, 1925.

TRANSLATOR'S PREFACE

This translation of *"San Min Chu I[1]"* is made from the tenth edition of the Chinese book issued by the New Age Publishing Company in May, 1927. The text in recent editions is more accurate, as several typographical errors of earlier editions have been corrected.

The extemporaneous style of Dr. Sun's lectures, the constant repetition for sake of emphasis and the looseness of Chinese Pai-hua (spoken language) construction make the original quite a lengthy book. A complete translation will seem redundant to many Western readers ; yet it has seemed wise, in view of the prominent and influential place which *The Three Principles of the People* holds in the Chinese Nationalist movement and because of the difficulty involved in making a fair selection of passages for an abridged edition, to translate the entire book. A full translation will also be of assistance, I hope, to some Westerners who are reading the book in Chinese and to Chinese students who are interested to know English equivalents for Dr. Sun's phrases and terms.

I have tried to make the translation faithful to the original and yet clear to the English reader. This is not an easy task, as many terms and expressions do not have exact English equivalents and a phrase is frequently used in different senses. *Min-ts'u*, for example, is used by Dr. Sun in the sense of nation, nationality, or race, depending upon the context. *Ch'uan* sometimes means sovereignty, sometimes rights, and at other times power or authority. Some terms have been transliterated as well as translated. Quotation marks usually mean that a Chinese idiom or proverb has been literally translated.

[1] Literally, "Three-People-Principles." The last two syllables are pronounced like "joo-ee."

The generally accepted Romanization of familiar Chinese proper names has been followed ; the Wade system has been used in the spelling of all other names. Geographical and historical references have been verified as far as possible.

Three features not in the original Chinese text have been added in the translation, for which the translator assumes full responsibility. The number of paragraphs has been increased. A few brief notes have been added to explain generally unfamiliar names and references. And in order to facilitate a rapid survey of the book and reference to various passages, a brief summary has been placed at the beginning of each chapter.

Many friends have aided in the production of this translation. Mr. L. T. Chen has edited it and has written an introductory biographical sketch of Dr. Sun Yat-sen. Dr. Fong F. Sec has taken a deep interest in the work and has given many valuable suggestions. I am especially indebted to Mr. Ho Ping-song (何 炳 松), formerly professor of history at the Peking National University and now head of the Chinese Literature Department of the Commercial Press, for his thorough and painstaking revision of the translation. His coöperation has been invaluable. The proof pages have been read by Mrs. O. D. Rasmussen and by Miss Alice M. Roberts of the Commercial Press staff, by Rev. Frank R. Millican, who has made a careful study of the Chinese text, and by my Hangchow College colleague, Professor C. B. Day. My wife helped me in the preparation of the typewritten copy for the press.

This translation is issued under the auspices of the China Committee, Institute of Pacific Relations, as a volume of the " International Understanding Series," with the hope that it will promote a better understanding abroad of the great forces that are now driving China forward.

FRANK W. PRICE.

Shanghai, August, 1927.

AUTHOR'S PREFACE

After the three volumes of my PLANS FOR NATIONAL RECONSTRUCTION — *Psychological Reconstruction, Material Reconstruction, Social Reconstruction* — had been published,[1] I devoted myself to the writing of RECONSTRUCTION OF THE STATE, in order to complete the series. This book, which was larger than the former three volumes, included *The Principle of Nationalism, The Principle of Democracy, The Principle of Livelihood, The Quintuple-Power Constitution, Local Government, Central Government, Foreign Policy, National Defense,* altogether eight parts. Part One, *The Principle of Nationalism,* had already gone to press; the other two parts on democracy and livelihood were almost completed while the general line of thought and method of approach in the other parts had already been mapped out. I was waiting, for some spare time in which I might take up my pen and, without much further research, proceed with the writing. Just as I was contemplating the completion and publication of the book, Ch'en Ch'iung-ming unexpectedly revolted, on June 16, 1922, and turned his guns upon Kwan-yin Shan.[2] My notes and manuscripts which represented the mental labor of years and hundreds of foreign books which I had collected for reference were all destroyed by fire. It was a distressing loss.

It now happens that the Kuomintang is being reorganized and our comrades are beginning to engage in a determined attack upon the minds of our people. They are in great need of the profound truths of *Sin Min Chu I* and the important ideas in the *The Quintuple-Power Constitution* as material

[1] In 1918.
[2] A hill in Canton near the headquarters of Dr. Sun.

for propaganda. So I have been delivering one lecture a week.
Mr. Hwang Ch'ang-ku is making stenographic reports of the
lectures and Mr. Tsou Lu is revising them. The *Principle
of Nationalism* series has just been completed and is being
published first in a single volume as a gift to our comrades.
In these lectures I do not have the time necessary for careful
preparation nor the books necessary for reference. I can
only mount the platform and speak extemporaneously, and
so am really leaving out much that was in my former manuscripts. Although I am making additions and corrections
before sending the book to the press, yet I realize that in
clear presentation of the theme in orderly arrangement of
the discussion and in the use of supporting facts, these lectures
are not at all comparable to the material which I had formerly
prepared. I hope that all our comrades will take the book
as a basis or as a stimulus, expand and correct it, supply
omissions, improve the arrangement and make it a perfect
text for propaganda purposes. Then the benefits which it
will bring to our people and to our state will truly be
immeasurable.

SUN WEN.

Canton, March 30, 1924.

BIOGRAPHICAL SKETCH OF
DR. SUN YAT-SEN

Dr. Sun Yat-sen, founder of the Chinese Republic and leader of the Revolution, was born of peasant parentage on November 12, 1866, in a little village near Hsiangshan, a small city in the province of Kwangtung. Here he spent an uneventful childhood attending the village school with the children of the neighborhood. At thirteen years of age he made a trip to Honolulu, where he remained for five years and completed his high school course. Here he breathed the spirit of liberty and absorbed freely the influences of American life. When he returned, therefore, to Hongkong and entered Queen's College, he was already dissatisfied with the political life of his own beloved country. Graduating at the age of twenty, he undertook to prepare himself for the medical profession and completed his training in the Hongkong Medical College in the year 1892.

His professional practice, however, was short-lived, for he gave it up to respond to a higher call following China's defeat in the Sino-Japanese War in the year 1894. This was by no means a new enthusiasm but rather a forward step in the career which he had chosen early in his college days. Every day he spent in Hongkong under British rule and every defeat China suffered at the hands of other countries added vigor to his conviction that the government of his own country was rotten to the core. Nothing short of a revolution would provide the remedy. He had dedicated himself to this cause, and among his fellow students he had found a few with whom he could share his deepest aspirations. The task of building up a free and enlightened China became his sole purpose in life.

From the very beginning the undertaking was fraught with dangers. After a hasty attempt at revolt that failed, he embarked in 1895 on his life of exile. Pursued by personal danger he went first to Japan, then to America, and was finally kidnaped on the streets of London and carried off to the Chinese legation, where he was kept hidden for twelve days. Thanks to the loyalty and ingenuity of his friend Dr. James Cantlie he escaped, and the scheme to smuggle him back to China for execution came to naught. He proceeded to Europe and spent the next few years studying the social and political institutions in the countries he visited. During this time he formulated his " Three Principles of the People " and spread his gospel of revolution among his compatriots wherever he went.

After the Boxer trouble in 1900 the cause of the Revolution gained in momentum. The overthrow of the Manchu régime had become a definite program and large numbers of Chinese men and women in all parts of the world joined in the crusade. A conference was held in Tokyo in 1905 at which two important resolutions were passed: (1) that the Revolutionists be united under the name of the Tung Meng Hui, and (2) that the reigning dynasty be deposed and China transformed into a republic. The membership of the conference included representatives from all the provinces of China and numerous persons from the ranks of Chinese merchants in other lands. The former engaged themselves in an active campaign of secret propaganda in the homeland and the latter opened their purses in unstinted support of these efforts. But for the generous giving of these patriotic businessmen abroad it is improbable that the Revolution could have materialized.

The culmination of these efforts came in the autumn of 1911, when the battle cry was sounded in Wuchang. This capital of Hupeh quickly fell to the Revolutionists. Although the outbreak was precipitated by mistake before the plans were completed, the response in other parts of the country was so widespread that the Revolution was a *fait accompli* in less than one hundred days! The effete Manchu government was overthrown, and Dr. Sun's dream of years had become a reality. His undaunted spirit had won the day and his weary body had earned a momentary rest. He was called upon, however, to become the first president of the new Republic, and hopes ran high that a rejuvenated China would turn a new page in history.

But the events of 1911 proved to be only the beginning of a long process. Broadly speaking, two schools of thinking came to dominate the minds of young China, the one led by Yüan Shih-kai and the other by Sun Yat-sen. The former believed in military force, the latter pinned his hope on the awakening of the masses of the people. In order that he might better accomplish his purpose Dr. Sun yielded the presidency to Yüan after he had held it for only three months. He chose to devote himself to the task of educating the people to an understanding of the fundamentals of democracy and of uplifting their economic standards. The Tung Meng Hui was reorganized as a political party with a broader program under the name Kuomintang, and a nation-wide plan of railroad building was undertaken as the first step towards the industrialization of the country. But the personal ambition of Yüan Shih-kai interfered. Instead of giving himself unselfishly to the political reconstruction of the country, he saw in the situation an opportunity for self-aggrandizement. He disregarded Parliament and set out to make himself emperor. Dr. Sun realized too late that his

confidence had been misplaced and that the Revolution had
been smothered by treason.

This fatal mistake delayed the Revolution until last autumn
(1926), when Chiang Kai-shek finally stepped into the shoes
of his deceased leader and led the Nationalist forces on their
victorious march from Canton toward the north. Yüan
meanwhile had left a legacy of militaristic oppression under
which China continues to groan.

But it would be a mistake to think that these sixteen years
following the initial success of the Revolution were wasted.
Dr. Sun's untiring efforts guided the people of China into
a constantly growing patriotism and national consciousness.
He attracted to his side many leaders and numberless patriots
eager to undertake the task of carrying on the Revolution
to a finish. The more he met with reverses the stronger
became his hold on his followers. Several times he set up a
separate government in Canton and as often his plans were
frustrated, until finally in 1923 a stable régime was established
and a demonstration of efficient and effective government
was made. During this period he reorganized the Kuomintang for the third time and made clear the practice
of party government. He elaborated his political philosophy
of the Three Principles in a series of popular lectures, sounded
the clarion call with respect to the unequal treaties, and
concluded an alliance with Russia. These achievements
constitute the basic ideals and policies of the Revolutionary
movement. The Three Principles inspired the people with a
political ideal, the denunciation of the unequal treaties
released a latent force in the hearts of the people nurtured
by the inarticulate desires of many years, and the alliance
with Russia determined a method of procedure for the dis-
entanglement of China's complex diplomatic problems. Sun
Yat-sen was a diligent student, a farsighted statesman, an
indefatigable worker, an irrepressible optimist and, above

all, he was China's beloved leader, clear of vision and stead-
fast in purpose. He not only blazed the trail in the reconstruction of new China, but he also laid down the highways
leading towards the successful consummation of his ideals
in the future. Out of his years of trial and travail he discovered for coming generations a sure way for the recovery
of national freedom.

On March 12, 1925, when the unification of China was apparently within reach, he died in Peking. For a short while
rumors were rife reporting the disintegration of the party
which he had founded and had taken pains to build up.
But the fact was quickly revealed that the party was stronger
than ever after his death. His indestructible spirit gripped
the lives of his followers even more powerfully than before.
It is sometimes even suggested that his death has actually
served to accelerate the progress of the Revolution.

But in the thinking of Dr. Sun the Revolution is a continuous
process. This " period of military achievement" represents
only its beginning and is of less importance than the " period
of training " which is to follow. Only when the training
process is completed can the Revolution bring the country to
the full enjoyment of democracy. In his own words uttered
on his deathbed, "The Revolution is not yet completed.
All my comrades must strive on."

Dr. Sun died a comparatively poor man, leaving behind no
property except a house which his adherents overseas had
bought for him over ten years ago, and a library said to be
one of the best on social and political sciences in existence.
For forty years he toiled " in order to achieve freedom and
equality for China." He is the father of new China, taking
his place among the foremost leaders in history.

L. T. CHEN.

CONTENTS

PART I

THE PRINCIPLE OF NATIONALISM

THE PRINCIPLE OF NATIONALISM

LECTURE 1

Lack of nationalism in China — Difference between nationality or race and the state — Factors in the development of a race: blood kinship, common language, common livelihood, common religion, common habits — The Chinese a homogeneous race but not united — Dangers to the Chinese race: more rapid increase of other populations — Progress within the last century of other nationalities: British, Japanese, Russian, German, American, French — Significance for China of Japan's modernization and of the Russian Revolution — Chinese have absorbed their conquerors in the past but cannot continue to do so — Birth control a pernicious doctrine for China.

———

Gentlemen: I have come here to-day to speak to you about the *San Min* Principles. What are the *San Min* Principles? They are, by the simplest definition, the principles for our nation's salvation. What is a principle? It is an idea, a faith, and a power. When men begin to study into the heart of a problem, an idea generally develops first; as the idea becomes clearer, a faith arises; and out of the faith a power is born. So a principle must begin with an idea, the idea must produce a faith, and the faith in turn must give birth to power, before the principle can be perfectly established. Why do we say that the *San Min* Principles will save our nation ? Because they will elevate China to an equal position among the nations, in international affairs, in government, and in economic life, so that she can permanently exist in the world. The *San Min* Principles are the principles for our nation's salvation; is not our China to-day, I ask you, in need of salvation ? If so, then let us have faith in the *San Min* Principles and our faith will engender a mighty force that will save China.

To-day I shall begin the discussion of the Principle of Nationalism. When the recent reorganization of the Kuomintang took place, the plans for national salvation laid stress upon propaganda. Widespread propaganda among the people needs, first of all, a clear exposition of the Principles. During the last ten or more years, thoughtful people have become accustomed to hearing about the Three Principles of the People, but many are still unable to comprehend them fully. So I shall first discuss with you in some detail the Principle of Nationalism.

What is the Principle of Nationalism ? Looking back over the history of China's social life and customs, I would say briefly that the Principle of Nationalism is equivalent to the "doctrine of the state." The Chinese people have shown the greatest loyalty to family and clan with the result that in China there have been family-ism and clan-ism but no real nationalism. Foreign observers say that the Chinese are like a sheet of loose sand. Why ? Simply because our people have shown loyalty to family and clan but not to the nation—there has been no nationalism. The family and the clan have been powerful unifying forces ; again and again Chinese have sacrificed themselves, their families, their lives in defense of their clan. For example, in the Kwangtung feuds between two clans, neither one will yield, no matter what the struggle costs in life or property, all because of the clan idea which is so deeply imbedded in the minds of the people that they are willing to sacrifice anything for their fellow clansmen. But for the nation there has never been an instance of the supreme spirit of sacrifice. The unity of the Chinese people has stopped short at the clan and has not extended to the nation.

My statement that the principle of nationality is equivalent to the doctrine of the state is applicable in China but not in the West. Foreigners make a distinction between the nation and the state. The English word for *min t'su* is "nation"; the word "nation" has two meanings, race and state. Although this word has two meanings they are very distinct and must not be confused. Many

Chinese words have double meanings: for example, *she-hui* (society) is used to designate a group of people and also an organized body. Nation and state are, of course, very closely related, and no separation seems necessary; but there is a clear line between them and we must distinguish carefully between the state and the nation. But when I say that the nation is equivalent to the state, why is this true only of China ? For the reason that China, since the Ch'in and Han dynasties, has been developing a single state out of a single race, while foreign countries have developed many states from one race and have included many nationalities within one state. For example, England, now the world's most powerful state, has, upon the foundation of the white race, added brown, black, and other races to form the British Empire; hence, to say that the race or nation is the state is not true of England. Again, Hongkong, which is British territory, includes among its population many ten thousands of Chinese ; if we say that the British state in Hongkong means the British nation, we miss the mark. Or, look at India, now British territory: within this British state are three hundred fifty million Indian people. If we say that the British state of India means the British nation, we are off the track. We all know that the original stock of England was the Anglo-Saxon race, but it is not limited to England; the United

States, too, has a large portion of such stock. So
in regard to other countries we cannot say that
the race and the state are identical; there is a
definite line between them.

How shall we distinguish clearly between the
two? The most suitable method is by a study of
the forces which molded each. In simple terms, the
race or nationality has developed through natural
forces, while the state has developed through force
of arms. To use an illustration from China's
political history: Chinese say that the *wang-tao*,
royal way or way of right, followed nature; in
other words, natural force was the royal way.
The group molded by the royal way is the race,
the nationality. Armed force is the *pa-tao*, or the
way of might; the group formed by the way of
might is the state. For example, Hongkong was
not built up because thousands of Hongkongese
wished the British to do it; Hongkong was
taken by the British by armed force. Because
China had been defeated in a war with England,
the Hongkong territory and its people were ceded
to England and, in time, the modern Hongkong
was built up. England's development of India is
a similar story. The territory of Great Britain
now spreads over the whole earth; the English
have a saying: "The sun never sets upon the
British Empire." In other words, wherever the sun
shines in a revolution of the earth, there lies some

British territory. If we of the Eastern Hemisphere should start with the sun, we would see it shining first upon New Zealand, Australia, Hongkong, and Singapore; as it turned westward it would shine on Ceylon and India; farther west, upon Aden and Malta; and yet farther, upon England itself; moving into the Western Hemisphere the sun would reach Canada and then complete its revolution at Hongkong and Singapore. So, wherever the sun shines in twenty-four hours, there is sure to be British territory. A great territory like Great Britain's has been developed entirely by means of force; since of old, no state has been built up without force. But the development of a race or nationality is quite different: it grows entirely by nature, in no way subject to force. The thousands of Chinese at Hongkong, for instance, are united in one race — by nature; whatever force England may employ cannot change the fact. Therefore, we say that a group united and developed in the royal way, by forces of nature, is a race; a group united and developed by the way of might, by human forces, is a state. This, then, is the difference between a race or nationality and a state.

Again, as to the origin of races. Man was originally a species of animal, yet he is far removed from the common fowl and the beasts; he is "the soul of all creation." Mankind is divided first into the five main races — white, black, red, yellow, brown. Dividing further, we have many sub-races, as the Asiatic races—Mongolian, Malay, Japanese, Manchurian, and Chinese. The forces which developed these races were, in general, natural forces, but when we try to analyze them we find they are very complex. The greatest force is common blood. Chinese belong to the yellow race because they come from the blood stock of the yellow race. The blood of ancestors is transmitted by heredity down through the race, making blood kinship a powerful force.

The second great force is livelihood ; when the means used to obtain a living vary, the races developed show differences. The Mongolians' abode followed water and grass; they lived the life of nomads, roaming and tenting by water and grass, and out of these common nomadic habits there developed a race, which accounts for the sudden rise of Mongol power. In their most flourishing days, the armies of the Yüan (Mongol) dynasty conquered Central Asia, Arabia, and a part of Europe in the west, united China in the east, and almost subjugated Japan — bringing together Europe and Asia. Compare the most prosperous days of other races, as of the Chinese in the great military age of the Han and T'ang dynasties, when the western frontiers of the empire reached only to the Caspian Sea; or of the Roman state at the

summit of its military power when the eastern
limits of the empire did not go beyond the Black
Sea. Never before had a nation's armed forces
occupied the two continents of Europe and Asia
as did the Mongol armies of the Yüan dynasty
in their prime. The reason for this great strength
of the Mongol race was their nomadic life and daily
habit of marching far without fear of miles.

A third great force in forming races is language.
If foreign races learn our language, they are more
easily assimilated by us and in time become
absorbed into our race. On the other hand, if
we know the language of foreign countries, we
are in turn easily assimilated by foreigners. If
two peoples have both common blood and common language, then assimilation is still easier.
So language is also one of the great forces for the
development of a race.

A fourth force is religion. People who worship
the same gods or the same ancestors tend to form
one race. Religion is also a very powerful factor
in the development of races. Look at the kingdoms of Arabia and Judea which perished long ago,
yet the Arabian and the Jewish people still survive.
The reason for the preservation of these races, in
spite of the destruction of their states, is their religion. The Jews to-day, we all know, are scattered
in large numbers in all lands. Some of the greatest
scholars, as Marx and Einstein, are Jews. In

England, America, and other countries, financial interests are largely controlled by Jews. To the Jew's natural gift of keen intelligence has been added religious faith, so that, although scattered all over the earth, they have been able to preserve their race up to the present time. The reason for the Arabian's survival is also religion — Mohammedanism. Another case is the Indian people with their deep faith in Buddhism, whose country is lost to Great Britain but whose race can never perish.

A fifth force is customs and habits. If people have markedly similar customs and habits they will, in time, cohere and form one race. When, therefore, we discover dissimilar peoples or stocks amalgamating and forming a homogeneous race, we must attribute the development to these five forces — blood kinship, common language, common livelihood, common religion, and common customs — which are products not of military occupation but of natural evolution. The comparison between these five natural forces and armed force helps us to distinguish between the race or nationality and the state.

Considering the law of survival of ancient and modern races, if we want to save China and to preserve the Chinese race, we must certainly promote Nationalism. To make this principle luminous for China's salvation, we must first understand it clearly. The Chinese race totals

four hundred million people; of mingled races
there are only a few million Mongolians, a million
or so Manchus, a few million Tibetans, and over
a million Mohammedan Turks. These alien races
do not number altogether more than ten million,
so that, for the most part, the Chinese people are
of the Han or Chinese race with common blood,
common language, common religion, and common
customs — a single, pure race.

What is the standing of our nation in the world?
In comparison with other nations we have the
greatest population and the oldest culture, of four
thousand years' duration. We ought to be advancing in line with the nations of Europe and
America. But the Chinese people have only family
and clan groups; there is no national spirit. Consequently, in spite of four hundred million people
gathered together in one China, we are in fact but a
sheet of loose sand. We are the poorest and weakest
state in the world, occupying the lowest position in
international affairs; the rest of mankind is the
carving knife and the serving dish, while we are the
fish and the meat. Our position now is extremely
perilous; if we do not earnestly promote nationalism
and weld together our four hundred millions into a
strong nation, we face a tragedy — the loss of our
country and the destruction of our race. To ward
off this danger, we must espouse Nationalism and
employ the national spirit to save the country.

If we are to do this, it is essential first to know wherein the danger to our nation lies, and the best way to make this danger clear is to compare the Chinese people with the peoples of the Great Powers. Before the European War there were seven or eight so-called Great Powers: the largest was Great Britain; the strongest, Germany, Austria, and Russia; the wealthiest, the United States; and the youngest, Japan and Italy. After the European War occurred the fall of three nations, and of the first-class powers only Great Britain, the United States, France, Japan, and Italy were left. Great Britain, France, Russia, and the United States had each developed their states out of a race. The original race from which Great Britain developed was the Anglo-Saxon; and the original territory, England and Wales, with a population of only thirty-eight millions which may be called pure Anglo-Saxon. Yet this race has become the most powerful in the world and the state it has created is the strongest. A hundred years ago, the population was only twelve millions; now it is thirty-eight millions, an increase of 300 per cent in a century.

We have in the East an island state which might be called the Great Britain of the East. This is Japan. The Japanese state has also developed from one race, known as the Yamato (Great Peace) race. From the beginning of the empire until

the present, Japan has never been seized by a
foreign power. Even the wide conquest of the
Yüan dynasty Mongols did not reach Japan. The
population to-day, excluding the Koreans and the
Formosans, is fifty-six millions. The exact number
a hundred years ago is difficult to ascertain, but
judging by the recent rate of increase, there has
been a growth of 300 per cent in the century,
which would make the early figure about twenty
millions. The genius of the Yamato race has
shown no decay; riding upon the advance of
European civilization, and acclimatizing themselves to the culture of the West, they have
employed the new methods of science to further
their state, and have become so modernized in half
a century that they are now the strongest nation
in the East, on a par with the nations of Europe
and America. Europeans and Americans dare not
look down upon them. Our country has a larger
population than theirs, but we are despised. Why?
One people has a national spirit; the other has
none. Before her modernization the power of
Japan was also very weak. With area and population not so large as those of Szechwan Province,
the Japanese, too, endured the shame of Western
domination. But because of their national spirit,
which has called forth a fiery heroism, they have,
in a period of less than fifty years, transformed
Japan from a weak into a powerful state. If we

want China to become strong, Japan is an excellent model for us.

Now compare the Europeans and the Asiatics. Formerly the white peoples, assuming that they alone possessed intelligence and ability, monopolized everything. We Asiatics, since we could not in a moment learn the strong points of the West and the secret of building strong nations, lost heart — not only the Chinese but every Asiatic people. In recent years, however, suddenly a new Japan, transformed into a first-class power, has risen, and Japan's success has given the other nations of Asia unlimited hope. They know that the Japanese state was once as weak as Annam and Burma to-day; now those countries are far behind Japan. Japan has been able to learn from Europe and, since her modernization, to catch up with Europe. At the Versailles Peace Conference, after the European War, Japan sat as one of the Five Great Powers. She was spokesman for the affairs of Asia, and the other powers listened to her proposals, looking upon her as the "leading horse." We may infer, therefore, that what the white races can do, Japan can evidently also do; although the races show variations of color, there are no marked differences in intelligence and ability. Because Asia possesses a strong Japan, the white races now dare not disparage the Japanese or any Asiatic race. So

Japan's rise has brought prestige not only to the Yamato race, but it has raised the standing of all Asiatic peoples. We once thought we could not do what the Europeans could do; we see now that Japan has learned from Europe and that, if we follow Japan, we, too, will be learning from the West as Japan did.

During the European War, a revolution broke out in Russia, overthrowing the old imperial order. Now Russia has become a new state, a socialist state, quite different from the old. The Russian people are of the Slavic race; a century ago they numbered forty millions, now the population is one hundred sixty millions, an increase of 400 per cent. The power of their state also increased fourfold, and for the past hundred years Russia has been one of the world's strong powers, her aggressions feared not only by Asiatic Japan and China but also by European England and Germany. During her period of imperalism, Russia adhered to a policy of aggression and strove to expand her territory, with the result that it now occupies half of Europe and half of Asia, bestriding two continents. At the time of the Russo-Japanese War, the world feared a Russian invasion of Chinese territory, all the more because this might be a step towards world aggression. The Russian people once did have an ambition to conquer the world, and other nations were considering ways to thwart them. The Anglo-Japanese Alliance was one counterblow to the Russian policy. When, as a result of the Russo-Japanese War, Japan drove Russia out of Korea and southern Manchuria, smashed the Russian dream of world domination, and maintained the integrity of Eastern Asia, a profound change took place in international life. And when, after the European War, Russia overthrew her own imperialism and substituted a new socialist state for her old imperialistic state, another greater change occurred. It is only six years since this revolution began, but in these six years Russia has reorganized herself within and has changed her old policy of force to a new policy of peace. This new policy not only harbors no wild design of world aggression; it aims to check the strong and to help the weak; it advocates justice. But a new fear psychology has developed in the world towards Russia, more desperate than former fears, because Russia's new policy aims not only at the destruction of Russian imperialism but also at the overthrow of imperialism in the whole world. Furthermore, it aims at the overthrow of the capitalism of the world. For, in every country, although the apparent power is in the hands of the government, real control is with the capitalists; the new Russian policy would smash this control, and so the capitalists of the world are panic-stricken. This is why a profound change has been produced in world affairs by which all future world currents will be affected.

In the history of Europe, international wars have been common: the most recent, the European War, was between the Allied Powers — Germany, Austria, Turkey, Bulgaria — and the Entente Powers — England, France, Russia, Japan, Italy, and the United States.[1] Exhausted by four years of bitter warfare, both sides finally desisted. Some world prophets are saying that there will never be spark enough to light another such international conflagration, but that, in the future, an inter-racial war is inevitable, as of the white against the yellow races. As I study forces in history and foresee the tendencies of the future, I am convinced that there will be more international conflicts. But these will not arise between two different races; the wars will be within races. The white races will divide and the yellow races will divide into a class war of the oppressed against tyrants, of right against might. Since the Russian Revolution, the Slavic race has dreamed of checking the strong and aiding the weak, of crushing the rich and relieving the poor, of lifting up justice and overthrowing inequality for the sake

[1] In Chinese, even after the war, the term "Allied Powers" was used to designate the Central Powers, and the term "Entente Powers" to designate the "Allies."

of mankind. As these ideas have penetrated
Europe, they have met a warm welcome from the
weaker and smaller peoples, especially from
the Turks. Before the European War, Turkey
was exceedingly poor and weak and seemed
incapable of revival; Europeans called Turkey
the "sick man of the East," and said she deserved
to perish. When she had been defeated on Germany's side in the European War, the other
nations wanted to dismember her, and her very
existence was threatened. Then Russia came
forth in the campaign against inequality and
helped Turkey to drive out the Greeks and to
revise her unequal treaties. Now Turkey, although
not a first-class power, has become one of Europe's
second- or third-class powers — thanks to Russia.
Judging by this, there will be a definite tendency
in the future for oppressed or wronged nations
or states to unite in opposing force.

At that time, which state was being oppressed?
When England and France in the European War
were out to destroy Germany's imperialism, Russia joined their side and made untold sacrifices of
men and property. But halfway in the war, she
withdrew her armies and proclaimed a revolution.
Why? Because the Russian people had been so
cruelly oppressed that they had to revolt in order
to put a socialist theory into effect against a policy
of might. The European powers opposed the

Russian theory and even sent common armies to
fight Russia. Fortunately, Russia with her old
Slavic spirit was able to withstand the Powers.
The Powers to-day are unable to meet Russia
with force, so they oppose her in a negative way
by refusing to recognize her government. (England now has formally recognized Soviet Russia.)
Why do the European nations oppose Russia's
new theory? Because they are advocates of
aggression and force without justice, while Russia
is fighting for justice and striking at the rule of
might; no wonder the Powers are trying to destroy
a policy so diametrically opposed to theirs! Before the revolution Russia was also a most reac-
tionary state and stood for might rather than
right; now, because she opposes the policy of
might, the other powers are mobilizing to fight
her. Hence, I say, the war of the future will be
between might and right. To-day Germany is the
oppressed nation of Europe. The small and weak
nations of Asia (excepting Japan) are all subject
to bitter oppression and to all kinds of suffering.
With the mutual sympathy of fellow sufferers they
will some day unite and take the field in a life
and death struggle against the oppressive states.
Throughout the world white and yellow defenders
of right will unite against white and yellow
defenders of might. With such a realignment,

towards which the signs of the times are pointing, another world war cannot be avoided.

Germany a hundred years ago had a population of twenty-four millions. Although the European War has drained the population, yet Germany to-day has sixty million people, a gain in a century of 250 per cent. The Germans belong to the Teutonic race, which is closely related to the English. They are very intelligent and their state has been very strong. After going through the European War and suffering a military defeat, they are naturally advocates of right rather than might.

The population of the United States a hundred years ago was not more than nine millions; now it is over one hundred millions. The rate of increase has been very high, 1,000 per cent in a century, and has been due largely to immigration from Europe and not merely to procreation of the native stock. People have moved from every country of Europe to the United States to seek a living there because of the limited area, crowded population, and difficulty of subsistence in their homelands. Consequently, the population of the United States has grown with amazing rapidity ; other countries have grown by normal increase in births, while the United States has grown by assimilation. The American race is more heterogeneous than any other race, including as it does immigrants from all lands, who upon arrival are being absorbed, fused in the melting pot. The race thus evolved is different from its original elements — English, French, German, Italian, and other southern European. It is a new race, which may well be called the American race. The United States with this independent race has become an independent state of the world.

The French belong to the Latin race. The Latin peoples are scattered over many countries of Europe — Spain, Portugal, Italy — and, by immigration, over the American continent — Mexico, Peru, Chile, Colombia, Brazil, Argentina, and other small republics in Central America. Because of its Latin population, South America is often called Latin America. The population of France has grown very slowly. A hundred years ago it was thirty millions; to-day it is thirty-nine millions, an increase of only 25 per cent in a century.

Now compare the rate of increase of the world's populations during the last century : the United States, 1,000 per cent ; England, 300 per cent; Japan, also 300 per cent; Russia, 400 per cent; Germany, 250 per cent; France, 25 per cent. The large gain has been due to the advance of science, the progress of medicine, and yearly improvement of hygienic conditions, all of which tend to reduce the death rate and augment the birth rate. What is the significance for China of this rapid growth of other populations ? When I compare their increase with China's, I tremble. Look at the United States: a hundred years ago it had a population of only nine millions, now it has over one hundred millions; at the same rate it will have one thousand millions at the end of another century. We Chinese are constantly boasting of our large population which cannot easily be destroyed by another. When the Mongols of the Yüan dynasty entered China, they not only failed to destroy the Chinese race but were absorbed by the Chinese. Chinese not only did not perish, they even assimilated their Mongol conquerors. The Manchus subjected China and ruled over her for more than two hundred sixty years; they not only did not wipe out the Chinese race, but were, on the contrary, absorbed by them, becoming fully Chinese. To-day many Manchus have Chinese surnames. Hence, many students of history say that, even if Japan or a white people should subject China, China could absorb them too, and so there is no cause for anxiety. Little do they consider that in another century the population of the United States will be one billion — two and a half times as much as ours. The reason why the Manchus could not subjugate China was because they numbered only a little over a million, such a small number in comparison with China's population that they were naturally absorbed. But if the United States, a hundred years hence, should try to subjugate China, there would be ten Americans to four Chinese and the Chinese would be absorbed by the Americans.

Gentlemen, do you know when China's four hundred million census was taken? — In the reign of Ch'ien Lung[1] in the Manchu dynasty. Since Ch'ien Lung, there has been no census. In this period of nearly two hundred years our population has remained the same—four hundred millions. A hundred years ago it was four hundred millions; then a hundred years hence it will still be four hundred millions.

France, because of her too small population, has been rewarding the bearing of children : a man with three children receives a prize; a man with four or five children, a special prize; and one with twins, extra prizes. Young men who reach the age of thirty or young women who reach twenty without marrying are fined. Thus France is trying to stimulate her birth rate. As a matter of fact, the population of France is not diminishing; only the rate of increase is not up to that in other countries. Then, too, France is primarily an agricultural nation; the state and the people are prosperous, the citizens enjoy peace and plenty, and make much of everyday pleasures. A hundred years ago an English scholar named Malthus,

[1] A.D. 1734–1795.

bewailing the world's overcrowded condition and the limited supply of natural resources for its use, advocated a reduction of population and proposed the theory that "population increases in a geometrical, food in an arithmetical, ratio." Malthus' theory appealed to the psychology of the French and to their love of pleasure. They began to propose that young men should not be embarrassed with family cares and that young women should not bear children; the methods they used to reduce the birth rate were not only the natural ones but also artificial ones. A century ago, France's population was larger than any other European country, but because of the spread of Malthus' ideas to France and their reception there, the people began to practice race suicide, and to-day France is suffering from too small a population, all because of the poisonous Malthusian theory. China's modern youth, also tainted with Malthus' doctrine, are advocating a reduction of the population, unaware of the sorrow which France has experienced. Our new policy calls for increase of population and preservation of the race, so that the Chinese people may perpetuate their existence along with the French race and other races of the world.

What is the actual population of China to-day? Although our rate of increase does not equal England's or Japan's, yet we should have five hundred millions by now, estimating from the Ch'ien Lung census. Nevertheless, a former American minister, Rockhill,[1] who made an investigation throughout China, concluded that China had at most a population of three hundred millions. If in the reign of Ch'ien Lung we had four hundred million people, then according to the American minister's estimate we have lost one fourth. Let us say that we have four hundred millions to-day, then on the above basis we shall still have four hundred millions after another century!

The population of Japan is now sixty millions; a hundred years from now it should be two hundred forty millions. But because of the difficulty of supporting her population, Japan is complaining to the world that her islands are too crowded, and she must expand to other countries. The Japanese turn eastward to the United States and find California closing her gates to them; they go south to Australia and find the English there talking of a "white man's Australia" not open to other races. Excluded thus from every country, the Japanese have made it clear to the world that they have no way but to enter and develop southern Manchuria and Korea. The other nations have understood Japan's purpose and have acquiesced in

[1] W. W. Rockhill, *Inquiry into the Population of China* (Washington, 1904).

her demands. The movement of Japanese into
Chinese territory would not affect them!

Within the next century the world's population
will surely multiply several times. Germany
and France in their desire to recover from war
losses will certainly stimulate their birth rate
and will no doubt increase their populations two
or three times. But when we compare the total
surface of the earth with the number of inhabitants,
we see that the world is already suffering from
overpopulation. The recent European War, some
have said, was a fight for a "place in the sun."
The European powers, to a large extent, are near
the frigid zone, so one of the causes of the war
was the struggle for equatorial and temperate land,
a struggle indeed for more sunlight. China has
the mildest climate and the most abundant natural
products of any country in the world. The reason
why other nations cannot for the present seize
China right away is simply because their population is yet smaller than China's. A hundred
years hence, if their population increases and ours
does not, the more will subjugate the less and
China will inevitably be swallowed up. Then China
will not only lose her sovereignty, but she will
perish, the Chinese people will be assimilated, and
the race will disappear. The Mongol and the Manchu conquerors of China used a smaller number to
overcome a larger and tried to make the larger

number their slaves. If the Powers some day subjugate China, it will be large numbers overcoming a smaller number. And when that time comes, they will have no need of us; then we will not even be qualified to be slaves.

January 27, 1924.

LECTURE 2

The Chinese people now subject not only to forces of natural selection but also to pressure of political and economic domination — China's territorial losses — Economic control intangible but dangerous — China a "hypo-colony" — Foreign control of China's customs — Economic loss to China through invasion of foreign goods, foreign paper money, foreign bank exchange, foreign freight charges, concession profits, and speculation business.

———

From ancient times, the increase and the decrease of population has played a large part in the rise and fall of nations. This is the law of natural selection. Since mankind has not been able to resist the forces of natural selection, many ancient and famous nations have disappeared without leaving a trace. Our Chinese nation is one also of great antiquity, with four thousand years of authentic history, and so at least five or six thousand years of actual existence. Although during this time we have been profoundly affected by natural forces, yet Nature has not only perpetuated the race but has made us extremely prolific. We have grown to four hundred millions and are still the world's most numerous and largest nation; we have enjoyed the blessings of Nature in greater measure than any other nation, so that through four millenniums of natural experiences, human movements, and varied changes we see our civilization only advancing and our nation free from decay. One generation has succeeded another and we are still the world's most cultured people. Hence a certain class of optimists, just because the Chinese nation has survived innumerable disasters in the past, hold that the nation cannot perish in the future, come what may. This sort of talk and hope I think is wrong. If it were a matter merely of natural selection, our nation might survive; but evolution on this earth depends not alone on natural forces, it depends on a combination of natural and human forces. Human agencies may displace natural agencies and " the work of man overcome Heaven." Of these man-made forces the most potent are political forces and economic forces. They have a greater influence upon the rise and fall of nations than the forces of Nature, and our nation, caught in the current of modern world movements, is not only feeling the pressure of these two forces but is being overwhelmed in the evils that result from them.

China in these thousands of years has been twice crushed by political power to the point of complete subjection, during the Mongol and Manchu dynasties. But both these times we lost our

country to a smaller not a larger people and these
smaller peoples were inevitably absorbed by us.
Hence, although China has been twice subjected
politically, the race has not been seriously injured.
But the situation now with the Great Powers is
very different from anything we have known before. In my last lecture, I compared the growth
of population among the Powers during the past
century: England and Russia have gained 300 to
400 per cent; the United States has gained 1,000
per cent. Calculating from our own increase during
the past hundred years, our race will have great
difficulty in advancing equally with other races
during the next century, no matter how richly
Nature blesses us. For example, the population of
the United States a century ago was not over nine
millions; now it is over one hundred millions, and
in another century will be over one billion. The
population of England, Germany, Russia, and Japan
will increase several fold. At this rate of gain, another century will find us in the minority and other
races in the majority. Then, even without political and economic pressure but only in the process
of natural evolution, the Chinese people are likely
to perish, to say nothing of the fact that a hundred
years from now we shall be subject not only to
forces of natural selection but also to the domination of political and economic forces which are
far more rapid and severe in their effects.

Although natural forces work slowly, yet they can exterminate great races. There was striking evidence of this about a hundred years ago among the red races of North and South America. Two or three hundred years ago, the American continent was entirely the land of the red aborigines. They were scattered everywhere in large numbers, but after the arrival of the white man on the continent they slowly disappeared until now they are almost extinct. Here we see natural selection exterminating a great race.

But political and economic forces work more rapidly than the forces of natural selection and can more easily extirpate a great race. China, if she were affected only by natural selection, might hold together another century; but if she is to be crushed by political and economic power, she will hardly last ten more years. Hence the next decade is the time of crisis for China. If during this period we can find some way to free China from her political and economic yoke, then our nation may have a chance to survive along with other nations; otherwise, we are doomed to annihilation by the peoples of the Great Powers. And should the whole number not perish this way, there are still the natural forces to wipe us out. From now on the Chinese people will be feeling the pressure simultaneously of natural, political, and economic forces. So you see what a critical time it is for our race!

China has been under the political domination of the West for a century; before this period, when the Manchus had a firm grip on us, our country was still very strong. England was then conquering India and did not dare to attempt the conquest of China for fear that China might stir up trouble in India. But during the past century China has lost a huge amount of territory. Beginning with recent history : we have lost Weihaiwei, Port Arthur, Dairen, Tsingtau, Kowloon, Kwangchow-wan. After the European War, the Powers thought to return some of the more recent cessions and gave back Tsingtau and just lately Weihaiwei. But these are only small places. The Powers' attitude was formerly something like this: since China would never awaken and could not govern herself, they would occupy the points along the coast like Dairen, Weihaiwei, and Kowloon as bases for " slicing up " China. Then when the Revolution broke out in China, the Powers realized that China still had life, and have given up, but only lately, the idea of partitioning her. When the Powers had their greedy eyes on China, some counter-revolutionists said that revolution would only invite dismemberment ; but the result was just the opposite, the Revolution frustrated foreign designs upon China. Further back in history, our territorial losses were Korea, Taiwan (Formosa), the Pescadores, and such places, which, as a result of the Sino-Japanese War, were ceded to Japan. It was this war which started the "slicing of China" talk among the Powers.

Still further back in the century, we lost Burma and Annam. China did put up a slight opposition at the time to giving up Annam. In the battle of Chen-nan-kuan (Southern Frontier) China was really victorious but was so overawed later by France that she made peace and was compelled to cede Annam to France. Only a few days before the peace the Chinese armies had won a great victory at Liang-shan (Langson) on the Southern Frontier [1] and almost annihilated the whole French army. When China followed this up by begging for peace, the French were astounded, and some of them said: "There is certainly no calculating what you Chinese will do. It is generally the custom for the conquering nation to boast of its victory and to demand territory and indemnities from the defeated nation; you in your day of triumph have given up territory, have cried for peace, gave Annam to France, and accepted all sorts of severe conditions. This is really an unprecedented example of the conqueror's suing the conquered for peace!" The reason for this breaking of historical precedent by a victorious nation was the utter stupidity of the Manchu government.

11885

Annam and Burma were both formerly Chinese
territory; as soon as Annam was ceded to France,
England occupied Burma, and China did not dare
to protest. Still earlier in the history of territorial losses were the Amur and Ussuri river
basins and before that the areas north of the Ili,
Khokand, and Amur rivers — the territory of
the recent Far Eastern Republic — all of which
China gave over with folded hands to the foreigner
without so much as a question. In addition there
are those small countries which at one time paid
tribute to China — the Loochoo Islands, Siam,
Borneo, the Sulu Archipelago, Java, Ceylon,
Nepal, Bhutan.

In its age of greatest power, the territory of the
Chinese Empire was very large, extending northward to the north of the Amur, southward to
the south of the Himalayas, eastward to the China
Sea, westward to the T'sung Lin. Nepal in the
first year of the Republic was still bringing
tribute into Szechwan, and then stopped because
of the impassability of the roads through Tibet.
When China was strongest, her political power
inspired awe on all sides, and not a nation south
and west of China but considered it an honor to
bring her tribute. At that time European imperialism had not invaded Asia, and the only country
of Asia that deserved to be called imperialistic
was China. The weaker and smaller nations were

afraid of China and her political domination and to this day are suspicious of her. When we held our recent Kuomintang Conference in Canton, Mongolia sent some delegates to observe whether the Southern Government was continuing the imperialistic tradition towards other countries. When they saw that the political principles adopted by the conference were not imperialistic, but favored the smaller, weaker peoples, they heartily approved and proposed that all unite to form a great Eastern state. And not only Mongolia, but all the small peoples in the East have commended this policy of ours. Now the European powers are crushing China with their imperialism and economic strength, so that China's territory is gradually being reduced, and even within the eighteen provinces she has had to give up many places.

After the Chinese Revolution, the Powers realized that it would be exceedingly difficult to dismember China by political force. A China which had learned how to revolt against the control of the Manchus would be sure some day to oppose the political control of the Powers. As this would put them in a difficult position, they are now reducing their political activities against China and are using economic pressure instead to keep us down. They think that to give up political methods in the division of China will obviate conflict among the Powers, but though conflict is avoided in China it is still inevitable in Europe. The Balkan question started the Great European War, and although the Powers suffered terrific losses, and states like Germany and Austria were overthrown, yet there has been no change in the imperialistic policy. England, France, and Italy are still continuing on the road of imperialism, while the United States throws away the Monroe Doctrine and keeps step with them. And though, after the experience of the war, they may suspend their imperialistic policy for a while in Europe, towards China, as one can see from the recent naval demonstration at Canton by a score or more gunboats of various Powers, there has been no change of heart. They are still using imperialism to forward their economic designs, and economic oppression is more severe than imperialism or political oppression. Political oppression is an apparent thing; when the twenty-odd foreign gunboats made their demonstration here, the people of Canton felt an immediate irritation and were stirred with popular indignation, and indeed the whole nation was angered. The common people are easily provoked by political oppression but are hardly conscious of economic oppression. China has already endured several tens of years of economic domination from the Powers and nobody has felt irritated at all.

The result is that China is everywhere becoming a colony of the Powers. The people of the nation still think we are only a "semi-colony" and comfort themselves with this term, but in reality we are being crushed by the economic strength of the Powers to a greater degree than if we were a full colony. For example, Annam and Korea are protectorates of France and Japan and their people are slaves. We taunt the Koreans and Annamese with the name "*wang-kuo nu*" (slaves without a country), yet while looking at their position we seem unaware that our own position is lower than theirs. Whose "semi-colony" is China? China is the colony of every nation that has made treaties with her, and the treaty-making nations are her masters. China is not the colony of one nation but of all, and we are not the slaves of one country but of all. Would it be better to be the slaves of one nation or of many nations? If we were slaves of one certain nation, and some natural calamity, as a flood or a drought, befell China, the master-nation would appropriate funds for relief as an obligation and distribute the funds as a duty, while the subject people would expect this relief of their master. When, a few years ago, North China experienced a natural disaster for which the foreign nations did not feel they had any obligation to send relief, and only those foreigners who were in China were raising funds for the sufferers, Chinese observers talked of the munificent philanthropy of other countries so far removed from the treatment which would be accorded a subject people! This shows that we are not yet up to Annam and Korea and that subjection to one power is a far higher and more advantageous position than subjection to many powers. So "semi-colony" is not the right designation for China; I think we ought to be called a "hypo-colony." The prefix "hypo" is taken from chemistry, as in the word "hypophosphite." A chemical which contains the element phosphoric compound but is of a lower grade than pure phosphoric compound is called a phosphorous compound. A still lower degree of compound is called a hypophosphorous compound, just as an organization has its second degree of office. We formerly thought China was a semicolony and that was shame enough. Alas, we did not realize that our real place is below Annam and Korea. We are not a semi-colony but a hypo-colony.

There is in Kwangtung a struggle with the foreign powers over the customs surplus. The customs surplus is rightfully ours, so why should there be a dispute? Because China's customs has been taken over by other countries. There was a time when we knew nothing about customs; we simply closed our ports and kept to ourselves. Then England came to China and sought entrance for purposes of trade ; China shut the door and denied her access. With imperialism and economic force combined England forced the barriers and broke open China's gates. At the same time the British army occupied Canton, but finding it untenable they withdrew and took Hongkong. They also demanded indemnities, but since China then did not have enough ready money to pay, she gave the maritime customs to England as security and allowed England to collect the duties. The Manchu government calculated that it would take a long time to pay in full, but the British, after securing control of the customs, surprised the Manchus by paying themselves all the indemnity in a few years ; the Manchu government then realized how rotten their own officials had been. The great weakness in the previous collection of customs duties had been the "squeezing." So the maritime customs of the whole country was turned over to British management and British were always selected for commissioners of customs. Later, other nations who had trade relations with China disputed with England over the control of the customs, and England compromised by giving them a share in the appointments according to their proportion of trade. As a result, the nation's maritime customs are now entirely in the hands of foreigners. Every new treaty which China concludes with a foreign power means another loss of some kind and the rights accorded in the treaties are always unilateral. The customs duties are fixed by the foreign powers and China cannot freely alter them; China cannot collect and use her own tariff — these are the reasons for the struggle over the customs.

Now how do other countries meet foreign economic pressure and check the invasion of economic forces from abroad? — Usually by means of a tariff which protects economic development within these countries. Just as forts are built at the entrances of harbors for protection against foreign military invasion, so a tariff against foreign goods protects a nation's revenue and gives native industries a chance to develop. For instance, the United States, after the extermination of the red aborigines, began to open up trade with European countries. The United States was then an agricultural nation, while the European nations were all industrialized. Since in international trade an industrial nation has an advantage over an agricultural nation, the United States set up a protective tariff to shield her native industries and trade. The idea of a protective tariff is to put a heavy duty on imports: for instance, if an imported article is worth a hundred dollars, the customs office will collect, say, eighty or a hundred dollars. The average tariff in the various countries is fifty or sixty per cent of the value. The high duty makes foreign goods expensive so that they cannot circulate, while native goods free from duty are reasonably priced and widely distributed.

What is the situation now in China ? Before China had a foreign trade, the goods used by the people were hand-manufactured by themselves. The ancient saying "man tills and woman weaves" shows that agriculture and cloth making are old industries in China. Then foreign goods began to come in. Because of the low tariff, foreign cloth is cheaper than native cloth. Since, moreover, certain classes of the people prefer the foreign to the native cloth, native industry has been ruined. With the destruction of this native hand industry, many people have been thrown out of work and have become idlers. This is a result of foreign economic oppression. Now although China still uses the hand loom, the raw material used is foreign cotton. Only in recent years has native cotton begun to be used in foreign machine looms. In Shanghai are many large cotton and cloth mills which might enable us to compete gradually with imported goods but for the fact that the customs is still in foreign hands. Not only is native cloth charged with high export duty, but when it is distributed within the country it meets heavy likin charges. Thus China not only has no protective tariff, but she even increases the tariff on native goods to protect foreign goods !

During the European War, when foreign countries could not manufacture goods to export to China, the Shanghai cotton and cloth mills enjoyed a temporary boom. Enormous profits were made, dividends of 100 per cent were declared, and capitalists multiplied. But after the war foreign goods flooded China and the Shanghai mills which had made so much money went into debt. While native goods are thus being worsted in the struggle against foreign goods, China's customs not only offers no relief but even protects the foreign merchants! It is as if one should dig a war trench and not only be unable to use it against the enemy but find the enemy using it to fight oneself. So, I say, political oppression can be easily seen even by the ignorant classes, but economic oppression is an intangible thing which none of us can easily perceive. One can even load heavy burdens on oneself.

Since China opened foreign trade, the balance of trade has swollen like a river torrent. Ten years ago, investigations showed that the balance amounted to $200,000,000. From a recent customs report we find that in 1921 imports exceeded exports by the value of $500,000,000, a 250 per cent increase in a decade. At this rate, after another ten years the balance of trade will be $1,250,000,000. In other words, ten years hence China will be paying in the mercantile field alone a tribute of

$1,250,000,000 to foreign countries. Doesn't this seem a terrible leakage to you ?

Then there is the economic domination of foreign banks. The Chinese psychology now is one of distrust toward the native banks and of extreme confidence in the foreign banks. In Kwangtung, for example, the foreign banks are widely depended upon, while the native banks inspire no confidence whatever. Formerly the paper money issued by our Kwangtung Provincial Bank could still be used, but now it is of no value at all and we are using only silver. Native bank notes have always been valued below the foreign bank notes, but now even the native silver is worth less than foreign paper. To-day the total number of foreign bank notes circulating in Kwangtung Province probably runs into tens of millions. Some people are even willing to store up foreign paper currency in preference to Chinese silver currency. In Shanghai, Tientsin, Hankow, and other trading ports we would find the same condition. And when we study into the reason we find it is because the people are poisoned by the foreign economic grip upon them. We are all accustomed to thinking of the foreigner as wealthy and do not take it in that he is exchanging paper for our commodities. The foreigners did not have much money to begin with ; most of their wealth has been practically given to them by us. They only have to issue

several million bank notes which we accept and
then they have millions of dollars to use. One
of those bank notes issued by a foreign bank only
costs a few cash to print, but the piece of paper is
stamped with the value of one, ten, or a hundred
dollars. Thus the foreigner at a very small expense
can print millions upon millions of paper dollars
and can exchange these paper millions for millions
of dollars' worth of our goods. Gentlemen, isn't
this a frightful loss? And the reason why they
can issue paper money this way and we cannot is
because the common people have been poisoned
by the influence of foreign economic domination
to trust the foreigner and to distrust themselves,
with the result that our own paper is unable to
circulate.

Besides the foreign bank notes, there is bank
exchange. We Chinese in the ports trust the
foreign banks also in the exchange of our money.
But, in making exchange for Chinese, the foreign
bank charges not only the customary bank rate
of one half per cent but seizes profits in other ways.
In paying a bank draft, they charge a discount
on the exchange from taels into dollars and the
loss from this discount at the place of remittance
and the place of payment amounts to two or three
per cent at least. For instance, if a foreign bank
in Kwangtung makes out a bank draft on Shanghai
for $10,000, it charges $500; besides this, in

changing small silver into the Shanghai tael they always put the Kwangtung small silver price low and the Shanghai tael price high and realize a profit, according to their own voluntary estimate, of at least one or two hundred dollars. Then, in cashing the draft at Shanghai, they pay not taels but dollars; in changing the Shanghai taels into dollars, they must lower the tael price and raise the dollar price, making another profit of at least one or two hundred dollars. So in remitting $10,000 back and forth between Canton and Shanghai there is a loss each time of two or three hundred dollars; in not more than thirty drafts the whole amount would be used up! And the reason why the people endure these losses is because they are filled with the poison of foreign economic domination.

The power of the foreign banks in China is seen also in their bank deposits. If a Chinese has money and wants to deposit it in a bank, he does not wait to ask whether the Chinese bank has a large or small capital or gives high or low interest. As soon as he knows that the bank is managed by Chinese, he immediately feels that it is probably not safe and that it would not do to risk his deposits there. He does not ask whether the foreign bank is reliable or not, whether it pays high or low interest; if he hears that the bank is run by foreigners and hangs out a foreign sign, he swallows the sedative, feels very safe, and invests his money. Even if the interest is very low, he is quite satisfied.

A remarkable thing happened in 1911. After the Revolutionary movement had started at Wu-chang, almost all members of the Manchu royal house and Manchu officials, fearing that the Revolution would mean the confiscation of their property, deposited all their gold, silver, and treasure in different foreign banks. They were perfectly happy not to draw any interest so long as the foreigners accepted their deposits. During the days when the Manchu troops were being defeated by the Revolutionary army at Wu-han, the foreign banks in the Legation Quarter at Peking received deposits of gold, silver, and treasure in countless amount from the Manchus until they were glutted with money[1] and had no more room to store it. The foreign banks not only paid the depositors no interest but charged them storage. All the depositors wanted was for the foreign banks to accept their deposits, and they paid whatever the banks asked. The foreign banks at that time received in Chinese deposits a total of twelve billion dollars. Although some of this has been withdrawn, yet in the past ten or more years a group of militarists and officials, like Feng Kuo-chang, Wang Chan-yuan, Li Shun,

---

[1] In Chinese, a play on words. The character for "Manchu" and "full" is the same.

and Tsao Kun, have been squeezing the country and each one has made a dishonest fortune of perhaps tens of millions. Because they want to secure their ill-gotten wealth as a perpetuity, they, too, deposit it in foreign banks. So since 1911 there has not been any considerable increase or decrease in the amount of Chinese deposits in foreign banks. The interest which the foreign banks pay for these twelve billions of deposits is very small, certainly not over four or five per cent, while the banks loan out the amount to small businesses in China at high annual interest, seven, eight, and even over ten per cent. Thus the foreign banks, with no trouble except that of handling the money, take Chinese capital and earn interest from it.

This yearly profit of millions from Chinese deposits in foreign banks is an intangible loss. The psychological reason for the common man's investment in foreign banks is his feeling that Chinese banks are not safe, while foreign banks are. He is not afraid that the foreign bank will fail; but, pray tell, is the Banque Industrielle de Chine, which has just suspended with its Chinese deposits unreturned, a foreign bank or not? Are the foreign banks entirely secure? If not, why do we Chinese still patronize them so willingly and eagerly? The reason for all this loss of interest to foreigners is again the vitiating influence of foreign economic control. The total profits of the foreign banks alone, in paper money issues, in exchange and deposit banking, must be around $100,000,000 a year.

Besides the foreign banks, there are freight rates. Chinese goods sent abroad have to depend on foreign bottoms, and even goods sent to interior points, as Hankow, Changsha, and Canton, are carried largely by foreign ships. The Japanese shipping business has flourished in recent years. Yet Japan at the start had only one company, the Nippon Yusen Kaisha (Japan Mail Steamship Company); later, the Toyo Kisen Kaisha, the Osaka Shosen Kaisha, and the Nisshin Kisen Kaisha (Sino-Japan Steamship Company) developed and began to provide communication to inland China and to points all over the world. The reason for this growth of the Japanese merchant marine has been the government subsidies and special protection. From the Chinese viewpoint there is no advantage to a government in subsidizing commercial steamship companies, but Japan wanted to compete with the economic power of other nations. So in the matter of marine transportation she also made treaties with other countries, fixing ocean freight rates at so much per ton. Freight shipped from Europe to Asia goes first to Shanghai and then to Nagasaki and Yokohama, Shanghai being much nearer to Europe than the Japan ports. But freight rates per ton from

Europe to Nagasaki and Yokohama are quite reasonable, while rates to Shanghai, because there is no Chinese merchant marine to compete with, are very high, which makes it cheaper to ship goods from Europe to Japan than to Shanghai. The result is that European goods can be sold more reasonably in Japan than in Shanghai. In the same way, if Chinese goods are shipped from Shanghai to Europe, freight rates are much higher than from Nagasaki and Yokohama. If China exports $100,000,000 worth of goods to Europe, she must pay $10,000,000 for freight. At this rate, since the value of China's exports and imports now exceeds $1,000,000,000 annually, the loss (through freight rates paid to foreign steamship companies) is not less than $100,000,000.

Again, there are the three items of taxes, land rent, and land prices paid in the foreign settlements and ceded territories, which amounts to not a little. For example, Chinese living in Hongkong, Formosa, Shanghai, Tientsin, Dalny, Hankow, and other settlements and cessions pay to foreigners each year in taxes upward of $200,000,000. Formerly Formosa paid to Japan only $20,000,000; now the taxes have increased to $100,000,000. Hongkong taxes paid to the British were formerly only a few million dollars annually; now they amount to $30,000,000 and will increase proportionately each year.

Rent money is taken by both foreigners and Chinese, and in the absence of any careful survey the exact proportion of each group's receipts cannot be determined, but there is no doubt that the foreigners get more. Rent payments are certainly ten times as much as taxes. Land values are rising every year; since foreigners control the economic situation it naturally follows that " wealth makes skillful merchants " and land within the settlements is cheaply bought and dearly sold. In these three ways the concession Chinese lose an annual amount of not less than four or five hundred million dollars.

Further, there are the countless foreign companies and individuals carrying on business within the country who, holding to special treaty privileges, rob rights from us. It is still more difficult to estimate the losses from this condition, but judging from the South Manchuria Railway Company alone, which is making a clear profit of over $50,000,000 a year, the profits of various foreign business enterprises must reach hundreds of millions.

There is yet one more loss to consider — that from the speculation business. Foreigners in the concessions take advantage of a weak point — avarice — in the Chinese character and provide daily opportunities for small speculation, and every few years some big opportunity which arouses the gambling passion of the Chinese to fever heat.

On each occasion of speculation over the mark or the rubber market, Chinese have lost tens of millions. And the ordinary small speculative businesses amount, in the end, to high figures.

Our various war indemnities — 250,000,000 taels to Japan in 1894, 900,000,000 taels to the Powers in 1900 — are part of our political and military oppression and cannot be put in the same class with economic domination. Indemnities are transient and inconsequential as compared with economic control. Consider the losses not only in China but also in our former feudatories and among our emigrants in other lands, and they become yet more incalculable. What a deadly thing this economic yoke is!

To sum up. In money value of stolen rights and privileges we lose every year: first, through invasion of foreign goods, $500,000,000; second, through the invasion of foreign paper money into our money market, along with foreign bank discounts on exchange and interest on our deposits, about $100,000,000; third, through freight charges on our exports and imports, up to $100,000,000: fourth, through taxes, rents, and land sales in the settlements and ceded areas at least, $400,000,000 or $500,000,000; fifth, through special privileges and private business of foreigners $100,000,000; sixth, through the speculation business and various other fleecing games, hundreds of millions.

These six kinds of economic domination cost us an annual loss of not less than $1,200,000,000. And unless we can find a remedy, the losses will only increase each year; certainly they will not diminish of their own accord. China has reached a state of national bankruptcy, and unless we can save her, economic domination will spell the loss of our country as well as the annihilation of our race.

In the days of China's glory, her neighbors brought tribute and paid yearly visits to the imperial court; although the annual tribute only amounted to a little over a million dollars, yet we considered it a great honor. When the Chinese Empire of the Sung dynasty declined and had to pay tribute to the Kin Tartars, the total amount was only around a hundred million, yet we considered it a terrible disgrace. Now our tribute to foreign countries is one billion, two hundred millions a year, or twelve billions in ten years. Such economic subjugation, such an enormous tribute, was not in our wildest dreams and even now is hard to visualize. Hence we do not feel the awful shame of it. If we had this tribute of $1,200,000,000 as a national income, what could we not do with it! What progress our society would make! But because of this economic mastery of China and the consequent yearly damages, our society is not free to develop and the common people do not have the means of living. This economic control alone is worse than millions of soldiers ready to kill us. And while foreign imperialism backs up this economic subjugation, the living problems of the Chinese people are daily more pressing, the unemployed are daily increasing, and the country's power is, in consequence, steadily weakening.

Within the last hundred years, China has begun to suffer from the population problem: the Chinese people are not increasing, while other populations are growing. Now we are suffering also from political and economic domination. If we can no longer find a solution for these three pressing problems, then, no matter how large China's area or how great her population, another century will see our country gone and our race destroyed. Our four hundred millions are not everlasting. Look at the red aborigines, once all over the American continent, now extinct. Now that we realize the seriousness of political domination and the even greater seriousness of economic domination, we cannot boast that China's four hundred millions will not be easily exterminated. Never before in all her millenniums of history has China felt the weight of three such forces at one and the same time. For the future of the Chinese nation we must find a way to break them!

February 3, 1923.

LECTURE 3

China has lost her national spirit for centuries—Opposition to nationalistic propaganda and to the Revolution — Old revolutionary movement against the Manchus had died out— The *literati* supported the Manchus, but nationalism was kept alive in secret societies among lower classes—Manchu efforts to destroy Chinese national spirit — Failure of the secret societies in the Taiping Rebellion — Why China has lost her national spirit: subjection to alien races — The seeds of decay in China's ancient imperialism and theory of cosmopolitanism — Cosmopolitanism developing in the West to camouflage imperialism, a danger to China — Origin of the Chinese race in the Yellow River valley — Story of a coolie throwing away a treasure hidden in his bamboo pole to illustrate China throwing away her nationalism—Development of nationalism essential to continued existence of the Chinese nation.

Nationalism is that precious possession which enables a state to aspire to progress and a nation to perpetuate its existence. China to-day has lost that precious possession. Why? To answer that question and to study whether we have really lost our national spirit is my theme to-day.

To me it is clear that we have lost it not for a day but for centuries. Just look at the anti-revolution articles which came out before the Revolution, all opposing nationalism! For hundreds of years the idea of nationalism had been dead in China; in all the literature of this time one can hardly catch any note of nationalism, only chants of praise to the "virtuous Manchus"—"great kindness and rich benefits"; "we are devouring your produce and trampling on your soil." No one dared to say anything against the Manchus. Even since the rise of revolutionary ideas in recent years, self-appointed scholars and *literati* of China have been speaking daily in behalf of the Manchus. At the time that we were publishing the *Min Pao* (*People's Daily*) in Tokyo and advocating nationalism, those who took issue with us argued that we did not become a subject people when the Manchus subjugated China ! Since the right to rule China had been conferred on the Manchus by the fact that the title of Lung-hu (general) was given them by the Ming emperor, the Manchus did not overthrow the Ming dynasty but merely succeeded to the hereditary throne,—a new dynasty, it is true, but not over a subject nation ! Yes, the former British inspector general of customs, Hart, was also breveted minister of the Board of Finance; if he had come to conquer China and be emperor, could we say that China was not a subject nation ? These critics not only used catchwords to uphold the Manchus but even organized a pro-monarchist society called *Pao-huang-tang* to defend the Manchu emperor and to crush the national spirit of the Chinese people. These monarchists were not Manchus, mind you; they were all Chinese, and they found the greatest welcome among Chinese living abroad. Later, when revolutionary ideas began to flourish, these emigrants gradually changed their attitude to support of the revolution, and revolutionary societies multiplied overseas.

The *Hung-mên San-ho-hui* (also called *Chih-kung-tang*) was one among them whose aim was to oppose the Manchus and restore the Mings. It cherished a strong nationalistic spirit. But when the pro-monarchy idea spread overseas, these societies became pro-monarchial and only thought of keeping the "Great Pure"[1] emperor on his throne. This reversion of nationalist societies to pro-monarchical societies shows how China had entirely lost her national spirit.

While speaking about these secret revolutionary societies, we ought to know something of their origin. They were most powerful during the reign of the Manchu emperor K'ang Hsi.[2] After Shun Chi had overthrown the Mings and had become master of China, the loyal ministers and scholars of the Ming dynasty rose everywhere to oppose him. Even up to the first years of K'ang Hsi there was still resistance and China was not yet

[1] Title taken by the Manchu dynasty.
[2] 1661–1722.

completely subjugated by the Manchus. In the latter years of K'ang Hsi, when the veterans of the Ming dynasty were slowly passing off the stage, a group of intense nationalists, who realized that their day was over and that not enough power was left to fight the Manchus, looked out upon society and conceived a plan to organize secret revolutionary societies. They were men of far-seeing vision and profound judgment and keen observers of society. Just at the time when they were organizing the various societies, K'ang Hsi inaugurated the *Po-hsüeh Hung-t'zŭ* examinations which caught almost all the old Ming scholars in the net of the Manchu government service. The thoughtful group among them saw that they could not depend upon the *literati* to keep alive the national spirit, so they turned to the lower strata of society, to the homeless class upon the rivers and lakes. They gathered these people together, organized them into groups, and gave to them the spirit of nationalism to preserve and perpetuate. Because these people came from the lowest class of society, because of the rude behavior which made them despised, and because they used a language not spoken by the educated to spread their doctrines, their part (in the anti-dynastic movement) attracted little attention. Those Ming veterans showed true knowledge and discernment in their plan for saving the nationalistic ideal. Just as wealthy men, whose treasures have in time of peace naturally been kept in expensive iron chests, when they see looters breaking into their homes, are afraid that the costly chests will be the first things opened, and therefore bury their treasures in places that will not be noticed, and possibly, during times of extreme danger, in the midst of the worst filth, so the Ming veterans, seeking to preserve China's treasure, sought to hide it in the roughest and lowest class of society. Thus, no matter how despotic the Manchu government became in the last two centuries, the national spirit was kept alive in the verbal codes transmitted by these secret societies. When the Hung-mên Society wanted to overthrow the Manchus and restore the Mings, why did they not plant their nationalist ideas among the intellectuals and transmit them to posterity through literature, in the phrase of the well-known historiographer, Ssŭ Ma Chien, "store them in famous mountains and bequeath them to worthy men" ? Because, when the Ming veterans saw the Manchus inaugurating their examination system and almost all the men of wisdom and learning enticed by it, they perceived that the intellectual class was not dependable, that "treasure could not be stored in famous mountains and bequeathed to worthy men," and must therefore be hidden in the lower class of society.

So they rallied the secret societies, whose organization and initiations were simple and adaptable, and intrusted to them the preservation of nationalism, not through literature but through oral language. So it is very difficult for us to-day to discuss the history of the origin of these societies, because we have only scraps of stories handed down by oral tradition. Even if the societies had had a literature, it would have been destroyed in the reign of Ch'ien Lung.

During the reigns of K'ang Hsi and Yung Chêng, the antidynastic agitation was still strong, and the government issued a great many books, such as *Ta-i-chio-mi-lu*. These argued that Chinese should not oppose Manchu rule on the ground that Shun[1] was an eastern "barbarian" and Wên Wang a western "barbarian," and so the Manchus, although they were "barbarians," might also be emperors of China. This shows that K'ang Hsi and Yung Chêng were at least honest in acknowledging themselves Manchus. But at the time of Ch'ien Lung, the words *Man* and *Han* (Manchu and Chinese) were banned, histories were revised, and everything pertaining to the relationship between the Sung and the Mongols or between the Ming and Manchu dynasties was deleted; all histories of the Manchus, Huns, and Tartars

---

[1] Emperors of early Chinese history.

were condemned, destroyed, and forbidden to be stored away or read. After several instances in which many lives were sacrificed on account of writing or reading the prohibited books, the Chinese national spirit, which had been kept alive in literature, was gradually crushed out. Up to the midday of the Manchu dynasty, the only society with any nationalistic ideas left was the Hung-mên secret order.

When Hung Hsiu-ch'uan[1] raised his revolt, the Hung-mên members all responded, and nationalism flared up again. It should be borne in mind that the name Hung-mên did not come from Hung Hsiu-ch'uan but probably from either Chu Hung-wu or from Chu Hung-chu (under whom a revolt started in the reign of K'ang Hsi). After the fall of Hung Hsiu-ch'uan, the current of nationalism flowed on through the army and the vagrant class. Troops of that time, as the Hunan and Huai River divisions, all belonged to the societies, and the Ching-pang and Hung-pang fraternities of to-day have come down from the army societies. The Ming veterans spread the ideas of nationalism through the lower classes; but, on account of their childish understanding, the lower classes did not know how to take advantage of the ideas, but were, on the contrary,

---

[1] Leader of the Taiping Rebellion.

made tools of by others. In the time of Hung
Hsiu-ch'uan, when the restoration idea was pene-
trating the armies, the Hung-mên failed to turn
this to good account and they remained in the
employ of the Manchus as soldiers. The following
incident will prove my statement.

In this same period, when Tso Tsung-t'ang was
leading troops to suppress Sinkiang, he started
from Hankow across the Yangtze River in the
direction of Sian, with a large number of Hunan
and Huai valley troops. At that time the revolutionary societies in the Pearl River valley were
called the San-ho-hui (Triad Order) and the
societies in the Yangtze valley the Ko-lao-hui
(Order of Brothers and Elders). The leader of
the latter order had the title of " Great Dragon
Head." A certain Great Dragon Head com-
mitted a lawless deed in the lower Yangtze and
fled to Hankow. The Manchu post-couriers carried news very fast, but the Ko-lao-hui horsemen
were still faster. When General Tso Tsung-t'ang
was on his way, he one day noticed his army falling
in of its own accord and forming a long line of
several miles. He was much puzzled. Before
long, he received a communication from the
viceroy of the two Kiangs (Kiangsu and Kiangsi),
saying that a notorious bandit chief was fleeing
from Hankow to Sian and asking him to arrest
the fugitive. General Tso had no way to carry

out the order immediately, so he considered it as
so much official paper and put the matter aside.
Then he observed a serious commotion in the long
army line and heard all the soldiers saying that
they were going to welcome the "Great Dragon
Head," which nonplused him all the more.
But when he found out that the Great Dragon
Head whom the soldiers were getting ready to
meet was none other than the bandit chief that
the viceroy wanted him to arrest, he became
extremely agitated and at once asked his secretary:
" What is this Ko-lao-hui I hear about? And
what is the relation of its Great Dragon Head
with the bandit chief?" The secretary answered:
" In our army, from private soldier up to highest
officer, every man is a member of the Ko-lao-
hui. And this Great Dragon Head whose arrest
is sought is the leader of our Ko-lao-hui."
General Tso asked, "Then how can I keep my
army together?" His secretary replied: "The
only way to keep the army intact is for you to
become the Great Dragon Head. If you refuse,
there is no hope of our marching on Sinkiang."
General Tso could think of no better method;
moreover, he wanted to get the most out of his
army, so he called an outdoor council and became
the Great Dragon Head, bringing all the secret
society under his command. From this it is
evident that General Tso's subsequent pacification

of Sinkiang was not by means of the redoubtable Manchu authority but rather through the ideas and spirit of the old Ming veterans. Nationalism had been conserved since the beginning of the Manchu dynasty; but when Tso Tsung-t'ang became the Great Dragon Head and learned the inner workings of the revolutionary society, he broke up their warrior leadership and destroyed their organization, so that at the time of the recent Revolution we had no organized body to get hold of. The Hung-mên Society had been made a tool and China's national spirit had long since been lost.

To-day I want to talk to you about some of the reasons for this loss of our nationalism. There are many reasons, of which the greatest is our subjection to alien races. When one race conquers another, it naturally does not allow the subject people to have independent thought. Japan, for example, now that it has control of Korea, is trying to convert the minds of the Koreans. All nationalistic ideas are expunged from Korean school texts, so that thirty years from now Korean children will not know there is a Korea or that they are Koreans. Manchuria once had the same design on us. The conquering people tries to destroy that precious possession of the subject people. The Manchus, with this purpose in mind, used the most artful methods. K'ang Hsi imposed the ban on certain books, but Ch'ien Lung

was more tricky in crushing the national spirit.
K'ang Hsi said that he was born of Heaven to be
emperor of China and urged the people not to
resist Heaven; but Ch'ien Lung wiped out all
distinctions between Manchus and Chinese, so
that the intellectual class for the most part had
after that no more national consciousness. That
was bequeathed to the lower classes, but although
they knew they ought to kill the Tartars they did
not know why. So China's nationalistic ideals
have disappeared for hundreds of years, due to
the craftiness of the Manchus.

China's nationalism was originally crushed out
by alien rule, yet there have been other subjugated
races than the Chinese. The Jews lost their
country and before Jesus' day had become a
conquered people. When Jesus was preaching,
his followers took him for a revolutionist and
wanted him to become a revolutionary leader; he
was called the "King of the Jews." The parents
of two disciples once said to Jesus, "Lord, if
you accomplish your purpose, let our elder son
sit at your left hand and our second son on your
right," corresponding to the positions of left and
right prime minister in China, which shows that
the disciples thought of Jesus as a revolutionist.
It is probable that Jesus' religion did contain
some ideas of political revolution, yet one of his
disciples thought the political revolution had failed

and betrayed his teacher. He did not comprehend that Jesus was a religious revolutionist who called his country the Kingdom of Heaven. So, although their state was destroyed, the Jewish race itself has survived since the time of Christ. Or consider India, also a conquered nation, whose national spirit has not been immediately destroyed by alien conquest as China's was. Or Poland, which, although it was a subject nation for a hundred years, has an unquenchable national consciousness; so after the European War the Poles revived their old state, and have now become one of the second- or third-class powers of Europe.

Thus compared, China is seen to be a subject nation similar to Judea, India, and Poland; then, why have they not lost their national spirit while China, after two periods of subjugation, has had all her national pride crushed out? It is a very strange fact and the study of its causes is very interesting. Before China was subjugated, she had a very cultured people and a powerful state. She called herself the "majestic nation," the "land of famous letters and objects," and looked on other countries as barbarian; she thought she was situated in the center of the world and so named herself the "Middle Kingdom." Other expressions, as the "Great Unifier," "Heaven has but one sun, people have but one King," "Gentry of all nations bow before the crown and pearls," date from before the period of China's subjection, when her nationalism was slowly evolving into cosmopolitanism and succeeding generations were employing imperialism to subdue other races. Chang Po-wang and Pan Ting-yuan of the Han dynasty destroyed thirty states in the same way that Clive, manager of the East India Company, brought scores of Indian states together under his rule. For thousands of years, China had been trying to effect a conquest of the world and had subjected all the small states of Asia, but China's methods were not cruel as the Europeans' methods. China used peaceful means to influence others and what was called the "royal way " to bring the weaker and smaller states under her rule. If we follow out this line of thought, we will begin to see why China has lost her national spirit while other races, as the Jews, have kept theirs for two thousand years, and why China has been a subject nation for only three hundred years, yet all her nationalism has vanished.

To study the cause is like diagnosing a sick man. Whatever disease a man contracts can be traced back either to a poor constitution or to some weakness before he was taken sick. Before China lost her sovereignty, there were already roots of disease in her system which, as soon as she suffered conquest, caused her national mind to decay. The hidden causes lie in the fact that China was for millenniums an imperialistic state like Great Britain and pre-revolution Russia, which have been among the world's most powerful states. China's ancient imperialism probably outstripped Great Britain's flourishing modern imperialism.

A new theory is emerging in England and Russia, proposed by the intellectuals, which opposes nationalism on the ground that it is narrow and illiberal — simply a doctrine of cosmopolitanism. England now, and formerly Russia and Germany, together with modern young advocates of new culture in China, support this doctrine and decry nationalism. I constantly hear young men saying, "The *San Min* Principles are not adapted to the tendencies of modern times; the latest and best doctrine is that of cosmopolitanism." Is it really ? Then why did China, as soon as she was conquered, lose all her national spirit ? Cosmopolitanism is the same thing as China's theory of world empire two thousand years ago. When we study this theory, do we find it good or not ? Theoretically we might call it a good theory, yet because the intellectual class in China held it, the Manchus were able to cross China's frontiers and the whole nation was lost to them. K'ang Hsi talked cosmopolitanism, saying that Shun was an eastern " barbarian," Wên Wang a western " barbarian," and since the barbarians of east and west could become emperors of China,

there was no distinction between barbarian and
Hua-hsia [1] — this is cosmopolitanism. We cannot
decide whether an idea is good or not without
seeing it in practice. If the idea is of practical
value to us and to the world, it is good; if the idea
is impractical, it is no good.

The nations which are employing imperialism to
conquer others and which are trying to maintain
their own favored positions as sovereign lords
of the whole world are advocating cosmopolitanism and want the world to join them. China
once wanted to be sovereign lord of the earth and
to stand above every other nation, so she espoused
cosmopolitanism. Because the common people
were influenced by this conception, the Manchus
entered the Great Wall without opposition, and
China fell. The Manchus came in with very small
numbers, not more than a hundred thousand.
How could these few conquer hundreds of millions?
Because most of the Chinese of that day believed
in cosmopolitanism rather than nationalism and
welcomed anyone as emperor of China. So,
although Shih K'o-fah opposed the Manchus,
he had too few followers to resist them successfully, while the majority of Chinese welcomed
the Manchus and let them sit securely on the
throne. And, not only did they give the Manchus

[1] Old name for China.

a welcome, but many enlisted under the Manchu banner, becoming Manchus in the so-called Chinese division of the Manchu army.

The most powerful states in the world to-day are Great Britain and the United States. There are several great states, the so-called Great Powers, whose policies and character have not yet undergone any marked change. But in the future, England and the United States may be able to break up the group of powers and become the only great powers. Suppose that should happen, and then that England should subjugate China and our people become English — would that be good for us? If Chinese should become naturalized British or Americans and help England or America to destroy China, saying that we were but following out the principle of cosmopolitanism, would our consciences, let me ask you, be at rest? If our consciences hurt us at all, it would be because we had some nationalistic feelings; so, I say, nationalism is that precious possession by which humanity maintains its existence. Just as the scholar uses the pen in his hand as an instrument of livelihood, so the human family employs nationalism as a means of its subsistence. If nationalism decays, then when cosmopolitanism flourishes we will be unable to survive and will be eliminated, in the process of natural selection, by other races. The ancient Chinese said, "Banish the three Miao tribes into Three Wei," and drove them to the borders of Yünnan and Kweichow, so that now they have almost disappeared without hope of maintaining their existence. These three Miaos were China's earliest inhabitants; some day we Chinese may be just like them.

With regard to the origin of the Chinese race, some say that the "hundred families" of our people came from the west, trekking over the T'sung-ling to T'ien-shan, across Sinkiang and into the Yellow River valley. As far as the birth-place of Chinese culture is concerned, this seems a reasonable theory, for if Chinese culture had not come from outside but had developed within the country, then, according to all natural principles, the Pearl River valley [1] would have been its cradle and not the Yellow River valley. The Pearl River valley had a temperate climate, rich prod-ucts, and easy living conditions; it should have produced a civilization. But if we study history, we find that Yao, Shun, Yu, T'ang, Wên, and Wu were not born in the Pearl River valley but in the northwest of China. In the time of the Han dynasty [2] the Pearl River valley was still barbarian country, so Chinese civilization must have sprung from northwest China and from other countries. The Chinese speak of their "hundred family

[1] In Kwangtung Province.
[2] 206 B.C. to A.D. 25.

surnames." Foreign students say that in ancient times a "hundred surname" race lived far west, which later moved to China and either destroyed the Miao race or became amalgamated with them, forming the present Chinese race.

According to natural laws of evolution, the fit survive and the unfit perish, the strong win and the weak lose. Have we a strong or a weak race, a fit or an unfit race ? Not one of us is willing to see our race perish or fail ; everyone wishes the race to survive and to win out — these are natural, instinctive feelings. But our country to-day is in a very perilous position. It seems that our race will certainly perish because of three destructive forces—growth of other populations; alien, political, and economic domination. Political and economic control is now pushing us to the wall, but our country is still large and we are not easily made conscious of the pressure of increasing populations in the rest of the world. But a hundred years hence we will feel it. Because we have lost our national spirit, we have opened the gates for political and economic forces to break in, which never would have happened if we had preserved our nationalism.

It is difficult to explain just how we have lost our nationalism. To illustrate I will tell a story which may seem off the point and unrelated to our thesis, but perhaps it will make clearer the causes of which we are speaking. It is an incident which I personally witnessed in Hongkong. There was a coolie who worked daily at the steamer jetties carrying passengers' baggage with his bamboo pole and two ropes. Each day's load was his means of livelihood for that day, but he finally managed to save more than ten dollars. The Luzon lotteries were flourishing at that time and this coolie used his savings to buy a Luzon lottery ticket. He had no home and no place to keep his things or the lottery ticket which he had bought. All his tool of trade was his bamboo pole and two ropes which he carried about with him everywhere he went. So he hid the lottery ticket inside of his bamboo pole, and since he could not always be pulling out the ticket to be looking at it, he fixed the number indelibly on his mind and thought about it all the time. When the day for the drawing came, he went to the lottery shop to match this number, and as soon as he saw the list of numbers he knew that he had won first prize, acquiring a wealth of $100,000. He was in ecstasy, almost insane with joy. Thinking that he would no longer have to be a coolie and use his bamboo pole and ropes, that he would be a rich man forever, he gleefully took the pole and ropes and threw them into the sea !

The coolie's bamboo pole may represent nation-alism — a means of existence; the winning of the first prize may represent the time when China's flourishing imperialism was evolving into cosmopolitanism and when our forefathers, believing that China wast he world's great state—that "Heaven has but one sun, people but one king"; that "gentry of all nations bow before the crown and pearls"; that universal peace would henceforth prevail and that the only thing necessary was a world harmony in which the world would bring its tribute to China—threw away nationalism as the coolie threw his bamboo pole into the sea. Then when China was overcome by the Manchus, she not only failed to become the master of the world, but even failed to keep her small family property intact. The national spirit of the people was destroyed, just as the bamboo pole was thrown into the sea.

When the Manchu soldiers entered the Great Wall, Wu San-kuei was their guide; and when Shih K'o-fah tried to espouse the nationalist cause, proposing the election of a Chinese prince, Fuh-wang, to the throne and the restoration of the Mings at Nanking, the Manchu To-erh-k'un[1] said to him, "We did not take these rivers and mountains of ours from the great Ming dynasty but from the rebel Li Ch'uang," meaning that the rivers and mountains of the Mings had been thrown away by the Mings themselves, just as that coolie threw away his bamboo pole. Those young

[1] Durgan.

students who prate about the new culture and espouse cosmopolitanism, saying that nationalism is out of date, might have some ground if they spoke for England and America or even for our forefathers, but if they think they are speaking for Chinese to-day, we have no place for them. Before Germany was hemmed in, she talked of not nationalism, but a world state — cosmopolitanism. I suspect that Germany to-day is ceasing to preach cosmopolitanism and is talking nationalism a bit! If our forefathers had not thrown away the bamboo pole, we might have won first prize, but we threw away the pole too early, forgetting that the ticket was hidden inside. As soon as we felt the yoke of foreign political and economic domination and encountered the forces of natural selection, we came face to face with the tragic possibility of a lost nation and a vanishing race.

If we Chinese can in the future find some way to revive our nationalism, can discover another bamboo pole, then no matter what foreign political and economic forces oppress us, we will survive through the ages. We can overcome the forces of natural selection ; Heaven's preservation of our four hundred millions of Chinese till now shows that it has not wanted to destroy us ; if China perishes, the guilt will be on our own heads and we shall be the world's great sinners. Heaven has placed great responsibilities upon us Chinese;

if we do not love ourselves, we are rebels against Heaven. China has come to the time when each one of us has a great responsibility to shoulder. If Heaven does not want to eliminate us, it evidently wants to further the world's progress. If China perishes, she will perish at the hands of the Great Powers; those Powers will thus be obstructing the world's progress. Yesterday a Russian said to me: "Why has Lenin been attacked by all the Powers? Because he dared to say that the people of the world were divided into two classes — the twelve hundred fifty millions and the two hundred fifty millions; the twelve hundred fifty millions are being oppressed by the two hundred fifty millions, and the oppressors are moving not in harmony with but in defiance of Nature. Only when we resist Might are we moving with Nature." If we want to resist Might we must unite our four hundred millions and join the twelve hundred fifty millions of the world. We must espouse nationalism and in the first instance attain our own unity, then we can consider others and help the weaker, smaller peoples to unite in a common struggle against the two hundred fifty millions. Together we shall use Right to fight Might, and when Might is overthrown and the selfishly ambitious have disappeared, then we may talk about cosmopolitanism.

February 10, 1924.

LECTURE 4

Expansion of the white races — Dominance of the Anglo-Saxons—Causes of the World War: racial rivalries and struggle for territory — United States entered the war because of racial affinity with England — Effect of President Wilson's principle of " self-determination " upon the smaller nations — Betrayal of this ideal after the war — The war really a conflict of imperialisms — One hopeful result of the war, the Russian Revolution — The coming world struggle between oppressed and oppressors — China's ancient, benevolent imperialism compared with modern imperialism — American rule in the Philippines — Conversation with British consul during the Great War regarding China's entry — Hypocritical aims of the Allies — Parallels in ancient China with modern political ideas — European civilization superior to China's only on material side — Western science a recent achievement — China must cherish her ancient ideals — Nationalism precedes internationalism.

The population of the world to-day is approximately a billion and a half. One fourth of this number live in China, which means that one out of every four persons in the world is a Chinese. The total population of the white races of Europe also amounts to four hundred millions. The white division of mankind, which is now the most flourishing, includes four races : in central and northern Europe, the Teutons, who have founded many

states, the largest of which is Germany, others
being Austria, Sweden, Norway, Holland, and
Denmark; in eastern Europe, the Slavs, who also
have founded a number of states, the largest being
Russia, and, after the European War, the new
countries of Czecho-Slovakia and Jugo-Slavia; in
western Europe, the Saxons or Anglo-Saxons, who
have founded two large states — England and the
United States of America; in southern Europe,
the Latins, who have founded several states, the
largest being France, Italy, Spain, and Portugal,
and who have migrated to South America forming
states there just as the Anglo-Saxons migrated
to North America and built up Canada and the
United States. The white peoples of Europe,
now numbering only four hundred million persons, are divided into four great stocks which have
established many states. Because the national
spirit of the white race was highly developed, when
they had filled up the European continent they
expanded to North and South America in the
Western Hemisphere and to Africa and Australia
in the southern and eastern parts of the Eastern
Hemisphere.

The Anglo-Saxons at present occupy more space
on the globe than any other race. Although this
race originated in Europe, the only European
soil it holds are the British Isles — England,
Scotland, and Ireland — which occupy about the

same position in the Atlantic that Japan occupies
in the Pacific. The Anglo-Saxons have extended
their territory westward to North America,
eastward to Australia and New Zealand, and
southward to Africa until they possess more land
and are wealthier and stronger than any other
race. Before the European War the Teutons and
the Slavs were the strongest races; moreover, by
reason of the sagacity and ability of the Teutonic
peoples, Germany was able to unite more than
twenty small states into a great German confederation. At the beginning an agricultural
nation, it developed into an industrial nation
and through industrial prosperity its army and
navy became exceedingly powerful.

Before the European War all the European
nations had been poisoned by imperialism. What
is imperialism ? It is the policy of aggression
upon other countries by means of political force,
or, in the Chinese phrase, "long-range aggression."
As all the peoples of Europe were imbued with
this policy, wars were continually breaking out ;
almost every decade had at least one small war
and each century one big war. The greatest of all
was the recent European War, which may be
called the World War because it finally involved
the whole world and pulled every nation and peoples into its vortex. The causes of the European
War were, first, the rivalry between the Saxon

and Teutonic races for control of the sea. Germany in her rise to greatness had developed her navy until she was the second sea power in the world; Great Britain wanted her own navy to rule the seas so she tried to destroy Germany ,whose sea power was next to hers. From this struggle for first place on the sea came the war.

A second cause was each nation's struggle for more territory. In eastern Europe there is a weak state called Turkey. For the past hundred years the people of the world have called it the "sick man of Europe." Because the government was unenlightened and the sultan was despotic, it became extremely helpless and the European nations wanted to partition it. Because the Turkish question had not been solved for a century and every nation of Europe was trying to solve it, war resulted. The first cause of the European War, then, was the struggle between white races for supremacy ; the second cause was the effort to solve critical world problems. If Germany had won the war, she would have held the supreme power on the sea after the war and Great Britain would have lost all her territory, breaking into pieces like the old Roman Empire. But the result of the war was defeat for Germany and the failure of her imperialistic designs.

The recent European War was the most dreadful war in the history of the world. Forty to fifty million men were under arms for a period of four years, and near the end of the war they still could not be divided into conquerors and vanquished. One side in the war was called the Entente; the other side, the Allied Powers. The Allied Powers[1] at first included Germany and Austria; Turkey and Bulgaria later joined them. The Entente Powers[2] at first were Serbia, France, Russia, England, and Japan; Italy and the United States joined afterwards. The United States' entry into the war was due entirely to racial considerations. During the first two years of the war Germany and Austria were in the ascendancy. Paris and the English Channel were almost captured by the German and Austrian armies. The Teutons thought that Great Britain was certainly done for, and the British themselves were thoroughly alarmed. Seeing that the American people are of the same race as they, the British used the plea of race relationship to stir up the people of the United States. When America realized that England, of her own race, was in danger of being destroyed by Germany, of an alien race, inevitably " the creature sorrowed for its kind " and America threw in her lot with England to defend the existence of the Anglo-Saxons. Moreover, fearing that her own strength would be insufficient, America tried with all her

1 Central Powers.
2 " Allies."

might to arouse all the neutral countries of the world to join in the war to defeat Germany.

During the war there was a great phrase, used by President Wilson and warmly received everywhere — " self-determination of peoples." Because Germany was striving by military force to crush the peoples of the European Entente, Wilson proposed destroying Germany's power and giving autonomy henceforth to the weaker and smaller peoples. His idea met a world welcome, and although the common people of India still opposed Great Britain, their destroyer, yet many small peoples, when they heard Wilson say that the war was for the freedom of the weak and small peoples, gladly gave aid to Great Britain. Although Annam had been subjugated by France and the common people hated the French tyranny, yet during the war they still helped France to fight, also because they had heard of Wilson's just proposition. And the reason why other small peoples of Europe, such as Poland, Czecho-Slovakia, and Roumania, all enlisted on the side of the Entente against the Allied Powers was because of the self-determination principle enunciated by President Wilson. China, too, under the inspiration of the United States, entered the war; although she sent no armies, yet she did contribute hundreds of thousands of laborers to dig trenches and to work behind the lines. As a result of the noble theme propounded by the Entente all the oppressed peoples of Europe and of Asia finally joined together to help them in their struggle against the Allied Powers. At the same time, Wilson proposed, to guard the future peace of the world, fourteen points, of which the most important was that each people should have the right of self-determination. When victory and defeat still hung in the balance, England and France heartily indorsed these points, but when victory was won and the Peace Conference was opened, England, France, and Italy realized that Wilson's proposal of freedom for nations conflicted too seriously with the interests of imperialism; and so, during the conference, they used all kinds of methods to explain away Wilson's principles. The result was a peace treaty with most unjust terms; the weaker, smaller nations not only did not secure self-determination and freedom but found themselves under an oppression more terrible than before. This shows that the strong states and the powerful races have already forced possession of the globe and that the rights and privileges of other states and nations are monopolized by them. Hoping to make themselves forever secure in their exclusive position and to prevent the smaller and weaker peoples from again reviving, they sing praises to cosmopolitanism, saying that nationalism is too narrow; really their espousal of internationalism is but imperialism and aggression in another guise.

But Wilson's proposals, once set forth, could not be recalled ; each one of the weaker, smaller nations who had helped the Entente to defeat the Allied Powers and had hoped to attain freedom as a fruit of the victory was doomed to bitter disappointment by the results of the Peace Conference. Then Annam, Burma, Java, India, the Malay Archipelago, Turkey, Persia, Afghanistan, Egypt, and the scores of weak nations in Europe, were stirred with a great, new consciousness; they saw how completely they had been deceived by the Great Powers' advocacy of self-determination and began independently and separately to carry out the principle of the "self-determination of peoples."

Many years of fierce warfare had not been able to destroy imperialism because this war was a conflict of imperialisms between states, not a struggle between savagery and civilization or between Might and Right. So the effect of the war was merely the overthrow of one imperialism by another imperialism; what survived was still imperialism. But from the war there was unconsciously born in the heart of mankind a great hope — the Russian Revolution. The Russian Revolution had begun much earlier, as far back as 1905, but had not accomplished its purpose.

Now during the European War the efforts of the revolutionists were crowned with success. The reason for the outbreak of revolution again at this time was the great awakening of the people as a result of their war experience. Russia was formerly one of the Entente nations ; when the Entente Powers were fighting Germany, Russia sent over ten million soldiers into the field — not a puny force. Without Russia's part in the war, the Entente's line on the Western front would long before have been smashed by Germany ; because Russia was embarrassing the Germans on the Eastern front, the Entente Powers were able to break even with Germany for two or three years and finally turn defeat into victory. Just half-way through the war, Russia began to reflect, and she realized that in helping the Entente to fight Germany she was merely helping several brute forces to fight one brute force and that no good results would come of it in the end. A group of soldiers and citizens awoke, broke away from the Entente, and concluded a separate peace with Germany.

As far as their legitimate national interests were concerned, the German and the Russian people had absolutely no cause for quarrel; but when it came to imperialistic designs, they vied with each other in aggressions until conflict was inevitable. Moreover, Germany went so far beyond bounds that Russia, in self-protection, could not but move in accord with England, France, and the others. Later, when the Russian people awoke and saw that imperialism was wrong, they started a revolution within their own country, first overthrowing their own imperialism; at the same time, to avoid foreign embarrassments, they made peace with Germany. Before long, the Entente also signed a peace with Germany and then all sent soldiers to fight Russia. Why? Because the Russian people had awakened to the fact that their daily sufferings were due to imperialism and that, to get rid of their sufferings they must eliminate imperialism and embrace self-determination. Every other nation opposed this policy and so mobilized to fight Russia, yet Russia's proposal and Wilson's were undesignedly similar; both declared that the weaker, smaller nations had the right of self-determination and freedom. When Russia proclaimed this principle, the weaker, smaller peoples of the world gave their eager support to it and all together began to seek self-determination. The calamitous war through which Europe had passed brought, of course, no great imperialistic gain, but, because of the Russian Revolution, a great hope was born in the heart of mankind.

Of the billion and a half people in the world, the most powerful are the four hundred million whites on the European and American continents;

from this base the white races have started out to swallow up other races. The American red aborigines are gone, the African blacks will soon be exterminated, the brown race of India is in the process of dissolution, the yellow races of Asia are now being subjected to the white man's oppression and may, before long, be wiped out.

But the one hundred fifty million Russians, when their revolution succeeded, broke with the other white races and condemned the white man's imperialistic behavior; now they are thinking of throwing in their lot with the weaker, smaller peoples of Asia in a struggle against the tyrannical races. So only two hundred fifty millions of tyrannical races are left, but they are still trying by inhuman methods and military force to subjugate the other twelve hundred fifty millions. So hereafter mankind will be divided into two camps: on one side will be the twelve hundred fifty millions; on the other side, the two hundred fifty millions. Although the latter group are in the minority, yet they hold the most powerful positions on the globe and their political and economic strength is immense. With these two forces they are out to exploit the weaker and smaller races. If the political arm of navies and armies is not strong enough, they bear down with economic pressure. If their economic arm is at times weak, they intervene with political force of navies and

armies. The way their political power coöperates
with their economic power is like the way in which
the left arm helps the right arm; with their two
arms they have crushed most terribly the twelve
hundred fifty millions. But "Heaven does not
always follow man's desires." The Slavic race of
one hundred fifty millions suddenly rose up and
struck a blow at imperialism and capitalism,
warring for mankind against inequality. In my
last lecture I told of the Russian who said, "The
reason why the Powers have so defamed Lenin is
because he dared to assert that the twelve hundred
fifty millions' majority in the world were being
oppressed by the two hundred fifty millions' minority." Lenin not only said this, but also advocated
self-determination for the oppressed peoples and
launched a campaign for them against injustice.
The Powers attacked Lenin because they wanted
to destroy a prophet and a seer of mankind and
obtain security for themselves. But the people of
the world now have their eyes opened and know
that the rumors created by the Powers are false;
they will not let themselves be deceived again.
The political thinking of the peoples of the world
has been enlightened to this extent.

Now we want to revive China's lost nationalism
and use the strength of our four hundred millions
to fight for mankind against injustice; this is our
divine mission. The Powers are afraid that we will

have such thoughts and are setting forth a specious
doctrine.   They are now advocating cosmopolitanism to inflame us, declaring that, as the civilization
of the world advances and as mankind's vision en-
larges, nationalism becomes too narrow, unsuited
to the present age, and hence that we should espouse cosmopolitanism.   In recent years some of
China's youths, devotees of the new culture, have
been opposing nationalism, led astray by this
doctrine.   But it is not a doctrine which wronged
races should talk about.   We, the wronged races,
must first recover our position of national freedom
and equality before we are fit to discuss cosmopolitanism.   The illustration I used in my last lecture of the coolie who won first prize in the lottery
has already made this very clear.   The lottery
ticket represents cosmopolitanism; the bamboo
pole, nationalism.   The coolie, on winning first
prize, immediately threw away his pole just as
we, fooled by the promises of cosmopolitanism,
have discarded our nationalism.   We must understand that cosmopolitanism grows out of nationalism; if we want to extend cosmopolitanism we
must first establish strongly our own nationalism.
If nationalism cannot become strong, cosmopolitanism certainly cannot prosper.   Thus we see
that cosmopolitanism is hidden in the heart of
nationalism just as the ticket was hidden inside
the bamboo pole; if we discard nationalism and

go and talk cosmopolitanism we are just like the
coolie who threw his bamboo pole into the sea.
We put the cart before the horse. I said before
that our position is not equal to that of the
Annamese or the Koreans; they are subject peoples
and slaves while we cannot even be called slaves.
Yet we discourse about cosmopolitanism and say
that we do not need nationalism. Gentlemen, is
this reasonable ?

According to history, our four hundred millions
of Chinese have also come down the road of
imperialism. Our forefathers constantly employed
political force to encroach upon weaker and
smaller nations; but economic force in those days
was not a serious thing, so we were not guilty
of economic oppression of other peoples. Then
compare China's culture with Europe's ancient
culture. The Golden Age of European culture
was in the time of Greece and Rome, yet Rome at
the height of its power was contemporaneous with
as late a dynasty in China as the Han. At that
time China's political thinking was very profound;
many orators were earnestly opposing imperialism
and much anti-imperialistic literature was produced, the most famous being " Discussions on
Abandoning the Pearl Cliffs." Such writings
opposed China's efforts to expand her territory
and her struggle over land with the southern
barbarians, which shows that as early as the Han

dynasty China already discouraged war against outsiders and had developed the peace idea to broad proportions.

In the Sung dynasty, China was not only ceasing to encroach upon other peoples, but she was even being herself invaded by foreigners. The Sung dynasty was overthrown by the Mongols and the nation did not again revive until the Ming dynasty. After this restoration, China became much less aggressive. However, many small states in the South China Sea wanted to bring tribute and to adopt Chinese culture, giving voluntary adherence because of their admiration for our culture and not because of military pressure from China. The small countries in the Malay Archipelago and the South China Sea considered it a great honor for China to annex them and receive their tribute; China's refusal would have brought them disgrace.

The strongest powers in the world to-day have not succeeded in calling forth a praise like this. Take America's treatment of the Philippines: allowing the Filipinos to organize their own Assembly and to have a share in the government; allowing them to appoint delegates to the Congress in Washington; not only not requiring a money tribute but subsidizing their main items of expenditure, building roads, and providing education for them. Such benevolent and magnanimous treatment can be considered the limit of generosity, yet the Filipinos even now do not consider it an honor to be Americanized and are every day asking for independence. Or take Nepal in India. The people of Nepal are called Gurkhalis, a very brave and warlike race; although England has conquered India she still fears the Gurkhalis. She treats them very generously, sending them money each year, just as the Sung dynasty in China, fearing the Kin Tartars, sent them funds, with this difference, that what the Sungs gave to the Kin Tartars was called a tribute, while England's gift to the Gurkhalis is probably called a gratuity. But up to the first year of our Republic, the Gurkhalis were still bringing their tribute to China, which proves that the small nations around China have not yet lost their hope for or faith in her.

About ten years ago, on a visit to the Foreign Office in Siam, I had a conversation with the assistant secretary for foreign affairs. We were discussing various Asiatic problems when the secretary said, "If China could have a revolution and become a strong state and people, we Siamese would gladly renew our allegiance to China and become a province of China." The interview was held in a public office of the Siamese government and the speaker was the assistant secretary for foreign affairs, so he could not be said to be expressing his personal opinion only;

he was representing the sentiments of all his people. This shows that even then Siam thought highly of China. But in these last ten years, Siam has become an independent state of Asia, has revised her oppressive treaties with other nations, and has raised her own national standing; hereafter she would hardly be willing to return to China.

I can tell you another very interesting incident. When the European War was raging most fiercely, I was in Canton setting up the constitutional government. One day the British consul came to the headquarters of the commander in chief to see me and to discuss with me the possibility of the Southern Government joining the Entente and sending troops to Europe. I asked the British consul, "Why should we send troops?" He replied: "To fight Germany. Since Germany has invaded Chinese territory and has seized Tsingtau from you, you ought to fight her and recover your possessions." I said: "Tsingtau is rather far away from Canton. What about the place nearest to us — Hongkong — or a little farther away, Burma, Bhutan, Nepal, and such places which formerly belonged to China? And now you want to come and take Tibet from us. China hasn't sufficient strength at present to recover her lost territory; if she did, perhaps she might first take back what Great Britain has usurped. Tsingtau, which Germany seized, is comparatively small; Burma is larger and Tibet much larger. If we were out to recover our possessions, we would begin with the large ones." When he heard my argument, he could not control his anger and said, " I came here to discuss public affairs with you ! " Immediately I answered, "I am discussing public affairs ! " For a long time we argued face to face and neither would yield the stage.

Finally I said to him: "Our civilization has already advanced two thousand years beyond yours. We are willing to wait for you to progress and catch up with us, but we cannot recede and let you pull us down. Two thousand years ago we discarded imperialism and advocated a policy of peace, and to-day the thinking of the Chinese people has fully realized this ideal. You also set up peace as your goal, in the present war. At first we heartily approved, but really you are still fighting, not talking peace; you are talking force, not justice. I consider your characteristic appeal to force as extremely barbarous. Go ahead and fight. We will certainly not join you. When you are worn out with fighting and some day are ready to talk real peace, then we may enlist on your side and seek the world's peace with you. Another strong reason why we are opposing China's entry into the war and the sending of troops is that we are not willing for China to become an unjust power like you. If we followed your advice and joined the Entente, you could send officers to China to train up soldiers; with your experienced leadership and splendid military equipment besides, you could certainly within six months' time train three to five hundred thousand good soldiers and transport them to fight in Europe and defeat Germany. Then you would be bad off ! "

" Why bad off ? " the British consul asked. I replied: "After using several million soldiers and fighting for years you cannot overcome Germany, yet you think that adding a few hundred thousand Chinese soldiers would spell her defeat! A real result would be the awakening of the martial spirit in China; from the nucleus of these few hundred thousand soldiers the Chinese army would grow to millions and that would be greatly to your disadvantage. Japan is now on your side and is already one of the Great Powers of the world ; with her military prowess she domineers over Asia. Her imperialistic policy is just like that of the Powers and you are terribly afraid of her. Yet China's population and resources far exceed Japan's. If we should follow the plan you suggest and China should enter the war on your side, before ten years we would become another Japan. When you think of the size of China's population and territory, we could become ten Japans; then all your world power would hardly be enough for one fight with China. Because we have advanced two thousand years beyond you and have gotten rid of the old savage, pugnacious sentiments and have attained only lately to a true ideal of peace, and because we hope that China will forever cherish her moral code of peace, therefore we are not willing to enter this great conflict." After listening to my speech, the British consul who, half an hour before was ready to fight with me, was deeply impressed and said, "If I were a Chinese, I would undoubtedly think as you do."

Gentlemen, you know that revolution is naturally a thing of bloodshed. Thus, in the revolutions of T'ang and Wu, everyone said that the rebels were "obedient to Heaven and well-pleasing to men" but as to the fighting it was said that they experienced "battle 'staves floating on rivers of blood." In the Revolution of 1911, when we overthrew the Manchus, how much blood was spilled? The reason for the small bloodshed then was the Chinese people's love of peace, an outstanding quality of the Chinese character. The Chinese are really the greatest lovers of peace in the world. I have constantly urged the people of the world to follow China's example; now the Slavic people of Russia are keeping pace with us and espousing the cause of peace after us, and their one hundred millions want to coöperate with us.

Our four hundred millions are not only a most peaceful but also a most civilized race. The new cultures which have flourished of late in Europe and which are called anarchism and communism are old things in China. For instance, Hwang-Lao's [1] political philosophy is really anarchism and what is Lieh-tze's [2] dream of the land of the Hua-hsü people who lived in a natural state without ruler or laws but another theory of anarchism? Modern youths in China, who have not studied carefully into these old Chinese theories, think that their ideas are the newest things in existence, unaware that, though they may be new in Europe, they are thousands of years old here. What Russia has been putting into practice is not pure communism but Marxism; Marxism is not real communism. What Proudhon and Bakunin advocated is the only real communism. Communism in other countries is still in the stage of discussion; it has not been fully tried out anywhere. But it was applied in China in the time of Hung Hsiu-ch'uan; his economic system was the real thing in communism and not mere theory.

[1] Hwangti and Laotze.
[2] The name of a philosopher in the Chow dynasty.

European superiority to China is not in political philosophy but altogether in the field of material civilization. With the progress of European material civilization, all the daily provisions for clothing, food, housing, and communication have become extremely convenient and time-saving, and the weapons of war — poison gas and such — have become extraordinarily perfected and deadly. All these new inventions and weapons have come since the development of science. It was after the seventeenth and eighteenth centuries, when Bacon, Newton, and other great scholars advocated the use of observation, experiment, and investigation of all things, that science came into being. So when we speak of Europe's scientific progress and of the advance of European material civilization, we are talking about something which has only two hundred years' history. A few hundred years ago, Europe could not compare with China, so now if we want to learn from Europe we should learn what we ourselves lack — science — but not political philosophy. Europeans are still looking to China for the fundamentals of political philosophy. You all know that the best scholarship to-day is found in Germany. Yet German scholars are studying Chinese philosophy and even Indian Buddhist principles to supplement their partial conceptions of science. Cosmopolitanism has just flowered out in Europe during this generation, but it was talked of two thousand years ago in China. Europeans cannot yet discern our ancient civilization, yet many of our race have thought of a political world civilization; and as for international morality, our four hundred millions have been devoted to the principle of world peace. But because of the loss of our nationalism, our ancient morality and civilization have not been able to manifest themselves and are now even declining.

The cosmopolitanism which Europeans are talking about to-day is really a principle supported by force without justice. The English expression "might is right" means that fighting for acquisition is just. The Chinese mind has never regarded acquisition by war as right; it considers aggressive warfare barbarous. This pacifist morality is the true spirit of cosmopolitanism. Upon what foundation can we defend and build up this spirit?—Upon nationalism. Russia's one hundred fifty millions are the foundation of Europe's cosmopolitanism and China's four hundred millions are the foundation of Asia's cosmopolitanism. As a foundation is essential to expansion, so we must talk nationalism first if we want to talk cosmopolitanism. "Those desiring to pacify the world must first govern their own state." Let us revive our lost nationalism and make it

shine with greater splendor, then we will have
some ground for discussing internationalism.

February 17, 1924.

LECTURE 5

How to revive China's nationalism—Awakening the people
to an understanding of China's position — Disasters which
threaten China—The military danger, from Japan, the United
States, Great Britain, France — China cannot trust to the
"balance of power" of foreign nations — Diplomatic
victories over China — The danger of foreign economic dom-
nation — Danger of greater increase in other populations —
China must face the facts — China should build her new
national sentiment upon the foundation of existent family
and clan loyalties — The method of the ancients — If
India can unite on a program of noncoöperation, China
should be able to unite — Positive and negative resistance
to foreign aggression.

My subject to-day is: What means shall we use
to revive our nationalism? From my previous
lectures you have seen that the reason why
China has declined to her present state has been
the loss of national spirit. We have been subjugated by other races, being governed by aliens
for over two hundred years. Formerly we were
slaves of the Manchus; now we are slaves of all
nations and suffering more than ever before. If
we keep on in this way and do not find some means
to recover our lost nationalism, then China will
not only perish as a nation but also perhaps as

a race. So, if we want to save China, we must first find a way to revive our nationalism.

To-day I shall discuss two ways by which our nationalism can be revived : the first is by awakening our four hundred millions to see where we stand. We are at a crisis when we must escape misery and seek happiness, escape death and find life. First we must see clearly and then, of course, act. Gentlemen, if you want to appreciate how " understanding is difficult, action easy," study my thesis. China formerly did not know that she was in decline and so perished ; if she had seen ahead, she might not have perished. The ancient sayings " The nation without foreign foes and outside dangers will always be ruined," and " Many adversities will revive a state " are altogether psychological truisms. " Foreign foes and outside dangers," for example : if a nation thinks that it has no outside dangers, that it is perfectly secure, that it is the strongest country in the world and foreigners will not dare to invade it so defense is unnecessary, that nation will crumble. " Many adversities will revive a state," because, as soon as we understand what these adversities are, our energies will be aroused to heroic deeds. It is also a matter of psychology. If the situation which I have described in my first four lectures is true, then we must keep clearly in mind the perilous position which we now occupy and the critical period in which we are now living, before we can know how to revive our lost nationalism. If we attempt a revival without understanding the situation, all hope will disappear forever and the Chinese people will soon be destroyed.

Gathering up the points in my previous lecture, what are the disasters which threaten us and from what direction do they come? They come from the Great Powers, and they are: first, political oppression; second, economic oppression; and third, the more rapid growth of population among the Powers. These three disasters from without are already upon our heads, and our people are in a most dangerous situation. The first disaster, the destruction of the nation by political force, may happen in a day. China, now under the political yoke of the Powers, may go to smash at any moment; we are not sure we can live from one morning to another. There are two ways in which political force can destroy a nation: through military power and through diplomacy. To see how military power can destroy a nation in a day, look at history: in the one battle of Yaimên, China of the Sung dynasty was destroyed by the Mongols; in the one battle of Yangchow the Ming dynasty fell. In foreign history, the one battle of Waterloo was enough to overthrow the empire of Napoleon I, and the battle of Sedan to ruin the empire of Napoleon III. If, then, one battle is able to cause the downfall of a nation, China is in daily peril of her life, for our army and navy and strategic points are not prepared for defense, and foreign troops could break through at any time and defeat us.

The nearest nation that could destroy us is Japan; in peace times they have a million soldiers that can take the field, and in war, three million. Their navy is also very powerful and could almost compete with the navies of Great Britain and the United States until the Washington Conference, when their battleships were limited to three hundred thousand tons. Japan's men-of-war, such as cruisers, submarines, and destroyers, are exceedingly well built, and their fighting strength is tremendous. For instance, when Japan recently sent two destroyers to Pai-o-t'an,[1] China had no ships with such great fighting power to oppose them. Japan has more than one hundred destroyers like these. If Japan should come with these destroyers to fight us, she could break down our national defenses immediately and deal us a deathblow. Besides, the strategic points along our coast have no forts for strong defense. Thus Japan, our near Eastern neighbor, has an army and navy that can rush straight and far at a moment's

---

[1] A place near Canton.

notice. She is not striking just yet; perhaps because the suitable time has not arrived. But if she should strike, she could destroy China any day. Between the day of mobilization in Japan and the day of attack on China, not more than ten days would elapse. So if China should break off relations with Japan, Japan could destroy her within ten days.

Looking from Japan across to the eastern shore of the Pacific, we see the United States, the most powerful nation there. She formerly had a navy three times the size of Japan's, but as a result of the limitations set by the Washington Conference, she has reduced her battleship tonnage to five hundred thousand. Of the new types of ships, such as submarines and destroyers, she has more than Japan. As to their army, education is available for all in the United States. Primary education is compulsory and every boy and girl in the country has to go to school; most of the people have high school and college education. All their citizens have received military training in high school and college, so that the government can at any time add hosts of soldiers to the army. When the United States entered the European War, she was able to send two million soldiers in less than a year. So, although the American standing army is small, the potential strength of the army is tremendous ; in a short time millions of soldiers could take the field. If China and the United States should sever diplomatic relations, the latter would need only a month after mobilization to be ready for attack, so the United States could destroy China one month after a rupture.

Looking from the United States eastward toward the continent of Europe we see in the Atlantic the British Isles. England was once called the "mistress of the seas" when her navy was the strongest in the world, but since the Washington Conference her war vessels have also been limited to five hundred thousand tons. Of ordinary cruisers, destroyers, and submarines, she has a larger number than the United States. England is only forty or fifty days' journey from China; and, moreover, she already has bases in China, such as Hongkong, which she has been building up for several decades. Hongkong is only a small place, but it has a thriving trade and by its natural location it can exert a strangle hold on all the southern provinces of China. Soldiers drill there and marines stay there. Although an attack from the Hongkong army and navy would not crush us immediately, still we would have no power to resist. Besides Hongkong, there are India and Australia near by, and if the land and sea forces of those colonies were employed, it would take not more than two months from the day of mobilization for them all to get to China. So if China and England should sever relations, in two months, at the most, England could wipe out China.

Turn again to the continent of Europe, where France is now the strongest power and her army is the strongest in the world, with the addition of two or three thousand airplanes, which could be further increased in case of war. The French also have a base very close to China — Annam — and from Annam they have constructed a railway straight through to the capital of Yünnan Province. If China should break with France, French troops could attack China within forty or fifty days; so France, like England, could destroy China within two months.

This means that there is not a single one of the Powers but could, with military force, break up China. Why, then, has China survived till the present ? Not because of any defensive strength of her own, but simply because all the Powers want to exploit China; all are watchfully waiting, and each is unwilling to make concessions to the others. The strength of the various nations in China has become a balance of power, which makes it possible for China still to exist. There are some people in China who cherish foolish and exaggerated notions that the Great Powers, since they are now mutually jealous over their rights in China, will always be equally balanced in power and not united, and that as long as this is true,

China need not exert herself to resist and will not come to ruin. Isn't this sort of dependence on others rather than upon oneself just " gazing at heaven and casting lots " ? As divination is unreliable, so this silly optimism about China will bring us nothing in the end. The Great Powers still want to crush China, but they think that the use of military force may make the Chinese question the occasion of another great war like the recent European War, with results only of defeat and damage on all sides and no great gain in the end for themselves. Foreign statesmen see this clearly and are not employing merely military force, for that would make war between the Powers inevitable. Even if they could avoid conflict over the balancing of their other rights and privileges, the problem of governing China would certainly produce a clash. And since this unavoidable clash would be of great disadvantage to them, the Powers are facing the serious possibility and are now proposing a reduction of armaments instead of war. Japan's war vessel tonnage is limited to three hundred thousand tons; England's and the United States', to five hundred thousand tons. The conference was apparently called for reduction of armaments, but it really met to consider the Chinese question. In partitioning rights and privileges in China, how could the Powers avoid conflict with one another ?

As I just said, there have been two methods used by political powers in the destruction of states — military force and diplomacy. Military force means the use of gun and cannon, which we have some idea how to resist; diplomacy means the demolishing of China with paper and pen, which we have not learned how to counteract. Although China appointed delegates to the Washington Conference, and although it was said superficially that the resolutions regarding China were to her advantage, yet not long after the close of the conference the press in all foreign countries began to talk of international control of China, and such talk is certain to increase daily. The concentrated thinking of the Powers will certainly evolve some consummate method for overthrowing China. Hereafter they will not need to move their armies or to send their war vessels. Just a paper and pen and a mutually satisfactory agreement will spell our ruin. It is only necessary that the diplomats of the different countries meet in one place and make their signatures; in one day the signing of a document, in one day united political action, can wipe out China. Such a thing is not without precedent; Poland's dismemberment at the hands of Russia, Germany, and Austria was the consequence of one day's negotiation and agreement. So China, too, may perish as the result of a single day's joint decision by Great Britain, France, the United States, Japan, and other powers. Looking at the political forces which threaten a nation, China is now in a position of extreme peril.

The second disaster, the foreign economic domination which is corrupting China, I have already spoken of. Every year we are robbed by foreigners of $1,200,000,000, and the loss is increasing each day. The balance of trade ten years ago was $200,000,000; now it is $500,000,000; at this rate of increase, 250 per cent every ten years, another decade will find us losing $3,000,000,000 a year; divided among our four hundred million people, an annual amount of $7.50 per capita. This means that every one of us Chinese will be paying $7.50 a year to foreign countries; in other words, a head tax of $7.50. If we do not count the female population of two hundred millions, which, under present conditions, could not be responsible for the $7.50 a person, it is clear that the males would all have to double their quota and pay $15 apiece annually. Yet the males are divided into three groups : the aged and the young, those who share but do not bring in profits, and the productive group. The first two groups cannot be expected to bear the tax, which means that two thirds of the males who are to pay $15 each must be eliminated, leaving the youthful and middle-aged group which produces wealth to bear the burden for all the others. Each one in the latter group will then have to pay a forty-five-dollar yearly head tax to foreign countries.

Do you say this is a frightening prospect or not? And this head tax will increase, not decrease. So, as I see it, if we still do not awake but go on in the way we have been going, even though the foreign diplomatists should sleep on their job, our nation would be ruined in ten years. To-day our people are poor and our resources are exhausted; what the poverty of the people will be ten years hence can only be imagined. When our load of debt is two and a half times what it is to-day, do you think that our China can survive?

It may be that the Powers, after their experiences in the European War, will not want any more fighting and violent action, and that they will prefer quiet to excitement, in which case we might be able to escape military control. But we cannot so avert diplomatic oppression; granting that by some good luck we could escape it, how can we but be destroyed by this economic tyranny alone, which is day by day pressing in upon us and sucking at our very life blood?

Then there is a third disaster which threatens us. The population of China has not increased during the past hundred years, and it will hardly increase during the next hundred years unless we find some way to stimulate the growth. In the last century the United States has grown tenfold; Russia, fourfold; England and Japan, threefold; Germany, two and a half fold; and France, least of all, has, however, added one fourth to her population. While their populations are daily growing, ours is at a standstill, or, what is worse, is becoming smaller. Study our own history: as the Han (Chinese) race multiplied, the aboriginal races of China — Miaos, Yaos, Laos, Tungs, and others — disappeared; if we, instead, had been under pressure of population increase on their part, anyone can see that we would have been the ones to disappear. China, under the political domination of the Powers, has no assurance of existence from morning till night. Under foreign economic domination we have just estimated that ten more years will see our downfall, and under the pressure of population growth abroad, our future is one of great danger.

These three disasters are already upon us. We ourselves must first know the facts, we must understand that these disasters are imminent, we must broadcast them until everyone realizes what a tragedy would be our nation's downfall and with what difficulty China will escape from the perils that encompass her. When we know all these facts, what shall we do? The proverb says, "The desperate beast can yet fight." When we are driven to no place of escape, then we have to rouse our energies to a life and death struggle with our enemies. These calamities are already upon us. Can we fight? Certainly we can fight. But to be able to fight we must believe that our death hour is near. If we want to advance nationalism we must first make our four hundred millions know that their death hour is at hand, then the beset beast will still turn and fight. Do our people on the point of death want to fight? Gentlemen, you are students, soldiers, statesmen; you are all men of foresight and vision. You must lead our four hundred millions to see that our race is in dire peril; and if our four hundred millions understand the danger, then it will not be difficult to revive our nationalism.

Foreigners are constantly saying that the Chinese are a "sheet of loose sand"; in the matter of national sentiment it is true. We have never had national unity. Have we had any other kind of unity? As I said before, China has had exceedingly compact family and clan groups and the family and clan sentiment of the Chinese is very deep-rooted. For instance, when two Chinese meet each other on the road, they will chat together and ask each other's "honorable surname" and "great name"; if they happen to find that they are of the same clan, they become wonderfully intimate and cordial and look upon each other as uncle or brother of the same family.

If this worthy clan sentiment could be expanded, we might develop nationalism out of clanism. If we are to recover our lost nationalism, we must have some kind of group unity, large group unity. An easy and successful way to bring about the unity of a large group is to build upon the foundation of small united groups, and the small units we can build upon in China are the clan groups and also the family groups. The "native place" sentiment of the Chinese is very deep-rooted, too; it is especially easy to unite those who are from the same province, prefecture, or village.

As I see it, if we take these two fine sentiments as a foundation, it will be easy to bring together the people of the whole country. But to reach the desired end, it will be necessary for all to coöperate; if we can secure this coöperation, it should be easier for Chinese to revive their nationalism than for people of other countries. For in the West the individual is the unit, and laws regarding the rights of parents and children, brothers and sisters, husbands and wives, aim at the protection of the individual; in lawsuits, no questions are asked about family conditions, only the morals of the individual are considered. The individual expands immediately into the state; between the individual and the state there is no common, firm, social unit. So in welding the citizens together into a state, foreign countries

do not have the advantage that China has.   Because
China lays emphasis upon the family as well as upon
the individual, the family head has to be consulted
on all matters, a system which some approve and
some criticize.   But I think that in the relation
between the citizens of China and their state, there
must first be family loyalty, then clan loyalty,
and finally national loyalty.   Such a system,
expanding step by step, will be orderly and
well regulated and the relationship between
the small and large social groups will be a real
one.   If we take the clans as our social units
and, after improving their internal organization,
join them together to form a state, our task will
naturally be easier than that of foreign countries
which make the individual the unit.   Where
the individual is the unit, there will be at
least millions of units in a country, four hundred
millions in China; the knitting together of such a
huge number of separate units would naturally
be very difficult.

But suppose we make the clan our unit : the
Chinese surnames are commonly said to be only a
hundred in number ; different ancestors have
sometimes been honored in the same clan and the
number of clans has increased, yet at most there
are not over four hundred to-day.   All within
the clan are collateral kindred ; each family is
constantly revising its genealogical record, pushing

back its ancestry tens and hundreds of generations to the age-long past. The names of the first ancestors were often changed from other names and but few search as far back as these original surnames. This custom of tracing the ancestral line back to its earliest sources is thousands of years old and firmly rooted in Chinese social life. Foreigners think the custom a useless one, but this idea of "reverencing ancestors and being kind to the clan" has been imbedded for millenniums in the Chinese mind. So a Chinese ignored the downfall of his country; he did not care who his emperor was, and all he had to do was to pay his grain tax. But if anything was said about the possible extinction of his clan, he would be in terror lest the ancestral continuity of blood and food be broken, and he would give his life to resist that. Those former family feuds in Kwangtung and Fukien all originated because of some small insult or attack upon the reputation or property of a family or upon one of its members; the members of the family would not begrudge any sacrifice of money or life if they could only give vent to their feelings for the honor of their name. Although the custom seems barbaric, yet there are good elements in it worth preserving. Suppose we could make these people see that foreign oppression is before their very eyes, that the race will soon perish and that the family will then not have a chance to survive. China's aborigines, the Miaos, the Yaos, and other tribes, have long ago broken the blood and food line with their ancestors; unless we can unite the strength of our clans and become a nation that can resist other nations, then some day our ancestors, as those of the Miaos and the Yaos, will have no blood descendants and no offerings.

We could then, in the first place, transform the clan struggles into a struggle against alien races and eliminate the savage feuds within the country; in the second place, we could use the clan's fear of extinction to unite our race easily and quickly and form a nation of great power. Let us take the clans as small foundations and work at building up the nation upon these. Suppose China has four hundred clans: it would be just as if we were working with four hundred individual people. We would make use of the original organization that each family name already has, and, in the name of the clan, begin to rally the people together, first in the neighborhood and prefecture, then in the province, and finally throughout the country, until each family name had become a large united group. For instance, if all members bearing the surname of Chen, using the original organization as a basis, would rally together all those who bore the same surname in their neighborhood and prefecture, then in the province, within two or three years, I think, the Chen clan would become a very large body. When every clan was so organized upon a very large scale, we would next unite the clans that had some connection with each other to form larger groups, and we would make every group know that great disasters threaten us, that our death hour is approaching, but that if we all combined we could become a great national union—the Republic of China—and that with such a union we need not fear outside adversaries or our inability to revive the state.

The History Classic says of the days of Yao: "He was able to demonstrate eminent virtue by loving the nine degrees of kindred; when these were on friendly terms, he pacified the hundred families; when they were enlightened, he united the myriad states; then the black-haired race entered upon an era of harmony." His work of peaceful government also began with the family, gradually extended among the people until all the little states were united and the black-haired race enjoyed a period of unity. Has he not set us a good example of how we may revive the state and oppose our enemies? If we start with our four hundred million individual citizens instead of with our four hundred clans, we will not know where of begin in consolidating the sheet of loose sand. Formerly, Japan united the interests of her feudal princes to form the great Yamato race, and the reason why Japan wanted to make use of these feudatories is just the reason why I am advocating the union of clan interests to form the Chinese nation.

If all our people know that they are oppressed citizens, that we have come to a time when we are simply up against it, that if we combine we must first organize the various clans into clan groups and then these clan groups into a great national union, we will have some positive methods with which to combat the foreigner. As it is, we cannot fight because we have no united group ; if we had, resistance would be easy. For example, India now is under the domination of Great Britain and is governed absolutely by the British. The Indian people have no way of resisting the political oppression, but they are meeting the economic oppression with Gandhi's policy of noncoöperation. What is noncoöperation ? The people of India will not furnish what the British need, and what the British furnish the Indians do not want. For instance, if a Britisher wants a laborer, the Indian will not work for him; the British offer the Indian people all kinds of goods, but the Indians will not use them and they use their own native products instead. When Gandhi's plan was first announced, the British thought it of no importance and so ignored Gandhi. But

after a long time noncoöperation societies began
to appear in numbers all over India and British
business was seriously affected. So the British
put Gandhi in prison. If we seek the reason why
India could get results from her noncoöperation
policy, we will find it in the ability of the people
of the whole country to put the policy into practice.
If India, which is already a subject country, can
put noncoöperation into effect, certainly in China,
which is not at the present moment destroyed,
the common people, though they may not easily
perform other tasks, can do such things as these —
refuse to work for foreigners, refuse to be foreign
slaves or to use foreign goods manufactured
abroad, push the use of native goods, decline to
use foreign bank notes, use only Chinese government money, and sever economic relations with
foreigners. The other problem of population
growth will be easily solved; China's population
has always been large and her resources abundant,
and our past oppression can be attributed to the
ignorance of the masses, who are "born in a stupor
and die in a dream." If our whole body of citizens can practice noncoöperation as the people of
India, if also we can realize a great national unity
upon the basis of our clan groups, no matter
what pressure foreign nations bring upon us —
military, economic, or population — we will not
fear. So the fundamental way to save China

from her imminent destruction is for us first to attain unity. If three or four hundred clan groups will take thought for the state, there will be a way out for us and, no matter what nation we face, we will be able to resist.

There are two ways of resisting a foreign power. The first is the positive way — arousing the national spirit, seeking solutions for the problems of democracy and livelihood, struggling against the power. The second way is the negative way — noncoöperation and passive resistance — whereby foreign imperialistic activity is weakened, the national standing is defended, and national destruction is averted.

February 24, 1924.

LECTURE 6

How restore the standing of the Chinese nation? — China's ancient greatness due above all to her high moral standards— China must recover and use the best in her past — China's ancient morality: Loyalty, Filial Devotion, Kindness, Love, Faithfulness, Justice, Harmony, and Peace—How they should be preserved — China's ancient learning, deep political philosophy — Poor impression which China makes on average foreigner due to Chinese lack of personal culture — Personal refinement and culture the heart of real knowledge — China's ancient powers and abilities — Chinese inventions: compass, printing, porcelain, gunpowder — Chinese discovery of tea, silk, suspension bridges, etc. — China must also learn the strong points of the West, scientific knowledge and methods — Only the best and most advanced science should be brought to China, e. g., electric rather than steam power— The hope for China's future—China's responsibility to weaker nations when she becomes strong — "Manifest the true spirit of our race."

Gentlemen: My subject to-day is: How can we restore the standing of our nation? In studying this question we must not forget what has been said in the previous lectures. What is the present standing of our nation? What is the situation of our nation and state in the world of to-day? A group of very thoughtful people spoken of as prophets and seers have said that China is now in the position of a "half-colony." But as I pointed out in my former study of the problem, China is far more than a "half-colony." Annam is France's colony and Korea is Japan's colony; if China were a half-colony her standing would be a bit above that of Annam and Korea, which have become complete colonies. But as a matter of fact, how does our position compare with Annam's and Korea's? According to my observation, China is a step lower than a complete colony, so I have invented a new title for her — "hypo-colony." My argument for this description was given with great thoroughness and I need not repeat it to-day.

What kind of position in the world did China occupy in ancient times? China was once an exceedingly powerful and civilized nation, the dominant state of the world, with a standing higher than that of the modern Great Powers — Great Britain, the United States, France, and Japan. Because China was once the sole Great Power of the world and because our forefathers once reached a position of such eminence, therefore I say that we are now not even a colony. Why did China once occupy so exalted a place and then "fall ten thousand feet in one drop"? The chief cause I have already discussed with you: because we lost our national spirit, our state has day by day degenerated. So if we want to restore our national standing, we must first revive our national spirit. If we want to revive our national spirit, we must fulfill two conditions. First, we must understand that we occupy to-day a most perilous position; and second, knowing our danger, we must utilize China's ancient social groups, as the family and the clan, and consolidate them to form a great national body. When this is accomplished and we have the strength of four hundred millions united to fight, no matter how low our present position we should be able to lift it up. So, to know and to unite are the two essentials for reviving our nationalism. When all of you have come to understand these essentials, you must proclaim them among the four hundred millions of the whole country until everybody understands them. Then we can begin to revive our lost national spirit. Our old national spirit is asleep; we must awake it and then our nationalism will begin to revive. When our nationalism is revived, we can go a step farther and study how to restore our national standing.

China did not reach her former position of greatness by one road only. Usually a nation becomes strong at first by the expansion of its military power, then by the development of various forms of culture; but if the nation and the state are to maintain a permanent standing, moral character is essential. Only by attaining a high standard of morality can the state hope to govern long and exist at peace. In former times, Asia had no stronger people than the Mongols. In the east they overthrew China; in the west they subjugated Europe. China in her day of greatest glory could not reach her arm beyond the west shore of the Caspian Sea and hardly to the east shore, so never touched Europe. But during the Mongol dynasty, almost all of Europe was swallowed up by the Mongols, who were thus stronger than the Chinese in their strongest days. Yet the Mongol dynasty did not last long, while the other dynasties, although not so strong as the Mongol, lasted very long. We find the reason in the moral standards of the former, which were below those of other dynasties. Because the character of the Chinese race was higher than that of other races, the Mongols, although they conquered China during the Sung dynasty, were later absorbed by the Chinese; and the Manchus, although China of the Ming dynasty fell twice before them, were assimilated by the Chinese. Because of the high moral standards of our race, we have been able not only to survive in spite of the downfall of the state, but we have had power to assimilate these outside races. So, coming to the root of the matter, if we want to restore our race's standing, besides uniting all into a great national body, we must first recover our ancient morality — then, and only then, can we plan how to attain again to the national position we once held.

As for China's old moral standards, they are not yet lost sight of by the people of China. First come Loyalty and Filial Devotion, then Kindness and Love, then Faithfulness and Justice, then Harmony and Peace. The Chinese still speak of these ancient qualities of character. But since our domination by alien races and since the invasion of foreign culture which has spread its influence all over China, a group intoxicated with the new culture have begun to reject the old morality, saying that the former makes the latter unnecessary. They do not understand that we ought to preserve what is good in our past and throw away only the bad. China now is in a period of conflict between old and new currents and a large number of our people have nothing to follow after.

A few days ago I was in the country and entered an ancestral temple. On going to the innermost court to rest, I saw on the right-hand side the character for "Filial Devotion," but on the left side a blank where there must have been previously, I think, the character for "Loyalty." [1] This I have seen more than once; many ancestral or family temples are in the same condition. But the character for "Filial Devotion," which I

[1] See note at end of chapter.

observed the other day, was extra large, while
the marks on the left wall where the character
had been scratched off looked very recent. It
may have been the work of the country folk
themselves or of soldiers living in the temple, yet
I have seen many ancestral temples which had
not been billets for soldiers with the character for
" Loyalty " rubbed off the walls. This shows
the thinking of a certain type of people to-day:
because we have a republic, we need not talk
about loyalty. They say that in former days
loyalty was shown to princes, and that as there
are no princes in a democracy so loyalty is not
needed and can be cast aside. Such an argument
is certainly due to misunderstanding: we do not
want princes in the country, but we cannot
do without loyalty. If we say that loyalty is
outworn to-day, what about the nation ? Can
we not direct our loyalty towards the nation ?
Of course we cannot now speak of loyalty to
princes, but how about loyalty to the people and
loyalty to our tasks ? When we undertake a
task we should not falter from first to last until
the task is done; if we do not succeed, we should
not begrudge our very lives as a sacrifice — this
is loyalty. The ancient teaching of loyalty
pushed to its limit meant death. To say that
ancient loyalty was due to kings and, since
now we have no kings, we do not need loyalty

and can do as we please, is absolutely wrong.
Now everybody who talks about democracy
breaks down all the old moral standards, and
the fundamental reason is right here. In a
democracy it stands to reason that we should still
show loyalty, not to princes but to the nation and
to the people. Loyalty to four hundred millions
must naturally be on a much higher level than
loyalty to one individual; so I say that the fine
moral quality of loyalty must still be cherished.

Filial Devotion is even more a characteristic of
China, and we have gone far beyond other nations
in the practice of it. Filial duty as revealed in
the "Canon of Filial Piety" covers almost the
whole field of human activity, touching every
point; there is no treatise on filial piety in any
civilized country to-day that is so complete. Filial
Devotion is still indispensable. If the people of the
democracy can carry out Loyalty and Filial Devotion to the limit, our state will naturally flourish.

Kindness and Love are also part of China's
high morality. In the past no one discussed love
better than Motze. His "love without discrimi-
nation" is the same thing as Jesus' "universal
love." The ancients applied the principle of love
to government, saying, "Love the people as your
children," and, "Be kind to all the people and
love all creatures." Love was used to embrace
all duties, from which we can see how well they

put kindness and love into effect. Since our foreign intercourse began, some people have thought that the Chinese ideal of kindness and love was inferior to the foreigners' because foreigners in China, by establishing schools and carrying on hospitals to teach and relieve the Chinese, have been, practicing kindness and love. In the practical expression of the fine qualities of kindness and love, it does seem as though China were far behind other countries, and the reason is that the Chinese have been less active in performance. Yet Kindness and Love are old qualities of Chinese character, and as we study other countries let us learn their practical methods, revive our own kindness and love, the spirit of ancient China, and make them shine with greater glory.

Faithfulness and Justice. Ancient China always spoke of Faithfulness in dealing with neighboring countries and in intercourse with friends. In my estimation, the quality of faithfulness is practiced better by Chinese than by foreigners. This can be seen in business intercourse: Chinese in their business relations do not use ̦written contracts; all that is necessary is a verbal promise which is implicitly trusted. Thus, when a foreigner places an order for goods with a Chinese, no contract is necessary; there is simply an entry on the books and the bargain is closed. But when a Chinese places an order with a foreigner, there must be a detailed contract; if there is no attorney or diplomatic officer at the place, the foreigner may follow the Chinese custom and simply enter the transaction in his books. But such cases are rare; a contract is nearly always required. Suppose two parties had agreed without a written contract on a certain price to be paid upon delivery of goods; if the sale price of the goods drops and he still takes the consignment, he will naturally lose money. For instance, if, when the order is placed, the price of the goods is clearly agreed upon as $10,000, but at the time of delivery the goods are worth only $5,000, $5,000 will be lost in accepting the consignment. Although, since at the beginning of the transaction there was no written contract, the Chinese might feel like refusing the consignment, yet for the sake of fulfilling his pledge, he would rather lose $5,000 than decline to pay. As a result, foreigners who have done business for a long time in the interior of China invariably speak highly of the Chinese, saying that a Chinese will keep his word better than a foreigner his contract. In Japan, however, although foreign business men always make contracts when they take orders, yet the Japanese are constantly breaking them. If, for example, when the order is placed, the price agreed upon is $10,000, but at the time of delivery the value of the goods has fallen to $5,000, in spite of the original contract, the Japanese will refuse to take the goods. Consequently, foreigners are constantly filing lawsuits against Japanese. Foreigners who have lived a long time in eastern Asia and have done business with both Chinese and Japanese all praise the Chinese but not the Japanese.

Justice. China in her mightiest days never utterly destroyed another state. Look at Korea, which was formerly a tributary of China in name, but an independent nation in reality. Twenty years ago Korea was still independent; it is only within the last ten years or more that she has lost her freedom. One day, about the time that the European War was raging most fiercely, I was talking with a Japanese friend about world problems, when Japan had just joined the Entente in their fight against Germany. My Japanese friend said that he himself did not approve of Japan's going to war against Germany, that he favored Japan's remaining neutral or joining Germany against the Entente. But he went on to say that since Japan and England were allies and had signed an international treaty, Japan had to be "faithful and just" and keep the agreement, sacrifice her own rights and take the side of the Entente. I immediately asked that Japanese gentlemen: "Did not China and Japan sign the Treaty of Shimonoseki, the most important provision of which was a guarantee of absolute independence to Korea ? Why is Japan willing to sacrifice her national rights to keep a treaty with England while with China she is faithless and breaks the Treaty of Shimonoseki ? The independence of Korea was proposed and demanded by Japan herself and effected by threats of force; now Japan is fat from eating her own words. What kind of faithfulness and justice do you call that?" Indeed, Japan advocates keeping her treaty with England but not with China because England is strong and China is weak. Japan's entry into the European War is because of fear of compulsion, not because of any "faithfulness" or "justice." China was a strong state for thousands of years and Korea lived on; Japan has been a strong state for not over twenty years and Korea is already destroyed. From this one can see that Japan's sense of "faithfulness and justice" is inferior to China's and that China's standards have advanced beyond those of other nations.

China has one more splendid virtue — the love of Harmony and Peace. Among the states and the peoples of the world to-day China alone preaches peace; other countries all talk in terms of war and advocate the overthrow of states by imperialism. Only in recent years, since the experience of many great wars and the huge, tragic death losses, have they begun to propose the abolition of war.

Several peace conferences have been held, such as the former Hague Conference, the Versailles Conference following the war, the Geneva Conference, the Washington Conference, and most recently the Lausanne Conference. But the representatives of the various nations have met to discuss peace out of fear of war, out of a feeling of necessity rather than out of a natural desire on the part of all citizens for peace. The intense love of peace which the Chinese have had these thousands of years has been a natural disposition. In individual relationships great stress has been laid upon "humility and deference"; in government the old saying was, "He who delights not in killing a man can unify all men." All of this is very different from the ideals of foreigners. China's ancient virtues of Loyalty, Filial Devotion, Kindness, Love, Faithfulness, and such are in their very nature superior to foreign virtues, but in the moral quality of Peace we will further surpass the people of other lands. This special characteristic is the spirit of our nation and we must not only cherish it but cause it to shine with greater luster; then our national standing will be restored.

We must revive not only our old morality but also our old learning. Since our subjugation by the Manchus our four hundred millions have been asleep, our ancient morality has been asleep, our ancient learning has been asleep. If we want to regain our national spirit we must reawaken the learning as well as the moral ideals which we once possessed. What is this ancient learning ? Among the human theories of the state, China's political philosophy holds a high place. We think that the states of Europe and America have made great strides forward in recent years, yet their new culture is not so complete as our old political philosophy. China has a specimen of political philosophy so systematic and so clear that nothing has been discovered or spoken by foreign statesmen to equal it. It is found in the "Great Learning": "Search into the nature of things, extend the boundaries of knowledge, make the purpose sincere, regulate the mind, cultivate personal virtue, rule the family, govern the state, pacify the world." This calls upon a man to develop from within outward, to begin with his inner nature and not cease until the world is at peace. Such a deep, all-embracing logic is not found in or spoken by any foreign political philosopher; it is a nugget of wisdom peculiar to China's philosophy of state and worthy to be preserved.

The principles of " regulating the mind, making sincere the purpose, cultivating personal virtue, ruling the family," naturally belong in the field of morals, but to-day it will be more fitting to treat them as matters of knowledge. While our forefathers exercised their powers on the moral

side, since the loss of our nationalism the true
spirit of learning has likewise disappeared. The
common people who study the classics constantly use the passage that I quoted in a conven-
tional way, but they repeat the words without
seeking their interpretation and with no idea of
their deeper meaning. The knowledge of how to
"regulate the mind and make sincere the purpose"
springs from inward control and is difficult to
expound. The scholars of the Sung period paid
much attention to this mental training, and as
we study their books we can see how well they
succeeded. But the "cultivation of personal
virtue, ruling the family, governing the state,"
are outward reforms which we have not yet effected; on the surface, at least, we have not succeeded in any of them for the past hundreds of
years. As a result, we cannot govern our own
country, and foreigners, seeing that we cannot
do so, want to come and establish international
control over us.

Why can we not govern China ? What reveals
the fact to foreigners ? In my personal opinion,
foreigners have no way of observing whether we
rule our families well or not, but they can see
that we are very much lacking in personal culture.
Every word and act of a Chinese shows absence
of refinement; one contact with Chinese people
is enough to reveal this. The ordinary foreigner's

impression of the Chinese is that they are uneducated and quite uncivilized. The only exceptions are foreigners who have lived twenty or thirty years in China or great philosophers like Bertrand Russell, who have a wide view of life, and who, as soon as they come to China, are able to discern that Chinese civilization is superior to European or American civilization and give China her due praise. The reason for this common impression of China is the little attention which Chinese pay to personal culture. We will not speak of big offenses; just in the words and acts of everyday life Chinese are too careless. When Chinese first began to go to the United States, the American people treated them as equals and made no distinction between Americans and Chinese. Later the large hotels all refused Chinese guests and the large restaurants would not admit Chinese to meals, simply because of the Chinese lack of refinement.

I was talking once with an American captain on a steamer. He told me about a Chinese minister on a previous passage of the same steamer who blew his nose and spit everywhere about the ship, even upon the costly rugs. Disgusting, indeed ! I asked the captain what he did about it. He replied, "I could not think of any plan except to take out my silk handkerchief before his face and wipe his spittle off the rug, but even that seemed hardly to draw his attention."

Such behavior as that of the Chinese minister is common among Chinese, and the incident shows how deficient we are in personal culture.

Confucius said, "If the mat is not straight, do not sit down," which shows how much attention he paid to personal culture, even to the minute details of sitting and standing. The Confucian scholars of the Sung age were even more careful and strict in "regulating the mind, making the purpose sincere, and cultivating the person," but modern Chinese hardly give these matters a thought. Why do the large dining rooms in foreign countries not admit Chinese? Someone has told of an incident which may explain it. It was just at the dinner hour; ladies and gentlemen of refinement were thronging the dining room and enjoying themselves, when suddenly a Chinese present noisily let off some gas. The foreigners scattered with exclamations of disgust, while the proprietor put the Chinese out. Since that experience no other Chinese has been allowed to eat in the dining room. Once, in Shanghai, a big Chinese merchant invited some foreigners to a feast and passed gas right at the table until the foreigners' faces were red with embarrassment. He not only did not check himself but even stood up and slapped his clothes, loudly saying, "Ee-s-ko-s me." Such behavior is uncivilized and vulgar in the extreme, yet even scholars and students are constantly guilty of it and reform is certainly difficult. Someone says that the habit, as noisy as possible, is good for the health; such a mistaken notion is all the more reprehensible. May the people of our country quickly do away with the bad habits as a first step in personal culture.

Then the Chinese love to leave their finger nails long, as much as an inch or more, without being trimmed, and consider it a mark of refinement. The French also have the custom of letting their nails grow, but only to the length of one or two tenths of an inch; they think this is an evidence that they are not rough laborers. Probably Chinese have the same idea. But a general objection to rough labor would be in direct opposition to the respect for labor which is a principle of our Kuomintang. Again, the Chinese have very yellow or black teeth and never wash or brush them clean — another great defect in the care of the person. All these bad habits can be regulated by simple, everyday personal culture, yet Chinese do not seem to care. As a result, although we have the wisdom about "cultivating personal virtue, regulating the family, governing the state, pacifying the world," as soon as foreigners meet us they say that we are barbaric and they will not study deeply into our learning. With the exception of philosophers like Russell,

no foreigners can at first sight of China understand her civilization, and only those who have
spent ten or more years in China can appreciate
her age-long culture. If everyone would devote
some systematic effort to the culture of his person,
"let the character within be manifested without,"
pay attention to even the smallest matters of
conduct, on meeting foreigners not rudely trespass
upon their freedom, then foreigners would certainly respect the Chinese. That is why I am
speaking to-day on personal culture. You young
men should certainly learn from the modern culture
of foreigners and first cultivate your own persons,
then you can talk about "ruling families and
governing the state." Government is progressing
in every other country to-day; in China it is going
backward. Why? Because we are under the
political and economic domination of foreign
nations, yes; but if we search for the fundamental
reason we will find it in the Chinese failure to
cultivate personal virtue. We seem to forget
that the ancients of China related personal culture back to "regulating the mind, making sincere the purpose, searching into the nature of
things, and extending the boundaries of knowledge." What discriminating teaching, what
comprehensive philosophy! And it is China's
ancient wisdom. If now we want to rule our
families and govern our state and not be subject

to foreign control, we must begin with personal culture, we must revive China's ancient wisdom and comprehensive philosophy, and then we can reawaken the spirit and restore the standing of the Chinese nation.

In addition to our ancient learning there are likewise our ancient powers. When Chinese to-day see the development of foreign machinery and the glorious progress of modern science, they naturally think that our ability is not equal to the ability of foreigners. But what about the capabilities of the Chinese thousands of years ago? In olden times the Chinese were much superior to foreigners. Some of the most valued things in the West to-day were invented in ancient China. Take, for example, the compass, which, in this great age of shipping, cannot be dispensed with for an hour or a moment; we find that it was invented by the Chinese millenniums ago. Chinese could not have invented the compass without some sort of ability, and that foreigners are still using what China used in the distant past shows that the Chinese ability is superior. There is another thing which occupies an extremely important place in civilization — the art of printing. The modern improved printing presses of the West can turn out tens of thousands of newspapers in an hour, yet the history of printing begins with early Chinese inventions. Take, again, porcelain

ware, which mankind uses daily, another invention
and special product of China; foreigners are still
trying to imitate it but cannot match its delicacy
and beauty. In modern wars smokeless powder
is used, yet this is only an improvement upon
the smoke-producing black gunpowder which was
invented by Chinese. These important and
valuable inventions — the compass, printing,
gunpowder — are known and used by Western
nations to-day and are reasons for their greatness.

In the field of human food and clothing, shelter
and communication, China has also contributed
many discoveries for the use of mankind. Take
beverages: China discovered the tea leaf, which
is one of the great necessities in the modern world;
civilized countries to-day compete in the use of
it and are making it a substitute for liquors.
Thus tea is helping in the eradication of the drink
evil and is bringing not a few other benefits to mankind. Take clothing: foreigners place the highest
value upon articles made of silk and wearers of silk
garments are daily increasing; the silkworm which
spins the silk was first found in China thousands of
years ago. Or shelter: the modern houses built
by foreigners are of course complete in every way,
but the principles of building and all the important
parts of the house were first devised by Chinese.
The arched doorway, for example, was introduced
earlier in China than anywhere else. Study

methods of communication: Westerners think that their suspension bridges are extremely modern engineering and the result of great native ability, but foreigners who visit the interior of China and reach the borders of Szechwan and Tibet see Chinese traversing high mountains and crossing deep rivers by means of suspension bridges. They then realize that the credit for inventing suspension bridges belongs to China and not to the West as they had thought. All this goes to show that ancient China was not without capabilities, but these powers were afterwards lost, and consequently our national position has declined. If we want to restore our former standing we must also revive our ancient powers.

But even if we succeed in reviving our ancient morality, learning, and powers, we will still not be able, in this modern world, to advance China to a first place among the nations. If we can reproduce the best of our national heritage just as it was in the time of our forefathers when China dominated the world, we will still need to learn the strong points of Europe and America before we can progress at an equal rate with them. Unless we do study the best from foreign countries, we will go backward. Will it be difficult or not for Chinese to learn from other countries? We have always thought that foreign machinery was intricate and that the operation of it was not easy to learn. In the West air flying is considered the most difficult manipulation of machinery and flying machines are among the most recent inventions, yet every day now we can see airplanes flying up from Tai Shatow.[1] And are not the pilots Chinese?

If Chinese can learn to fly, what other difficult things can we not learn? With our own fine foundation of knowledge and our age-long culture, with our own native intelligence besides, we should be able to acquire all the best things from abroad. The strongest point of the West is its science. This has been three hundred years in the course of development, but it has made rapid strides forward only within the last half century. The advance of science has made it possible for man to " usurp the powers of nature " and to do what natural forces had done.

The most recently discovered natural power is electricity. Formerly power was gotten from coal, which in turn generated machine power. Now Western science has advanced to the second age — the age of electricity. There is a tremendous project on foot in the United States to link up all the electrical horse power of the factories throughout the country into one unified system. Since there are thousands of factories, if each one has its own generating plant and burns its own coal to generate electric power, an enormous

[1] In Canton.

amount of coal and labor is used. Because of this heavy consumption of coal by the factories, the hundreds of thousands of miles of railroad are not sufficient to transport the needed fuel. The result is that the railways are too busy to move the agricultural products of the various sections, and these do not find the wide market they should. Since the use of coal has two such serious disadvantages, the United States is now considering a great central power station which would unite the electric power used by the thousands of factories into one system. If this super-power project succeeds, then all the generating equipment of the thousands of factories can be consolidated into one central plant. The individual factory will not need to use coal and a lot of laborers to feed the fires; all it will need to carry on its work will be a copper wire to conduct the power. The advantages of this plan may be illustrated by the hundreds of people gathered in this lecture hall. If each one of us should have a small stove to cook a meal here, it would be troublesome and wasteful, but if all joined together and cooked a meal on a big stove, we would find it much more convenient and economical. The United States is just now considering this scheme of linking together all its factories in one great electric power system; if China wants to learn the strong points of the West, she should not start with coal power but with electricity, and give a single, great motive power to the whole country. This way of learning may be compared to what military men call a frontal attack, "intercepting and striking at the advance force." If we can learn from the advance guard, within ten years we may not be ahead of other nations, but we will be keeping step with them.

If we want to learn from the West, we will have to catch up with the advance line and not chase from behind. In the study of science, for instance, this will mean the saving of two hundred years. We are in such a position to-day that if we should still slumber on, not commence to struggle, and not know how to restore the standing of our state, our country would be lost and our race wiped out forever. But now that we know how, we ought to follow the world currents and study the best features of Western nations; we certainly should go beyond other countries in what we study and cause the "last to be first." Although we went backward for many centuries, yet now it should take us but a few years to catch up with the rest of the world. Japan is a good example. Her culture was formerly copied from China and was much inferior to ours, but recently Japan has studied only European and American civilization, and within a few decades has become one of the world's great powers. I do not think that our intellectual powers are below those of the Japanese, and it should be easier for us now than for Japan to learn from the West. So the next ten years is a critical period for us; if we can come to life as the Japanese did and all put forth a very sincere effort to elevate the standing of our nation, within a decade we should be able to get rid of foreign political and economic control, the pressure of foreign population increase, and all the various calamities that are now upon us. Japan studied from the West for only a few decades and became one of the world's great powers. But China has ten times the population and thirty times the area of Japan, and her resources are much larger than Japan's. If China reaches the standard of Japan, she will be equal to ten great powers. At present there are only five great powers — Great Britain, the United States, France, Japan, and Italy — and when Germany and Russia recover there will be only six or seven. If China gets only as far as Japan, she will have the strength of ten powers in her one state, and will then be able to recover her predominant national position.

After China reaches that place, what then? A common phrase in ancient China was, "Rescue the weak, lift up the fallen." Because of this noble policy China prospered for thousands of years, and Annam, Burma, Korea, Siam, and other small states were able ot maintain their

independence.   As European influence spread over
the East, Annam was overthrown by France, Burma
by Great Britain, Korea by Japan.   If we want
China to rise to power, we must not only restore
our national standing, but we must also assume
a great responsibility towards the world.   If China
cannot assume that responsibility, she will be a
great disadvantage not an advantage to the world,
no matter how strong she may be.   What really is
our duty to the world ?   The road which the Great
Powers are traveling to-day means the destruction of other states; if China, when she becomes
strong, wants to crush other countries, copy the
Powers' imperialism, and go their road, we will
just be following in their tracks.   Let us first of
all decide on our policy.   Only if we "rescue the
weak and lift up the fallen" will we be carrying
out the divine obligation of our nation.   We must
aid the weaker and smaller peoples and oppose the
great powers of the world.   If all the people of the
country resolve upon this purpose, our nation will
prosper; otherwise, there is no hope for us.   Let
us to-day, before China's development begins,
pledge ourselves to lift up the fallen and to aid
the weak; then when we become strong and look
back upon our own sufferings under the political
and economic domination of the Powers and see
weaker and smaller peoples undergoing similar
treatment, we will rise and smite that imperialism.

Then will we be truly "governing the state and pacifying the world."

If we want to be able to reach this ideal in the future, we must now revive our national spirit, recover our national standing, unify the world upon the foundation of our ancient morality and love of peace, and bring about a universal rule of equality and fraternity. This is the great responsibility which devolves upon our four hundred millions. You, gentlemen, are a part of our four hundred millions; you must all shoulder this responsibility and manifest the true spirit of our nation.

March 2, 1924.

Note to page 126. Filial Devotion, *hsiao*, and loyalty, *chung*, are constantly associated, being considered attributes of the same virtue. When manifested in the relationship between father and son, it is *hsiao;* when manifested in the relationship between emperor and officers, it is *chung*.

PART II

THE PRINCIPLE OF DEMOCRACY

THE PRINCIPLE OF DEMOCRACY

LECTURE 1

Definition of "people" and of "sovereignty"— Functions of sovereignty: protection and sustenance — Periods in human history: First, the age of wilderness, struggle of man with beast—Evolutionary theory of origin of universe and man— Geological contributions to ancient history — Second period: struggle of man with nature — Rise of civilization in favored regions — Early Chinese civilization in Yellow River valley — Theocracy — Third period: struggle of man with man, rise of autocracies — Modern period of struggle within states, rise of democracy — Is China ready for democracy? — Democratic ideas in ancient China — China must follow modern world tendencies — The struggle for democracy in the West — Cromwell's Commonwealth — American and French revolutions — Rousseau's false theory of "natural rights" of man — Facts must precede theory — The continual struggle for imperial power in Chinese history — Democracy the only remedy—Failure of Taiping Rebellion because of rivalries for power — Selfish opposition of Ch'en Ch'iung-ming and other military leaders to the Chinese Revolution.

Gentlemen: To-day I am opening the discussion of the People's Sovereignty. What is the People's Sovereignty? In order to define this term we must first understand what a " people " is. Any unified and organized body of men is called a " people." What is " sovereignty " ? It is power and authority extended to the area of the state. The states with the greatest power to-day are called in Chinese the "strong states," in foreign languages the "powers." Mechanical force is spoken of in Chinese as "horse strength," in other languages as "horse power." Thus strength and power are used interchangeably. The power to execute orders and to regulate public conduct is called "sovereignty," and when "people" and "sovereignty" are linked together, we have the political power of the people. To understand "political power" we must know what government is. Many people think that government is a very abstruse and difficult subject which ordinary persons cannot comprehend. Chinese military men are always saying, "We are soldiers and know nothing about politics." The reason why they are ignorant is because they consider government to be a deep and abstruse study. They do not know that it is a very clear and comprehensible thing. If military men say that they will not interfere with government, we can let them by; but if they say that they cannot understand government, they are foolish. Since the soldier is the driving force behind the government, he should certainly understand what government is. Briefly, government is a thing of the people and by the people; it is control of the affairs of all the people. The power of control is political sovereignty

and where the people control the government
we speak of the "people's sovereignty."

Now that we understand what the "people's
sovereignty" is, we must study its functions.
As we view life about us or study into the distant
past, we see that human power has been employed,
to put it simply, in maintaining the existence
of the human race. In order to exist, mankind
must have protection and sustenance and it is
daily engaged in meeting these two great needs.
Protection means self-defense : whether it is an
individual or a group or a state, the power of
self-defense is necessary to existence. Sustenance
means seeking food. Self-defense and food-
seeking are, then, the two chief means by which
mankind maintains its existence. But while man
is maintaining his existence, other animals are
also trying to maintain theirs; while man is
defending himself, other animals are also defending themselves; while man seeks food, other
animals are also seeking food; and so the protection
and the sustenance of man comes into conflict with
the protection and the sustenance of other animals,
and struggle ensues. To keep alive in the midst
of struggle man must fight, and so mankind has
not ceased to fight since the beginning of human
life. Thus the human race has used its strength
in combat, and since its birth upon the planet
until now has lived in the thick of strife.

This struggle of the human race may be divided into several periods. The first was the period of primeval and universal wilderness before the dawn of human history. We do not know how long that period was, but in recent times geologists have found, as they studied the rock strata, fossils of human beings in rocks not over two million years old. Rocks earlier than this age bear no human traces. The average man thinks of events several million years ago as being exceedingly vague and uncertain, but with the advance of modern geological science, geologists can now distinguish many different strata of rock, each representing so many generations, and can tell which strata belong to an early age and which are most recent, describing the various geological periods by their rocks. To us two million years seems a long time, but to the geologists it is a brief period. There are many rock layers which date back further than two million years, but there is no data for the study of the earth's history before the formation of rock. The general theory is that before the rocks there was a kind of liquid material, and before that some sort of gaseous matter. According to evolutionary philosophy, the earth was originally a gaseous body and part of the sun; in the beginning the sun and gaseous bodies formed a nebula in space; when the sun began to contract, many gaseous bodies broke off from it, which finally condensed into liquid bodies and from liquid bodies solidified into rock. The oldest rocks go back tens of millions of years; geologists now have definite evidence of rocks twenty million years of age, so they estimate that the condensation of vapor into liquid must have taken tens of millions of years; and the solidification of the liquid into rocks must have taken a similar length of time. From the earliest formed rocks to the present time is a period of at least twenty million years. Because we have no written record of this period it seems very long ago to us, but geologists think of it as a comparatively recent age.

What is the connection of all this geology with our subject to-day ? From the origin of the earth we can deduce the origin of man. The geologist has found that the history of man is within the last two million years, and that it was only two hundred thousand years ago that human civilization was born. Before that time man differed little from the animals, so philosophers say that man has evolved from animals and was not suddenly created. Man and all living beings have in these two hundred thousand years gone through a process of gradual evolution to form our present world. What age have we now reached ? The age of the people's power, the age of democracy.

While the germs of democracy were found in Greece and Rome two thousand years ago, yet only within the last one hundred fifty years has democracy become firmly rooted in the world. The preceding age was one of autocracy and the age before that one of theocracy. Before theocracy came the wilderness age when men fought with beasts. Man sought to live and the animal sought to live. Man had two ways of preserving his existence — through seeking food and through self-defense. In very ancient times men ate beasts and beasts also ate men; there was a constant struggle between them. The land was covered with venomous snakes and wild animals; man was beset by dangers and so had to fight for his very life. The warfare of that day was the irregular conflict between man and beast; there was no banding into groups, it was "each fighting for himself."

As to the orginial birthplace of man, some say that the human species originated in only a few places, but geologists assert that after man once appeared on the globe he was to be found everywhere, because no matter where we dig down we find some human relic. The struggle between man and the savage creatures has not yet ceased; if we go now to the uncultivated islands of Malaysia we will find this warfare still going on. If we penetrate into the wild mountains or go out into the great deserts, where no man and no smoke is to be seen, we can picture the environment which men and animals had in those old ages. The reason, then, why we can bring to light the history of the dim past is because we have found these human traces and relics; without these we could not possibly know anything that happened.

The usual method of studying events of the past is by reading history, but history is a written record and there is no history of civilization before the invention of writing. China has not more than five or six thousand years of recorded history; and Egypt, not more than ten thousand years. In the study of all kinds of knowledge China has depended solely upon books; but foreign countries do otherwise. Their pupils of the primary and secondary schools study from books, but university students make use also of actual investigation, and from rocks, animals, and the life of savage races as well as from books, they infer what kind of society our forefathers had. For instance, the observation of savage races in Africa or Malaysia helps us to know what were the conditions of ancient uncivilized man. So modern scientific students do not rely merely upon books in their researches, and the books which they put out themselves are the fruit of the investigating mind and but contributions towards our record

of the human race. Two methods of investigation
are used — observation, or the scientific method;
and judgment, or the philosophic method. The
principles of human evolution have been worked
out by these two methods. In the primitive
struggle between man and wild beasts, man used
only his individual physical strength or sometimes
the species would fight together; if, for instance,
in one place a few score men were battling with
a few score beasts, and in another place, another
group of men were doing the same thing, the men
of both places might perceive their own kinship
to each other and their difference from the animals, unite as fellow creatures, and fight together
against the other species. Certainly man would
not join with another species to fight and devour
man and injure his own kind. Such a banding
together of the species and unwitting alliance
against reptiles and beasts was a natural, not
an artificial thing; when the reptiles or beasts
were destroyed the men scattered. At that time
there was no such thing as popular sovereignty;
man, in fighting the animals, used simply his own
physical prowess and not any kind of authority.
It was an age of brute force.

Later, when man had about exterminated the
venomous reptiles and savage beasts, when his
environment was somewhat improved, and his
dwelling place was better suited to his type of

existence, then groups of people began to live in one place and to domesticate the tamer animals. This was the beginning of the pastoral age and also of civilization. The people of that time lived about like the Mongolians or Arabs in southwest Asia to-day, who are still in the pastoral stage. A great change now took place in man's living conditions: warfare with animals was about at an end, civilization was growing up, what we call the ancient period of human history had arrived. Man began to direct his warfare against the forces of Nature. Briefly, in the first stage man warred with beasts and employed his own brute force or the united strength of many to kill them off; in the second stage man warred with Nature. In the first stage, because man did not know when an animal would attack him, he was not sure whether he could live from one moment to another; he had only his two hands and two feet for self-defense, but he was wiser than the beasts and learned to use sticks and stones for weapons, so finally he won a complete victory over his wild enemies. Only then could man plan ahead for a day; while he was battling with the beasts his life was not secure for a moment.

When wild beasts no longer threatened, the human race began to multiply and the most favorable spots on the earth began to fill up with people. What were the favorable spots? — Places sheltered from wind and rain or regions which storms did not touch, such as the valleys of the Nile and Mesopotamia in Asia. Here the soil was exceedingly fertile and it hardly rained during the four seasons. The waters of the Nile rose once a year and as they receded rich alluvium was deposited on both banks of the river. Cultivation was easy and grain and rice grew in profusion. But only in the Nile valley and in Mesopotamia were such regions to be found, so it is commonly said that the Nile valley and Mesopotamia were cradles of the world's civilization. Because of the fertility of these two valleys and their freedom from storm and rain all the year round, which made cultivation of the soil and flock raising easy, and because of the abundant animal life in the rivers, living there was easy. Without much mental and physical labor men idly passed their days and their descendants quickly multiplied. When the race became too prosperous, there were not enough choice situations to go around and some people had to move to places not quite so favorable, where they were threatened by natural disaster like storms and floods.

The valley of the Yellow River was the cradle of Chinese civilization. Since this region is afflicted with storm and flood and is also very cold, since it would not naturally be the place to give birth to a civilization, how did China's

ancient civilization happen to originate there ?
Because the dwellers upon the Yellow River
banks came from other regions, such as, perhaps,
Mesopotamia, whose civilization antedated China's
by more then ten thousand years. Before the
time of the Three Emperors and the Five Kings
these progenitors of the Chinese race moved out
of Mesopotamia into the Yellow River valley
and began to develop the civilization of China.
After driving out the poisonous reptiles and
savage beasts they were faced with natural
disasters of storm and flood. Naturally they
would try to avert these disasters and to struggle
against Nature. As protection against wind and
rain, they had to build houses; as protection
against cold they had to make clothes; when
man had learned to do these things he was far
advanced in civilization. But natural calamities
did not come at regular times nor were they
easily prevented: a storm would blow their
houses down, a flood would overwhelm them,
a fire would burn them to the ground, or a stroke
of lightning would demolish them. These four
disasters — flood, fire, storm, and lightning —
the ancients could not understand. Their houses,
moreover, were constructed of grass and wood and
could not stand up against such catastrophes, so
there was no way of preventing their destruction.
In the age of warfare with the beasts man could

use his own physical strength to fight, but mere fighting was of no value in the day of struggle against Nature. Mankind then suffered many hardships until some wise men came forth with schemes for the welfare of the people. Thus the Great Yü [1] reduced the waters to order and averted the calamity of flood for the people, and Yu Ch'ao Shih (the Nest Builder) [1] taught the people how to build houses in trees and avert the disasters from wind and storm.

From this time on civilization slowly progressed, the people began to unite, and, as land was plentiful and the inhabitants were few, food was very easy to procure. The only problems were the catastrophes of Nature which could not be fought, as the wild beasts were, with bodily strength, and so there arose the idea of divine power. Men of deep wisdom began to advocate the doctrine of gods and divine teachings, and introduced prayers as a means of warding off evil and obtaining blessings. There was no way of telling at the time whether their praying was effective or not; however, since they were struggling against Heaven they had no other plan, when in extremity, but to appeal for the power of the gods. A man of profound insight would be chosen as leader, like the chiefs of savage tribes

[1] Legendary rulers of ancient Chinese history.

in Africa to-day, whose special duty it was to offer prayers. In the same way Mongolians and Tibetans now make a "Living Buddha" their ruler and are under a religious government. So the ancients used to say that the two great functions of the state were worship and war, praying and fighting.

The Republic of China has been established now for thirteen years; we have overthrown the monarchy and given up autocracy. Japan is even yet a monarchy and worships its gods; the Japanese give their emperor the title of *Tenno* ("Heavenly King"). We used to speak of the emperor of China as the "Son of Heaven" in the days when we still clung to theocracy, although autocracy had long before begun to flourish. The Japanese emperor was deposed several hundred years ago by the Bushi, but when the Meiji Restoration took place sixty years ago and the Tokugawa was overthrown, the "Heavenly King" was restored. So Japan is still both an autocratic and a theocratic state. Formerly, the Roman emperor was also the religious head of his state; when Rome fell and the emperor was deposed, the city lost its political power. Its religious authority was maintained, however, and people of all nations still pay homage to the Pope in Rome, just as the various states in the time of the *Spring and Autumn Annals* did reverence to the Chou dynasty.

Thus after the age of warfare with wild animals came the struggles with Nature and out of these struggles was born theocracy. The next step in history was autocracy, when mighty warriors and political leaders wrested the power away from the religious rulers or put themselves at the head of the churches and appointed themselves kings. A period of struggle between man and man thus evolved. When struggles between man and man began to take the place of struggles with Nature, people realized that simple dependence upon the power of religious faith could neither protect society nor aid in warfare and that an enlightened government and strong military power were necessary in order to compete with other peoples. Men have fought against men since the beginning of recorded history. At first they employed both the power of religion and the power of autocracy in their struggles; later, as theocracy weakened and, after the dissolution of the Roman Empire, gradually decayed, autocracy became stronger until, in the reign of Louis XIV of France, it reached the peak of its power. Louis XIV said that there was no difference between the king and the state — " I am the king, therefore I am the state." He took every power of the state into his own hands and exercised despotism to its limits, just as did Ch'in Shih Hwang of

China.[1] The absolute monarchy became more terrible every day until the people could bear it no longer. About this time science was beginning to make steady progress and the general intelligence of mankind was steadily rising. As a result, a new consciousness was born. The people saw that autocracy was something that only grasped for power, made private property of the state and of the people, contributed to the gratification of one individual and did not care about the sufferings of the many; as it became unbearable they realized with increasing clearness that, since the system was iniquitous, they should resist it, and that resistance meant revolution. So, during the last hundred years, the tides of revolutionary thought have run high and have given rise to democratic revolutions, struggles between people and kings.

This division into periods will help us in studying the origins of democracy. Summing up: the first period was one of struggle between man and beast in which man employed physical strength rather than any kind of power; in the second period man fought with Nature and called divine powers to his aid; in the third period, men came into conflict with men, states with states, races with races, and autocratic power was the chief

---

[1] Despot who united China and founded the Ch'in dynasty, 255 B.C.

weapon. We are now in the fourth period, of war within states, when the people are battling against their monarchs and kings. The issue now is between good and evil, between right and might, and as the power of the people is steadily increasing we may call this the age of the people's sovereignty — the age of democracy. This is a very new age. We have only recently entered upon it and overthrown the autocracy of the old age.

Is the change a good thing or not? When the masses were unenlightened and depended upon sacred kings and virtuous sages to lead them, autocracy was of considerable value. Before autocracies arose, holy men founded religion upon the way of the gods in order to conserve social values; at that time theocracy rendered a large service. But now autocracy and theocracy are things of the past and we have come to the age of democracy, the age of the people's power. Is there any just reason why we should oppose autocracy and insist upon democracy? Yes, because with the rapid advance of civilization people are growing in intelligence and developing a new consciousness of self, just as we, who as children wanted our parents to support us, cannot depend upon them further but must be independent when we grow up to manhood and seek our own living. Yet there are

intellectuals to-day who still defend autocracy
and decry democracy; Japan has many such,
Europe and America too.   Many old scholars in
China are still monarchists, and we have a group
of old officials who are even to-day advocating
the restoration of the emperor and the return to
monarchical government.   With part of our educated class supporting autocracy and another part
supporting democracy, no wonder our government
is still not settled.   We are advocating a democratic government, so we should make a study
of democracy as it exists in various countries of
the world.

From two hundred thousand years up to ten
or more thousand years ago, mankind lived under
theocracy, and theocracy was well suited to the
needs of the age.   If any attempt should now
be made in Tibet to substitute a king for the
church head there, the people would certainly
rise in revolt; because of their faith in the head
of the church, they have made the Living Buddha
their ruler, respecting his authority and obeying
his commands.   The situation in Europe was a
similar one a thousand or more years ago.   Chinese
culture flowered earlier than European culture,
so we have had more autocracy than theocracy;
the age of autocracy began long ago in China.
But even the word democracy — popular sovereignty — has only lately been introduced into

China. All of you who have come here to-day
to support my revolution are naturally believers
in democracy. Those old officials who want
to restore the monarchy and become emperor are
naturally opponents of democracy and believers
in autocracy. Which, autocracy or democracy,
is really better suited to modern China? This
is a question worthy of serious study. Fundamentally, both are methods of administering
government and of carrying on the affairs of state
for all the people, but as political conditions
vary in each age, so methods of government must
also vary.

The essential question is this: Is China to-day
ripe for democracy? There are some who say
that the standards of the Chinese people are too
low and that they are not ready for popular
government. Although the United States is
a democratic state, yet when Yüan Shih-kai was
trying to become emperor, an American professor
named Goodnow[1] came to China to advise a
monarchical form of government, saying that
the Chinese people were not progressive in their
thinking, that their culture was behind that of
Europe and America, and so they should not
attempt a democracy. Yüan Shih-kai made good
use of these arguments of Goodnow and overthrew
the republic, making himself emperor. Now if

[1] Dr. Frank J. Goodnow, of Johns Hopkins University.

we are going to advocate democracy for China, we should understand very clearly what it means. China from the beginning of her history has never put democracy into practice; even in the last thirteen years we have not had democracy. In all these four thousand years, through periods of order and of disorder, China has seen nothing but autocracy. If we ask history whether autocracy has really been a good thing for China or not, we find that its effects have been about half advantageous and half disadvantageous. But if we base our judgment upon the intelligence and the ability of the Chinese people, we come to the conclusion that the sovereignty of the people would be far more suitable for us. Confucius and Mencius two thousand years ago spoke for people's rights. Confucius said, "When the Great Doctrine prevails, all under heaven will work for the common good." [1] He was pleading for a free and fraternal world in which the people would rule. He was constantly referring to Yao and Shun simply because they did not try to monopolize the empire. Although their government was autocratic in name, yet in reality they gave the people power and so were highly reverenced by Confucius. Mencius said, "Most precious are the people; next come the spirits of land and grain; and last, the princes." Again: "Heaven sees as the

[1] 天下爲公, *t'ien hsia wei kung.*

people see, Heaven hears as the people hear," and "I have heard of the punishment of the tyrant Chou[1] but never of the assassination of a sovereign." He, in his age, already saw that kings were not absolutely necessary and would not last forever, so he called those who brought happiness to the people holy monarchs, but those who were cruel and unprincipled he called individualists whom all should oppose. Thus China more than two millenniums ago had already considered the idea of democracy, but at that time she could not put it into operation. Democracy was then what foreigners call a Utopia, an ideal which could not be immediately realized.

Because foreigners have received a poor impression of the Chinese and look down upon them as they would upon savages of Africa or of the South Seas, they express strong disapproval when Chinese talk to them about democracy. What right, they think, has China to talk about democracy at the same time with Europe and America ? This mistaken viewpoint comes from the fact that foreign scholars have not studied deeply into our history or into the conditions of our country, and do not really know whether China is ready for democracy or not. Even returned students from Europe and America

[1] Last ruler of the Shang or Yin dynasty which fell 1122 B.C. A cruel tyrant condemned by all Chinese historians.

have taken up the foreign tune about China not being fit for democracy. Such views are utterly misleading. As I read history, I find China making progress long before Europe and America and engaging in discussion of democracy thousands of years in the past. The democratic ideas appeared, it is true, only in theoretical discourses and did not develop into reality. Now that Europe and America have founded republics and have applied democracy for one hundred fifty years, we whose ancients dreamed of these things should certainly follow the tide of world events and make use of the people's power if we expect our state to rule long and peacefully and our people to enjoy happiness. But the rise of democracy is comparatively recent and many states in the world are still autocratic; those which have tried democracy have experienced many disappointments and failures. While democracy was discoursed upon in China two thousand years ago, it has become an accomplished fact for only one hundred fifty years in the West. Now it is suddenly spreading over the whole world on the wings of the wind.

The first instance of actual democracy in modern times was in England. A revolution of the people took place about the time of the close of the Ming dynasty and the beginning of the Manchu dynasty in China, under a leader named Cromwell, which resulted in the execution of King Charles I. This deed sent a thrill of horror through the people of Europe and America, who had never heard of the like in the world before and who thought that those responsible should be treated as traitors and rebels. The secret assassination of princes was common in every country, but Cromwell's execution of Charles I was not done in secret; the king was given a public trial and openly proclaimed guilty of disloyalty to the state and to the people, and so guilty of death. Europe thought that the English people would defend the rights of the people, and give a great impetus to democracy, but, to the surprise of all, the English preferred autocracy to democracy; although Charles I was dead, they continued to long for a king. Within less than ten years the restoration of the monarchy had taken place and Charles II was welcomed back as king. This happened just at the time when the Manchus were entering the Great Wall, before the downfall of the Mings, not much further back than two hundred or more years. Something over two centuries ago, England had this one period of democratic government, but it soon collapsed and autocracy again held sway.

A hundred years later the American Revolution took place when the colonies broke away from England and declared independence, forming the

federal government of the United States of
America. This state, which has now existed
for one hundred fifty years, was the first in the
modern world to carry out the principles of
democracy. Ten years after the establishment
of the American Republic, the French Revolution
was precipitated. The situation at the time
of the French Revolution was like this: Since
Louis XIV had seized all the power of the state
and exercised absolute despotism, the people
of France had suffered untold miseries; when
his heirs displayed an even greater cruelty and
wickedness, the people were goaded beyond
endurance and started to revolt. They killed
Louis XVI just as the English had killed Charles
I, after giving him a public trial and proclaiming
his disloyalty to the state and to the people.
But then all the other states of Europe arose to
avenge the death of the French king and war
was fought for over ten years, with the result
that the revolution failed and monarchy lifted
its head once more. From this time on, however,
democratic ideas flourished all the more among
the French people.

Everyone who discusses the history of democracy knows about the French philosopher Rousseau, who advocated popular rights in an extreme
form and whose democratic theories generated the
French Revolution. Rousseau's most important

work out of his lifelong thinking and writing upon democracy was his *Social Contract*. The idea upon which the book is built is this : Man is born with rights of freedom and equality, rights which were endowed by Nature but which he has thrown away. According to his theory, the people are given their sovereign rights by Nature; but, as we study the evolution of history, we see that democracy has not been Heaven-born but has been wrought out of the conditions of the times and the movement of events. We can find no facts in the evolution of the race to bear out Rousseau's philosophy, which, consequently, lacks foundation. Opponents of democracy take Rousseau's unfounded arguments as material for their case, but we who believe in democracy do not need to start with discussions about it; universal principles are all based first upon fact and then upon theory; theory does not precede fact.

Take, for example, the science of infantry tactics which has now become a systematized study. Did it begin with certain doctrines or with certain facts ? Modern military men say that you must enter a military school and study military science before you can go out to fight for your country, which seems to be putting theory before fact. But as we study the progress of the world, we find primitive man fighting with

the animals for a million or so years before he was
able to eliminate the venomous reptile and wild
beast.   Did the men of that time have any military science ?   They may have had, but since
they kept no written records, we have no way of
studying it.   Then, for two hundred thousand
or more years, men fought against each other and
country against country; since there was still no
recorded history we have no way of knowing how
many wars mankind passed through.   From
Chinese history, we find that the military writings
of two thousand years ago made up thirteen
books.   These books explained the principles of
warfare which were known at that time, and out
of them developed China's military philosophy.
As we look at these thirteen books, we realize
that actual warfare certainly preceded the writing
of them.

Modern military science is also based upon the
military experience of the past, together with the
advances which have been made steadily ever since.
Since the recent invention of smokeless powder, the
art of warfare has undergone a great transforma-
tion.   Formerly, when soldiers saw the enemy, they
would advance upon them in one even line after
another; in modern warfare troops who sight the
enemy immediately lie upon the ground to fire.
Is the use of smokeless rifles the real reason why
we lie down to fire?   Does the fact, the experience,

precede the book about it, or does the book precede the fact? The deploying of troops, shooting from a recumbent position, and such military methods in foreign countries date from the time of the Boer War in Africa. The British soldiers in fighting the Boers marched against them by columns, while the Boers lay on the ground; as a result the British suffered terrific losses. The art of fighting from the ground began with these Boers. When they originally migrated from Holland to Africa, they numbered only three hundred thousand and had to fight against the natives. When the Boers first arrived, they were at a great disadvantage because the natives fought them from a prone position; they then learned the methods of the natives. When the British fought against the Boers, they suffered greatly. The British troops then learned the Boer tactics and, when they returned to England, taught the whole army. The world learned from England and now every country employs the new method in its military science. This shows clearly that facts and experience give rise to theory and that theory does not come first.

The theory in Rousseau's *Social Contract* that the rights and the powers of the people are bestowed by Nature is fundamentally in conflict with the principle of historical evolution, and so the enemies of democracy have used Rousseau's unsound argument to stop the mouths of the supporters of democracy. Rousseau's idea that democracy is naturally endowed was unreasonable, but for opponents to use one false conclusion of his as an argument against all democracy is just as unreasonable. When we are studying the truths of the universe, we must begin by investigating the facts and not depend merely upon the treatises of scholars. Why, if Rousseau's philosophy was not based upon fact, did all the peoples welcome it? And how was Rousseau able to produce such a treatise? He saw the power of the people rising into a flood and espoused the people's sovereignty; his democratic proposals suited the psychology of the time and made the masses welcome him. So, although his theory of democracy conflicted with the principles of historical progress, the spirit of democracy which was already coming to be a reality in the life of his day caused him to be warmly received in spite of his faulty arguments. And it may be added that Rousseau's advocacy of the original idea of democracy was one of the greatest contributions to government in all history.

Since the beginning of human history, the kind of power which government has wielded has inevitably varied according to the circumstances and tendencies of the age. In an age which reverenced gods, theocratic power had to be used;

in an age of princes autocratic power had to be used. We may say that Chinese autocracy reached its limit in the reign of Ch'in Shih Hwang, yet later kings still tried to imitate him and no matter how much power the monarchy wielded, the people gladly assented. But now the currents of the world's life have swept into the age of democracy and it behooves us quickly to study what democracy means. Because some of the treatises upon democracy, such as Rousseau's *Social Contract,* have been a bit inconsistent with true principles, is no reason why we should oppose all that is good in democracy as well. Nor must we think that democracy is impracticable because the monarchy was restored after Cromwell's revolution in England or because the revolution stretched out for so long a time in France. The French Revolution lasted eighty years before it succeeded. The American Revolution accomplished its aims in eight years, but England after two hundred years of revolution still has a king. But if we observe the steady progress of the world from many angles, we are assured that the day of democracy is here; and that, no matter what disappointments and defeats democracy may meet, it will maintain itself for a long time to come upon the earth.

Thirty years ago, therefore, we fellow revolutionists firmly resolved that, if we wanted China to be strong and our revolution to be effective, we must espouse the cause of democracy. But in those days merely to make such a suggestion stirred up opposition not only from Chinese but also from foreigners. When the Chinese revolutionary movement was in its initial stages, the world still had some powerful despots who united in one person the supreme power of the state, such as the czar of Russia, and other despots who had brought mighty armies and navies under their single command, such as the emperors of Germany and Austria. With such strong monarchs in Europe, how could Asia possibly attain to democracy ? It was easy for Yüan Shih-kai's monarchic movement and Chang Hsun's attempt at restoration[1] to take place. But now the powerful rulers of Russia and Germany have been unseated from their thrones while the two countries have become republics, which shows that the world has entered upon an era of democracy. Chinese who opposed democracy used to ask what strength there was in our Revolutionary Party to be able to overthrow the Manchu emperor. But in 1911 he fell with one push, another victim of the world tide. This world tendency is like the Yangtze River, which makes crooks and turns, sometimes to the north and sometimes to the south, but in

1 Chang Hsun, the " pig-tailed bandit-general " succeeded in restoring the Manchus to power in Peking for ten days in July, 1917.

the end flows eastward and nothing can stop it.
Just so the life of mankind has flowed from theocracy on to autocracy and from autocracy now
on to democracy, and there is no way to stem
the current. If we try to do so, even though we
may have the power of Yüan Shih-kai or a barbaric, cruel army like Chang Hsun's, we will still
fail at last. The northern military despots are
now opposing the world trend, while we southern
supporters of democracy are going with the trend.
Although the southern government is weak,
although our army is inferior to the northern
armies in training, supplies, and ammunition,
still if we follow the current of the age we will,
in spite of temporary setbacks, eventually succeed
and succeed for all time. Since the North is
fighting the current and subverting all principles
of right, no matter what their present strength
is or how much they may by good luck succeed
for the moment, in the end they will fall and
never again be able to rise.

A revolution has already stirred in theocratic
Mongolia, to overturn the Living Buddha there,
and the theocracy is gone. The theocracy in
Tibet is also doomed to an early overthrow by
the people. In Mongolia and Tibet you see the
last days of theocracy; when the day comes,
no matter how hard it struggles to keep alive, it
cannot continue to exist. Autocracy in Europe

is on the wane. Great Britain uses a political party rather than a king to govern the country; it may be called a republic with a king. From all this we see that not only theocracy but also autocracy will soon crumble before the on-flowing world current. The present age of democracy is a sequence of the democratic ideas in the Greek and Roman age and, while it has been only one hundred fifty years since the beginnings of democracy, its future will be growing brighter day by day.

So we in our revolution have chosen democracy, first, that we may be following the world current, and second, that we may reduce the period of civil war. From ancient times in China, men of great ambition have all wanted to be king. Thus, when Liu Pang[1] saw Ch'in Shih Hwang riding out, he said, " That is the way for men of valor ! " and Hsiang Yü[2] also said, " Let me usurp his place ! " From one generation to another, there has been no end to this unscrupulous greed for power. When I launched the revolution, six or seven out of every ten who came to our support had imperialistic ideas, but after we made it known that our revolutionary principles aimed not only at the overthrow of the Manchus but also at the establishment of a republic, this group

1 The founder of the Han dynasty.
2 A rival of Liu Pang.

gradually got rid of their selfish ambitions. But there are still a few among them who, even in this thirteenth year of the Republic, cling to the old hope of becoming king, and this is the reason why even among our followers there were some who fought against each other. When we first proclaimed our revolution, we lifted up the rights of the people as the basis upon which to build our republic, with the hope that this would prevent the rivalry for imperial power. But, alas! there are some people who are stupid and unreformable ; you can do nothing with them.

The Taiping Rebellion was a warning to us. When Hung Hsiu-ch'uan first lifted his banner of revolt in Kwangsi, won over Hunan, Hupeh, Kiangsi, and Anhwei, and established his capital at Nanking, over half of the Manchu Empire was in his possession. Then why did the Taiping Rebellion fail in the end ? There are several reasons. Some say that the chief reason was that the Taipings did not understand diplomacy, because when Great Britain at that time sent her minister, Pottinger, to Nanking to negotiate a treaty with Hung Hsiu-ch'uan, he was allowed to see only the Eastern Prince, Yang Hsiu-ch'ing, and not the " Heavenly King," Hung Hsiu-ch'uan. To see Hung, Pottinger was required to kotow, which he refused to do ; he went on to

Peking and concluded a treaty with the Manchu government. Later he sent Gordon with troops to attack Soochow and Hung Hsiu-ch'uan was consequently defeated; hence some say that his failure was due to his ignorance of diplomacy. It may have been one of the reasons. Others say that Hung Hsiu-ch'uan failed because, when he reached Nanking, he did not follow up his opportunity and drive on toward Peking. This is also one of the reasons.

But as I study history, these two reasons seem to me to have played a very small part in Hung Hsiu-ch'uan's failure. The main cause was the struggle for the throne which began as soon as the Taipings reached Nanking. They closed the city gates and began to plot murder against each other. First, Yang Hsiu-ch'ing and Hung Hsiu-ch'uan fought for power; when the latter became king, the former also wanted to be king. Yang Hsiu-ch'ing had sixty or seventy thousand trained soldiers in the original army unit which he had brought to Nanking, but when the internal dissensions broke out he was killed by Wei Ch'ang-hwei and his army was destroyed. Then when Wei Ch'ang-hwei began to carry on with a high hand and challenged Hung Hsiu-ch'uan's authority, he was put to an end by all the rest. About that time Shih Ta-k'ai heard of the trouble in Nanking and hurried from Kiangsi to Nanking to offer his services as mediator. He saw that there was no way out of the difficulty and himself fell under suspicion of wanting to be king, so he fled from Nanking and took his army to Szechwan where, before long, he was wiped out by the Manchu troops. Simply because of the rivalry between Hung and Yang for the imperial throne the four armies of Hung Hsiu-ch'uan, Yang Hsiu-ch'ing, Wei Ch'ang-hwei, and Shih Ta-k'ai, the main units of the Taiping forces, were annihilated, and the power of the Taipings rapidly declined. So the failure of the Taiping cause was due fundamentally to Hung Hsiu-ch'uan's mistake in trying to be king. Hung Hsiu-ch'uan in his revolution had no idea of democracy, so, right at the beginning, he conferred the title of "prince" upon five men. After coming to Nanking and witnessing the struggle between Yang Hsiu-ch'ing and Wei Ch'ang-hwei, he decided that he would not create any more princes. Later Li Hsiu-ch'eng and Ch'en Yü-ch'eng so distinguished themselves that it was impossible not to confer titles on them; but Hung Hsiu-ch'uan, fearing that this would make them undependable also, created thirty or forty other princes at the same time, hoping that all these, since they were of equal rank, would serve as checks upon each other. But after that, Li Hsiu-ch'eng and Ch'en Yü-ch'eng and others found themselves unable to move the princes about, and so Hung Hsiu-ch'uan failed. The collapse of the rebellion can be traced back entirely to the ambition of all the leaders for the kingship.

Why did Ch'en Ch'iung-ming lead a revolt against us in Canton year before last? Many people said that he only wanted to seize Kwang-tung and Kwangsi for himself, but that is far from true. Before Ch'en Ch'iung-ming began his revolt, I had proposed the punitive expedition against the North and had worked unweariedly to impress him with the seriousness of our plan, but he always opposed it. Later I thought that perhaps, as he was fighting for the two Kwang provinces, our northern expedition might seem to be interfering with his domain, so on the last day of our conferences, I said to him with utter frankness, " If our punitive expedition against the North succeeds, our government will be moved to either Wuhan or Nanking and will certainly not come back here, in which case we will intrust the two Kwang provinces to you and ask you to be our rear guard. If the northern expedition should unfortunately fail, we will have no face to come back here and whatever diplomatic schemes you employ in dealing with the northern government, you will certainly be able to preserve your own sphere of influence. Even if you throw in your lot with the Northern side, we will not bother you nor criticize you." He seemed to be at a loss for an answer to this, which proved that his ambitions were not limited to the two Kwang provinces. Afterwards, when our expeditionary forces entered Kanchowfu (in Kiangsi), he launched his rebellion against us. Why did he do it just at that time? Because he wanted to become king and he had to destroy the revolutionary troops who were dead against kings before he could even lay a foundation for his scheme.

There is another thing which proves that Ch'en Ch'iung-ming coveted the throne. After the Revolution of 1911, he was constantly telling people of a dream he used to have in his youth in which he grasped the sun with one hand and the moon with the other. In one of his poems there was this line, "Failing to grasp the sun and moon I have been untrue to my youth," to which he added, in notes, the story of his own dream, and he used to show this to everybody. The name which he took for himself (meaning "Clear and Bright") also matched his dream. And look at the men under his command — Yin Chü, Hung Chao-lin, Yang K'un-ju, Ch'en Ch'iung-kwang and that group; not a member of the Revolutionary Party among them, except Teng K'eng, and he was secretly put to death long ago. Ch'en Ch'iung-ming was a party to the Revolution because he hoped to be king, and that ambitior

of his is not yet dead. Besides him, there were
others who used to cherish hopes of kingship;
I don't know what their attitude is now in the
thirteenth year of the Republic and I have no
time to find out.

To-day I am speaking about the people's
sovereignty and I want you all to understand
clearly what it really means. Unless we do
understand clearly, we can never get rid of imperial ambitions among us, ambitions which will
make even brethren in a cause and citizens of
the same country fight one another. The whole
land will be torn year after year with civil strife
and there will be no end to the sufferings of
the people. Because I wanted us to avert such
calamities, I lifted up the banner of democracy
as soon as the revolution began and determined
that we should found a republic. When we
have a real republic, who will be king? The
people, our four hundred millions, will be king.
This will prevent everybody from struggling for
power and will reduce the war evil in China.
The history of China shows that every change
of dynasty has meant war. When the people
were opposing Ch'in Shih Hwang's despotism and
Ch'en Che and Wu Kw'ang raised a revolt in
which all the provinces joined, there was the
beginning of a popular revolution. But then
Liu Pang and Hsiang Yü took the field and the

struggle between the Ch'u and Han states began. What were Liu Pang and Hsiang Yü fighting over ? — The throne. And from the Han and T'ang dynasties onward, not a dynasty has been free from the contests for imperial power. In Chinese history a peaceful period has always been followed by disorder, disorder over the rivalry for kingship. Foreign countries have had wars over religion and wars over. freedom, but China in her thousands of years has had but one kind of war, the war for the throne. In order to avert further civil war, we, as soon as we launched our revolution, proclaimed that we wanted a republic and not kings. Now the ^republic is established, but we still have men like Ch'en Ch'iung-ming in the south, Ts'ao K'un in the north, Lu Yung-t'ing in Kwangsi, and I don't know how many others who are plotting for the kingship. When the old dynasties of China changed their titles, the men with the greatest army strength sought to be king, those with fewer soldiers sought to become princes and marquises. That the militarists to-day are not aspiring to the ranks of prince or marquis shows that we are making some progress at any rate away from civil war !

March 9, 1924.

LECTURE 2

The watchword of the French Revolution: "Liberty, Equality, Fraternity"—Different attitude of Western peoples and of the Chinese people towards liberty—Passion for liberty in the West compared with the passion for wealth in China—The Western struggle for liberty against despotic oppressions of feudalism and autocracy — China's autocracy did not seriously affect the people — Achievement of personal liberty in the West — Early excesses and later limitations — Personal liberty has been taken for granted in China like fresh air — Western doctrine of liberty out of place to-day in China and generally misapplied — Abuse of liberty in schools and in the Party — Aim of Chinese Revolution should be unity and freedom for the nation — Need for individual sacrifice.

Foreign scholars always associate "democracy" with "liberty" and many foreign books and essays discuss the two side by side. The peoples of Europe and America have warred and struggled for little else besides liberty these past two or three hundred years and, as a result, democracy is beginning to flourish. The watchword of the French Revolution was "Liberty, Equality, Fraternity," just as the watchword of our Revolution is "*Min-tsʽŭ, Min-chʽuan, Min-sheng*" (People's Nationalism, People's Sovereignty, People's Livelihood). We may say that liberty, equality, and fraternity are based upon the people's sovereignty or that the people's sovereignty develops out of liberty, equality, and fraternity. While we are discussing democracy we must consider the meaning of the French watchword.

As revolutionary ideas have spread through the East, the word "liberty" has come too; many devoted students and supporters of the new movement have sought to explain in detail its meaning, as something of vital importance. The movement for liberty has played a large part in the history of Europe the past two or three hundred years, and most European wars have been fought for liberty. So Western scholars look upon liberty as a most significant thing, and many peoples in the West have engaged in a rewarding study of its meaning. But since the word has been brought to China, only a few of the intelligentsia have had time to study and to understand it. If we should talk to the common people of China in the villages or on the streets about "liberty," they would have no idea of what we meant. So we may say that the Chinese have not gotten anything yet out of the word: even the new youth and the returned students, those who have paid some attention to Western political affairs and those who have constantly heard "liberty" talked about or have seen the word in books, have a very hazy

conception of what it signifies. No wonder that
foreigners criticize the Chinese, saying that their
civilization is inferior and their thinking immature, that they even have no idea of liberty and
no word with which to express the idea, yet at
the same time criticizing the Chinese for being
disunited as a sheet of loose sand.

These two criticisms are absolutely contra-
dictory. What do foreigners mean when they
say that China is a sheet of loose sand ? Simply
that every person does as he pleases and has let
his individual liberty extend to all phases of life,
hence China is but a lot of separate sand particles.
Take up a handful of sand; no matter how much
there is, the particles will slip about without
any tendency to cohere — that is loose sand.
But if we add cement to the loose sand, it will
harden into a firm body like a rock, in which the
sand, however, has no freedom. When we compare sand and rock, we clearly see that rock was
originally composed of particles of sand; but in
the firm body of the rock the sand has lost its
power to move about freely. Liberty, to put
it simply, means the freedom to move about as
one wishes within an organized group. Because
China does not have a word to convey this idea,
everyone has been at a loss to appreciate it.
We have a phrase that suggests liberty — "running wild without bridle," but that is the same

thing as "loose sand" — excessive liberty for
the individual. So foreigners who criticize us,
who say on the one hand that we have no power
to unite, are loose sand and free particles, and
say on the other hand that we do not understand
the meaning of "liberty" — do they not realize
that it is everybody's liberty which is making
us a sheet of loose sand and that if all are united
in a strong body we cannot be like loose sand?
These critics are "holding their spear against their
own shield."

Within the last two or three centuries, foreign
countries have expended enormous energy in
the struggle for liberty. Is liberty really a good
thing? What is it? I don't think the common
people of China have the least conception of
what this "liberty," that the Westerners say
they have been fighting for, means. In their
wars, Westerners extolled liberty to the skies and
made it sacred; they even made a saying like
" Give me liberty or give me death " their battle
cry. Chinese students, in translating Western
theories, have introduced these words into China;
they have upheld liberty and determined to
fight for it. In their first enthusiasm they almost
equaled the Westerners in days past. But the
mass of the people in China do not understand
what liberty means; you must realize that liberty
develops as the power of the people develops.

So in speaking about democracy to-day, I cannot
but first speak of liberty. We must understand
that Europe and America have shed much blood
and have spent much life in the struggle for
liberty. As I said to you last time, we are now
in the age of democracy. Democracy has been
in existence for over a century in the West, but,
historically, it followed the fight for liberty.
Life was first poured out in order to attain liberty;
the fruit of liberty was democracy. In those
days the educated leaders of Europe and America
held up liberty as their banner just as we in our
revolution are holding up the Three Principles
of the People. From all this we can see that the
Western wars were first for liberty and when
liberty was attained the results were called by
scholars democracy. The term "democracy"
comes from an old Greek word. Even now
Westerners are not very much interested in the
term "democracy" and think of it more or less
as a technical term in political science; it is far
from being the matter of life and death which
liberty has been. Democracy had made its actual
beginnings in the time of Greece and Rome;
the government was then a republic controlled
by the nobility and there was a word signifying
the sovereignty of the people. Later, after Rome
and Greece fell, the word fell into oblivion; the
wars for liberty in the last two centuries have

brought it to light again and in recent decades it has been on the lips of many people; great numbers in China have taken it up and are talking about it.

But in the modern wars of Europe, liberty rather than democracy has been the aim proclaimed. Liberty was a word that everybody in Europe could easily understand. The Europeans' response to the word " liberty " is similar to the Chinese response to-day to the word " make a fortune " which is thought so much of in China. If you tell Chinese that you want them to fight for liberty, they will not understand you and will not take up your cause, but if you invite them to go and make a fortune, crowds will follow you. Liberty has been the rallying cry in modern European wars because Europeans understood the word and were willing to contend for it and to sacrifice for it; everyone worshiped liberty. Why have Europeans so cherished this word while the Chinese people pay no attention to it, yet welcome " making a fortune " ? There are many underlying causes which we must study carefully in order to appreciate. The Chinese respond to " making a fortune " because China now is bankrupt and her people are poor. What the people are suffering most from is poverty, and because " making a fortune " is the only way of relief from poverty, it is everywhere a

welcome word.   Relief from poverty means relief
from suffering, " rescue from misery and distress."
When the people in the misery of poverty suddenly
hear someone talk about getting rich and escaping
distress, they will naturally follow and risk their
lives in the struggle for fortune.   Westerners of
the last century or two have answered to the
call of " liberty " just as Chinese to-day answer
to the call of " fortune."

The peoples of the West sought liberty because
of the extremes to which autocracy had developed.
They were in a stage of civilization corresponding
to the close of the Chou dynasty and the period
of the coördinated states in China, about the time
of the Roman Empire.   Contemporaneously with
the Chou, Ch'in, and Han dynasties, Rome was
unifying Europe.   Rome at first established a
republic, but later became a monarchy.   After
the downfall of the Roman Empire several states
sprang up simultaneously in Europe, just as the
break-up of the Chou dynasty was followed by
the coördinated states.   So many scholars have
compared the conflict of the "Seven Leaders" at
the end of the Chou dynasty with the situation
after the fall of Rome.   After the Roman Empire
had broken up into small states, the feudal
system came into existence: the strongest leaders
became kings and princes; the next in power,
marquises; the least powerful, earls, viscounts,

and barons. They all held autocratic power and
the whole system of government was far more
despotic than the feudal régime during the Chou
dynasty in China. We to-day cannot imagine
what the people of Europe suffered under their
feudal rule; it was far worse than anything
Chinese have ever suffered under their autocracies.
The reason is this : the Ch'in dynasty in im-
posing its autocracy directly on the people would
make a human sacrifice of any who spoke evil of
the government and execute two people for even
talking together; soon afterwards the dynasty
rushed headlong into ruin. So the dynasties and
governments which followed the Ch'in adopted
a much more liberal policy towards the people ;
apart from paying the regular grain taxes the
people had almost no relation with the officials.
The European tyranny in one way and another
pressed directly down upon the shoulders of the
common people. As this lasted very long and
despotism developed more and more systematically,
conditions became worse than anything we have
ever experienced in China. So Europeans two
hundred years ago were groaning under the
painful yoke of autocracy just as Chinese to-day
are groaning under the yoke of poverty. Europeans, after such a long period of cruel tyranny,
felt keenly the distress which the lack of liberty
brought; the only way for them to get rid of

their misery was, therefore, to fight for liberty,
and when men spoke of liberty they joyfully
responded.

After the destruction of China's ancient feudal
system, the stately pomp of autocracy hardly
affected the common people. Since the Ch'in
dynasty, the aim of China's emperors has been
first to protect their own throne that they might
continue to keep the empire in their own family
and that their heirs might reign in peace forever.
So any activities of the people which seemed to
endanger the throne were repressed as strongly
as possible; if anyone started a rebellion, not
only he himself but his nine degrees of kindred
were punished, the sternest measures being employed to prevent a popular revolution. These
absolute monarchs simply wanted to keep their
thrones forever. In other words, as long as the
people did not offend against the throne, they
could do anything else without any interference
on the part of the government. So ever since
the Ch'in dynasty, succeeding emperors have
cared only for their own royal power and but
little about the lives of the people. As for the
happiness of the ·people, that was not in their
thoughts at all. The Republic has been in existence now for thirteen years; because our government is disorganized and we have not yet had
time to establish a good government, no attention

has yet been paid to the relations between the people and the state. What were the conditions under the Manchu dynasty, the relations between the people and the Manchu emperor before 1911? During the Manchu dynasty each province had a viceroy or governor at the top, below him taotai and prefects, and in the lowest rank various assistant magistrates and subordinates. The people had little direct relation to the emperor beyond paying him the annual grain tax—nothing more. Consequently, the political consciousness of the people has been very weak. The people did not care who was emperor. As soon as they had paid their grain tax they considered their duty as citizens done. The emperors wanted only the grain tax from the people and were not interested in anything else they did, letting them live and die to themselves. We can see from this that the Chinese people have not been directly subject to the oppression of autocracy; their sufferings have come indirectly. Because our state has been weak, we have come under the political and economic domination of foreign countries and have not been able to resist. Now our wealth is exhausted and our people are destitute, suffering poverty because of an indirect tyranny.

The Chinese people, therefore, felt very little resentment against their emperors. On the other hand, the autocracy of Europe was quite different from that of China. The despotism in Europe, from the downfall of Rome up to two or three centuries ago, had been developing rapidly and the people had suffered increasingly and unbearably. Many kinds of liberty were denied them, chiefly liberty of thought, liberty of speech, and liberty of movement. These restrictions are now things of the past in Europe and we cannot now see conditions as they once prevailed. But we still have a way of telling what non-freedom of movement means. We know something about the restrictions which Chinese emigrants to the Dutch or French possessions in Malaysia are called upon to endure. Take Java, for instance, which was once a Chinese dependency and brought tribute to China, but now belongs to the Netherlands. Since the Dutch took control of the island, every Chinese business man, student, or laborer who goes to Java must, as soon as the steamer docks, undergo a strict examination by the Dutch police. The Chinese is led to a small room and shut in there; he has to take off his clothes and be examined from head to foot by a doctor, have physical measurements and finger prints taken before he is allowed to go on shore. Even then, no matter where he goes, he has to register his name and in traveling from one place to another has to carry a pass. After nine o'clock at night, an ordinary pass is not sufficient; he must have a night pass and carry a lantern. This is the treatment which Chinese emigrants to Java receive from the Dutch government. Such infringements upon personal liberty of movement have certainly been carried over from the old autocratic days in Europe and are now directed by the Dutch against the Chinese. They suggest to us what the old European autocracy was like. There are many other kinds of restrictions upon freedom, upon freedom of business, freedom to work, freedom of belief and such. Take freedom of belief. When people who live in a certain place are forced to believe in a particular religion, whether they want to or not, the situation becomes very hard to bear. Europeans indeed suffered "deep waters and burning fires" from the denial of freedom. So, whenever they heard of anyone leading a struggle for liberty, they all rejoiced and espoused his cause. Such was the beginning of the European revolutionary idea.

The revolutions in Europe were struggles for liberty. In the cause of liberty the people poured out illimitable dark blood and sacrificed innumerable lives and homes. No wonder that when liberty was won, all accepted it as sacred and even to-day worship it. This conception of liberty has recently been introduced into China and a certain group of scholars have become its eager advocates; as a result many have the idea of fighting for liberty in China. To-day we are discussing democracy. The theory of democracy came from Europe and America and we should all understand clearly what it implies. We must also understand what sort of thing the kindred idea of liberty is. Europeans once suffered bondage until they could suffer no more, and millions with but one thought went out to fight for liberty; when liberty had been attained democracy developed. So, if we are to discuss democracy, we must first understand the history of the struggle for liberty.

As the revolutionary ferment of the West has lately spread to China, the new students and many earnest scholars have risen up to proclaim liberty. They think that because European revolutions, like the French Revolution, were struggles for liberty, we, too, should fight for liberty. This is nothing but "saying what others say." They have not applied their minds to the study of democracy or liberty and have no real insight into their meaning. There is a deep significance in the proposal of our Revolutionary Party that the Three Principles of the People, rather than a struggle for liberty, should be the basis of our revolution. The watchword of the French Revolution was "Liberty"; the watchword of the American Revolution was "Independence"; the watchword of our Revolution is the "Three

Principles of the People." We spent much time and effort before we decided upon our watchword; we are not merely imitating others. Why do we say that our new youth's advocacy of liberty is not the right thing, while the Europeans' cry of liberty was so fitting? I have already explained: when we propose an objective for a struggle, it must be relief from some suffering that cuts deep under the skin if we want all the people eagerly to take part in it. The peoples of Europe suffered so bitterly from despotism that as soon as the banner of liberty was lifted high, millions with one heart rallied about it. If we in China, where the people have not suffered such despotism, should make the cry of liberty, no attention would be paid to it. But if we should propose making fortunes, all the people would welcome the call. Our Three Principles of the People is in many ways like a theory of acquiring wealth. We must turn this statement over in our minds and interpret it carefully before we can appreciate what it implies. Why do we not speak directly about acquiring wealth? Because the acquisition of wealth does not embrace the whole of the Three Principles, but the Three Principles do include the acquisition of wealth. The communism which Russia put into effect early in her revolution was like fortune-making; it was a

direct and simple policy of getting wealth.   The
policy of our Revolutionary Party has more than one
aim, so "making a fortune " cannot sum it all up.
It is even more difficult for "liberty" to sum it up.

Modern European scholars who observe China all
say that our civilization is so backward and our
political consciousness so weak that we do not
even understand liberty.   " We Europeans," they
declare, " fought and sacrificed for liberty one or
two hundred years ago and performed no one
knows how many startling deeds, but Chinese still
do not know what liberty is.   This shows that the
political thinking of us Europeans is far superior to
the political thinking of the Chinese."   Because we
do not talk about liberty, they say that we are poor
in political ideas.   I don't think such an argument
gets anywhere.   If Europeans value liberty so
much, why do they call the Chinese a " sheet of
loose sand " ?   When Europeans were struggling
for liberty, they naturally took a strong view of
liberty, but since they have won liberty and have
reached their goal, their conception of liberty has
probably become weaker.   If the banner of liberty
should be raised again to-day, I don't think it
would call forth the same enthusiasm as before.
Moreover, struggles for liberty was the European
method of revolution two or three centuries ago
and could not be repeated now.   To use the figure
"loose sand," what is its chief characteristic?—Its

absolute freedom, without which there can be no such thing as loose sand. When European democracy was just budding, Europeans talked about fighting for liberty; when they had gained their end, everyone began to extend the limits of his individual liberty and soon the excesses of liberty led to many evil consequences. Therefore an English scholar named Mill[1] said that only individual liberty which did not interfere with the liberty of others can be considered true liberty. If one's liberty is incompatible with another's sphere of liberty, it is no longer liberty. Before that, Westerners had set no limits upon freedom, but when Mill proposed his theory of a limited freedom, the measure of personal liberty was considerably reduced. Evidently Western scholars had come to realize that liberty was not a sacred thing which could not be encroached upon, but that it must be put within boundaries. Foreigners who criticize the Chinese, saying that they do not understand what liberty is and that they are "loose sand," are certainly self-contradictory. If Chinese are like loose sand, they already have complete freedom; if our being like loose sand is not a good thing, we ought to add cement and water as quickly as possible, consolidate into rock, and become a firm body. When that takes place,

[1] Referring to John Stuart Mill.

the sand cannot move about and will no longer
be free. The trouble from which the Chinese
are suffering is not lack of liberty; if " loose
sand " describes our nature, then we have
long had enough freedom. What the Chinese
have not had is the word for " liberty " and
hence the idea of liberty. But what has the lack
of this idea to do with government ? Do Chinese
really have liberty ?

When we think about that " sheet of loose
sand " we realize that the Chinese have had a
great measure of liberty. Because we have so
much of it, nobody pays any attention to it, not
even to the name for it. Why is this ? Let
me illustrate from our everyday life. Our greatest daily needs are food and clothing, — at least
two meals a day and two suits of clothes a year.
But there is something else which is vitally more
important than food or clothing. The ordinary
person thinks that food is the most important
thing in his life, because if he does not eat he will
die, but this other thing is ten thousand times
as important as food. Because we are not immediately conscious of it, we do not appreciate how
important it is — breathing the fresh air. Why
is breathing in fresh air ten thousand times as
important as eating food ? If we eat two meals
or even one meal a day, we can keep alive, but
we need at least sixteen breaths of life-giving

fresh air every minute to be at all comfortable; we cannot stand to be without this amount of air. If you don't believe me, try holding your nose for one minute and shutting off these sixteen breaths. I cannot do it a minute now without feeling distress. A day has twenty-four hours, each hour sixty minutes, and each minute sixteen breaths, which means that we breathe nine hundred sixty times an hour, twenty-three thousand forty times a day; therefore, I say, unmistakably breathing is much more important than food. The reason why we do not appreciate the fact is that fresh air is all about us everywhere, limitless and inexhaustible. We breathe it all day long without waste of time and without expenditure of labor as in getting our food, and so we think that it is easy to get, while food is hard to get. Fresh air is so easy to obtain that we think nothing about it. Holding your nose to shut off your breathing is only a small experiment to prove the importance of fresh air. A larger experiment would be to close tight all the windows in this hall; the fresh air for breathing would gradually diminish in quantity and within a few minutes these hundreds of people would feel great discomfort. Or lock a person in a small room for a whole day; when he is first let out he feels greatly exhilarated — another illustration of our principle. Because Chinese have had an

excessive degree of liberty, they have given it no
concern, just as when there is plenty of fresh air
in the room we do not realize its value; but when
the doors and the windows are closed and no fresh
air can come in, we know its importance. Europeans under the despotism of two or three centuries ago had no liberty whatsoever, so every
man appreciated how precious a thing liberty
was and was ready to give his life for it. Before
they won liberty, they were like men shut up in a
small room; after they had won liberty they were
like men suddenly let out into the open air.
Naturally everyone felt that liberty was something
of wonderful value and was saying, "Give me
liberty or give me death."

But the situation in China is different. The
Chinese do not know "liberty," but only about
"making a fortune." To talk to the Chinese
about liberty is like talking to the aboriginal
Yao tribes deep in the mountains of Kwangsi
about making a fortune in money. The Yaos
frequently come from the heart of the mountains
and bring bear galls and deer horns to exchange
for other articles in the open-air marts of the outside world. At first the traders in the marts
wanted to give the Yaos money for their things;
the Yaos always refused money but were perfectly
happy to trade for salt or a piece of cloth. We
think nothing is better than to make a fortune

in money, but the Yaos are content to have usable
things. Since they do not know what it means
to make a fortune, they do not care for money.
Modern Chinese scholars who are offering liberty
to the Chinese people are like the traders who
talk about making a fortune to the Yaos.
The Chinese have no use for "liberty," yet the
students still preach about it. They certainly
don't know the "signs of the times." Europeans
and Americans risked their lives in the battles
for liberty a hundred and fifty years ago, because
liberty was rare for them. When nations like
France and the United States won liberty, they
became what we call the pioneers in democratic
government. Yet even in these two countries,
is everyone free? Many classes, such as students,
soldiers, officials, and persons under twenty years
of age, who have not reached maturity, do not
have liberty. The struggles for liberty in the
West two and three centuries ago were made
only by people over twenty and by those who
were not militarists, government officials, and
students. And after this freedom had been won,
only those who did not belong to these groups
were permitted to enjoy it. Even to-day citizens
of these groups are not entirely free. The students
of China, having absorbed these ideas of liberty
and having no other place to practice them, gave
expression to them in their schools. Student

insurrections and strikes followed, under the
dignified guise of fighting for "liberty." The
liberty which Westerners talk about has its strict
limitations and cannot be described as belonging
to everyone. Young Chinese students when they
talk about liberty break down all restraints. Because no one welcomes their theory in the society
outside, they can only bring it back into their own
schools, and constant disorders and strikes result.
This is abuse of freedom. That foreigners should
not be familiar with Chinese history and should
not know that since ancient times Chinese have
enjoyed a large measure of liberty, is not strange.
But that our own students should have forgotten
the Liberty Song of the ancient Chinese —

> "When the sun rises, I toil;
> When the sun sets, I rest;
> I dig wells for water;
> I till the fields for food;
> What has the Emperor's power to do with me?"

is surprisingly strange. We can see from this
Liberty Song that China, while she has not had
liberty in name, has had liberty in fact from days
of old, and so much of it that she need not seek
for more.

Since democracy grows out of liberty, we must,
in discussing democracy, explain clearly the history
of the Western struggle for liberty. Otherwise we
will not see that liberty is precious. The struggle
of the Europeans for liberty was a great passion

that has since cooled; this shows that liberty has both good and bad features and is not a holy thing. If foreigners say that we are a sheet of loose sand, we will acknowledge the truth, but we cannot accept their assertion that Chinese have no understanding of liberty and are weak in their political consciousness. Why has China become a sheet of loose sand ? Simply because of excessive individual liberty. Therefore the aims of the Chinese Revolution are different from the aims in foreign revolutions, and the methods we use must also be different. Why, indeed, is China having a revolution ? To put the answer directly, the aims of our revolution are just opposite to the aims of the revolutions of Europe. Europeans rebelled and fought for liberty because they had had too little liberty. But we, because we have had too much liberty without any unity and resisting power, because we have become a sheet of loose sand and so have been invaded by foreign imperialism and oppressed by the economic control and trade wars of the Powers, without being able to resist, must break down individual liberty and become pressed together into an unyielding body like the firm rock which is formed by the addition of cement to sand. Chinese to-day are enjoying so much freedom that they are showing the evils of freedom. This is true not merely in the schools but even

in our Revolutionary Party. The reason why,
from the overthrow of the Manchus until now,
we have not been able to establish a government
is just this misuse of freedom. For the same reason our Revolutionary Party was defeated by
Yüan Shih-kai.[1] In the second year of the Republic, Yüan Shih-kai contracted large foreign
loans without the approval of Parliament, killed
Sung Chiao-jen,[2] and did much else to injure the
Republic. I urged all the provinces to rise immediately and punish Yüan, but because everybody in the party was talking freedom, there
was no unity. In the southwestern provinces,
for example, from divisional commanders and
brigadier generals down to privates, there was not
one but talked about his individual liberty. None
of them would work together. Then this liberty
was extended to the provinces and each province
insisted on its own freedom and could not
coöperate with other provinces. The southern
provinces, which were enjoying some of the left-
over glory of the Revolution of 1911, displayed
great enthusiasm on the surface, but the party
within was split to pieces and could not agree upon
orders. As for Yüan Shih-kai, he had the old six-
army defense organization of the Peiyang Party;
the divisional commanders, brigadier generals, and

1 Second Revolution of 1913.
2 Speaker-elect of Parliament.

all the soldiers in these six armies were under splendid discipline and subject to one command. In a word, Yüan Shih-kai had a firm organization while we in the Revolutionary Party were a sheet of loose sand, and so Yüan Shih-kai defeated the party. This shows that a principle which suits other countries does not necessarily suit China. The revolutions in the West made use of the struggle for liberty, but the Chinese Revolution cannot be said to aim at liberty. If we declare that we are fighting for liberty, we will remain loose sand and not become unified; we will never attain to the desired end of our revolution.

Western revolutions began with the struggle for liberty; only after war and agitation of two or three centuries was the liberty realized from which democracy sprang. The watchword of the French Revolution was "Liberty, Equality, Fraternity." Our watchword is "People's Nationalism, People's Sovereignty, People's Livelihood." What relation do the two watchwords have to each other? According to my interpretation, our Nationalism may be said to correspond to their Liberty, because putting the People's Nationalism into effect means a struggle for the liberty of our nation. The Europeans fought for individual liberty, but to-day we have a different use for liberty. Now how shall the term "liberty" be applied? If we apply it to a person,

we shall become a sheet of loose sand; on no
account must we give more liberty to the individual; let us secure liberty instead for the nation.
The individual should not have too much liberty,
but the nation should have complete liberty.
When the nation can act freely, then China may
be called strong. To make the nation free, we
must each sacrifice his personal freedom. Students who sacrifice their personal liberty will be
able to work diligently day after day and spend
time and effort upon learning; when their studies
are completed, their knowledge is enlarged and
their powers have multiplied, then they can do
things for the nation. Soldiers who sacrifice
their personal liberty will be able to obey
orders, repay their country with loyalty and
help the nation to attain liberty. If students
and soldiers talk liberty, they will soon have
" unrestrained license," to use a Chinese phrase
for liberty. Schools will have no rules and the
army will have no discipline. How can you
have a school without rules ?   What kind of army
is that without discipline ?

Why do we want the nation to be free ? —
Because China under the domination of the Powers
has lost her national standing. She is not merely a
semi-colony; she has indeed become a hypo-colony,
inferior to Burma and Annam and Korea. They
are each the protectorate of one nation, the

slave of one master. China is the colony of all the nations and the slave of all. In fact, we are now slaves to over ten masters; our national freedom is terribly restricted. If we want to restore China's liberty, we must unite ourselves into one unshakeable body; we must use revolutionary methods to weld our state into firm unity. Without revolutionary principles we shall never succeed. Our revolutionary principles are the cement. If we can consolidate our four hundred millions and form a mighty union and make the union free, the Chinese state will be free and the Chinese people will be really free. Compare the watchword of the French Revolution with that of ours. "Liberty" in the French revolutionary watchword and "People's Nationalism" in our watchword are similar. The People's Nationalism calls for the freedom of our nation. "Equality" is similar to our "Principle of the People's Sovereignty" which aims to destroy autocracy and make all men equal. "Fraternity" originally meant brothers and has the same significance as the Chinese word *t'ung-pao* (compatriots). The idea in "Fraternity" is similar to our "Principle of the People's Livelihood," which plans for the happiness of our four hundred millions. I will explain this more in detail when I come to the discussion of The People's Livelihood.

March 16, 1924.

LECTURE 3

Equality — Equality not a natural endowment — Artificial inequalities which accentuate natural inequalities — Social and political classes in medieval Europe — The true meaning of equality — The theory of "natural equality" proposed in Europe to counteract the theory of "divine rights"— China does not need personal liberty and equality as Europeans did— The revolutions in England, America, France, Russia — The American struggle for independence based on theory of equality — America's second struggle against slavery within the nation — Causes of the Civil War — Freedom won for the negro slaves by the whites — Negro resentment towards the North which had emancipated them — The Three Principles will give China liberty and equality — Liberty and equality dependent upon democracy — The continued struggle for equality in the West — History of labor organization — Intellectual leadership necessary — Misunderstanding of equality among Chinese workers — Good government essential to labor progress — Selfish and altruistic philosophies of life contrasted — Coöperation between seers, promoters, and executives needed — The service aim.

Min-ch'uan, the People's Sovereignty, is the second part of our revolutionary watchword and corresponds to equality in the French watchword. So to-day let us take equality as the theme for our study. The word "equality" is usually associated with the word "liberty." During the former revolutions in the various countries of Europe, all the people expended an equal amount of strength and sacrificed to an equal degree in their fight for liberty and equality, and consequently they valued equality as much as they did liberty. Moreover, many people felt that if they could secure liberty, they would certainly attain to equality, and that if they did not become equal, there was no way to manifest their freedom; they regarded equality as being even higher than liberty. What is equality and whence does it come? The revolutionary philosophy of Europe and America spoke of liberty as something bestowed by Nature upon man. For example, the "Declaration of Independence" of the American Revolution and the "Declaration of the Rights of Man and of the Citizen" of the French Revolution both pronouncedly and emphatically proclaimed that liberty and equality were natural and inalienable rights of man.

Are men really born with the special right of equality? Let us first study this question carefully. In the First Lecture, we traced the history of people's rights from the age of primitive man millions of years ago down to the beginning of our modern democratic period, but we did not discover any principle of natural human equality. In the world of Nature we do not find any two things level, except upon the surface of water. On level ground there is no place truly level. The section of the Canton-Hankow Railway between Wongsha Station (Canton) and Yinchanghwan

runs through a natural plain; but if you look out
of your coach window along the way and observe
carefully the contour of the land, you will find that
there is not a mile of track but has required human
labor and engineering to make it level. Even what
we call a natural plain, then, is not perfectly level.
Or take the vase of flowers on this table. The
flower that I am now holding in my hand is a
locust. If you looked at it casually, you might
think that every leaf and every blossom was just
alike; but observe it carefully or put it under the
microscope and you will find that no two leaves
and no two blossoms are alike. Even in the
millions of leaves of a whole locust tree, you will
find no two leaves which are entirely alike. Project this dissimilarity into space and time. This
locust leaf here is not like any locust leaf anywhere else; this year's locust leaf is different from
last year's locust leaf. This shows that nothing
produced in the world is just like anything else,
and since all things are different, they naturally
cannot be called equal. If there is no equality
in the natural world, how can there be such a
thing as human equality?

Nature originally did not make man equal;
but when autocracy developed among mankind,
the despotic kings and princes pushed human
differences to an extreme, and the result was an
inequality far worse than Nature's inequality.

The inequality created by kings and princes was an artificial inequality. To illustrate the conditions it resulted in, let me draw a diagram on the blackboard here:

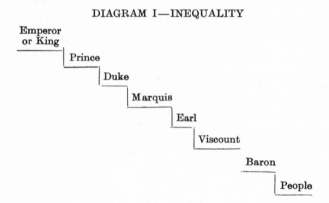

DIAGRAM I—INEQUALITY

Emperor or King

Prince

Duke

Marquis

Earl

Viscount

Baron

People

Study this diagram carefully and you will understand what artificial inequality meant. Because of these artificial ranks, the specially privileged classes became excessively cruel and iniquitous, while the oppressed people, unable to contain themselves, finally broke into rebellion and warred upon inequality. The original aim in the revolutions had been the destruction of man-made inequalities; when that was completed, men thought their revolution would be over. But the men who occupied the high stations of emperor and king all assumed a divine appointment as a shield for their office; they said that they had received their special position from God and that the people who opposed them would be opposing God. The ignorant masses, who did not study to see whether there were any truth or not in these words, followed on blindly and fought for more privileges for their kings. They even opposed the intelligent people who talked about equality and liberty. So the scholars who were supporting revolution had to invent the theory of nature-bestowed rights of equality and liberty in order to overthrow the despotism of kings. Their original purpose was to break down artificial, man-made inequalities. But in everything, certainly, "action is easy, understanding difficult"; the masses of Europe at that time believed that emperors and kings were divinely sent and had special "divine rights," and large numbers of ignorant folk supported them. No matter what methods or how much energy the small group of intelligent and educated people used, they could not overthrow the monarchs.

Finally, when the belief that man is born free and equal and that the struggle for freedom and equality is the duty of everybody had permeated the masses, the emperors and kings of Europe fell automatically. But after their downfall, the people began to believe firmly in the theory of natural equality and kept on working day after day to make all men equal. They did not know that such

a thing is impossible.   Only recently, in the light
of science, have people begun to realize that there
is no principle of natural equality.   If we acted
according to the belief of the masses at that time,
regardless of the truth, and forced an equality upon
human society, that equality would be a false one.

DIAGRAM II—FALSE EQUALITY

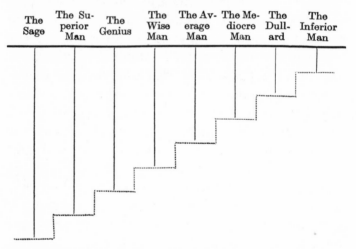

| The Sage | The Superior Man | The Genius | The Wise Man | The Average Man | The Mediocre Man | The Dullard | The Inferior Man |

As this second diagram shows, we would have to
level down superior position in order to get equality
at the top, but the line representing the standing
ground of these different types would still be uneven and not level.   The equality we secured would
be a false equality.   Equal position in human
society is something to start with ; each man
builds up his career upon this start according to his

natural endowments of intelligence and ability.
As each man has different gifts of intelligence and
ability, so the resultant careers will be different.
And since each man works differently, they certainly cannot work on an equal basis.   This brings
us to the only true principle of equality.   If we pay
no attention to each man's intellectual endowments
and capacities and push down those who rise to a
high position in order to make all equal, the world
will not   progress   and   mankind   will   retrocede.
When we speak of democracy and equality but yet
want the world to advance, we are talking about
political equality.   For equality is an artificial not
a natural thing, and the only equality which we
can create is equality in political status.

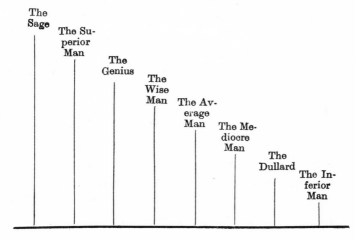

DIAGRAM III—TRUE EQUALITY

After the revolution, we want every man to have an equal political standing, such as is represented by the base line in Diagram III. This is the only true equality and true principle of nature.

In the revolutions of Europe, the people spent much effort and made untold sacrifices in their struggles for equality and liberty. In order to understand why they contended so fiercely and sacrificed so much, we must know something of the inequality which existed before the revolutions. The first diagram which I drew represents the condition in Europe before the revolutions and the political inequality which actually existed. The steps in the diagram — emperor, king, prince, duke, marquis, earl, viscount, baron — show the various classes in the former political system of Europe. China once had these class distinctions, and not until the revolution and overthrow of autocracy thirteen years ago were the unequal ranks made equal. But China's former inequality was not so serious as Europe's. Europe two hundred years ago was still in a state of feudalism similar to the feudalism of China more than two thousand years ago. Because of the earlier advance of government in China, the feudal system here was destroyed two thousand years ago, while in Europe it is not yet completely wiped out. Only two or three centuries ago did Europeans begin to realize the evils of inequality

and to have the ideas of equality which China had
two millenniums ago. China was advanced in her
political organization long before European nations, but within the last two centuries, Europe has
not only caught up with China, but she has progressed beyond China. "The last has become first."

The situation which existed under European
despotism before the days of revolution was far
more serious than the situation in China has
ever been. Why was this true? — Because of
the hereditary system in Europe. The European
emperors, kings, princes, dukes, marquises, and
other nobles passed their ranks on from generation
to generation; no one ever changed from his
inherited vocation. The occupations of the common people were also hereditary; they could never
do anything else. If a man was a tiller of the soil,
his children and grandchildren would be farmers.
A laborer's children and grandchildren would
have to do bitter toil. The grandson could not
choose a different occupation from his grand-
father's. This inability to change one's profession
was the kind of inequality which existed at that
time in Europe. Since the break-up of the
feudal system in China, these professional barriers
have also been entirely destroyed. Thus we see
that while China along with foreign countries
has had a class system and a kind of inequality,
yet China has had the advantage, since only the

emperor's rank was hereditary. Unless the emperor was overthrown, the right to reign was passed from one generation to another in the same family. Only when there was a change of dynasty did the line of emperors change. But as for dukes, marquises, earls, viscounts, and barons, these titles were changed from one generation to another even in olden days. Many commoners have become ministers of state or have been appointed princes and nobles ; these were not hereditary offices. There may have been a few commoners in Europe who became ministers of state or were appointed princes and nobles, but the majority of titles were hereditary and the common people were not free in choosing their occupations. This lack of freedom was what caused them to lose their equality. Not only were the political ranks not equal, but the social classes of the common people were unequal. Consequently, it was very difficult for the common people, first, to reach the position of duke, marquis, earl, viscount, or baron, and, second, to change their own occupations freely and thus rise in life. At last they came to feel that they could no longer endure the afflictions of this system, that they must throw their lives into a struggle for liberty, emancipate themselves from non-freedom of occupation and strive to progress. Such a war for liberty, such a demolishing of tyrannical class

inequality, has never been witnessed in China.
Although Chinese have experienced class distinctions, yet they have never sacrificed their own
lives or their families as a price for liberty.
The revolutions of the European peoples have
concentrated upon achieving liberty and equality,
but Chinese have never really understood what
these things mean. The reason for this is that
China's autocracy, in comparison with Europe's,
has not been at all severe. And although China's
government was autocratic in ancient times and
has not made any progress in the last two thousand years, yet before that period many reforms
had been made and the abuse of despotism had been
considerably reduced. Consequently, the people
have not suffered very much from the autocratic
system and have not fought for the principle
of equality.

Since European civilization has spread its
influence eastward, European political systems,
economics, and science have also penetrated
China. When Chinese hear European political
doctrines they generally copy them word for word
without any thought of modification. The
European revolutions two and three centuries ago
were "struggles for liberty," so China now must
struggle for liberty ! Europeans fought for
equality, so China must fight for equality also !
But China's weakness to-day is not the lack of

liberty and equality. If we try to arouse the
spirit of the people with "Liberty and Equality,"
we will be talking wide of the point. Our people
are not cut deeply enough by these things; they
are not sensitive to them, and so would certainly
not join our banner. But the people of Europe
two or three centuries ago suffered "waters of
tribulation and fires of torment" from the loss
of liberty and equality; they felt that unless they
could achieve liberty and equality, no question
could be solved, and so they hazarded their lives
in the struggle for them.

This agitation produced the three revolutions
of the past three centuries — the first in England,
the second in America, the third in France. The
American and French revolutions succeeded; the
English Revolution can be counted as a failure,
and consequently the English political system has
not yet changed very greatly. The English Revolution took place contemporaneously with the
close of the Ming dynasty and the beginning of
the Manchu dynasty. The English overthrew the
throne and killed the king, but in less than ten
years the monarchy was restored. So, until to-day,
the English government is still monarchical in
form, and the nobility still largely exists. The
American colonies, after breaking away from
England and becoming independent, did away
entirely with the old political classes and founded a

republican system of government. France followed
in their footsteps and overthrew the old class
system from the bottom up. Now just six years
ago Russia staged a revolution, also overthrowing
her class system and becoming a republic. The
United States, France, and Russia are all powerful states and we can trace their strength back
to their successful revolutions. Russia has effected the most recent revolution and also the
most successful one; she has leveled down not
only political classes but also all the capitalist
classes of society.

Take the United States again. The objective in
the minds of the American people during their
revolution was independence. Why? Because
their thirteen colonies were all British territory
and under British control. Great Britain was
a despotic monarchy and was oppressing the
American people much more severely than she
oppressed her own people. When the Americans
saw that they and the British were under the same
government, but that British citizens were treated
liberally while they themselves were so much
abused, they felt keenly the inequality in the
situation; they wanted to secede from Britain,
govern themselves, and establish an independent
state. For the sake of independence they resisted
Britain and engaged in war with her for eight
years until they achieved their purpose. The

American government has treated its white races alike, on a basis of equality, but its treatment of colored races has been very different. The African negroes, for instance, were looked upon as slaves. Although, after the American Revolution, the white people had an equal political standing, yet the whites and the blacks were not politically equal. This actual fact was inconsistent with the American Constitution and the Declaration of Independence, the opening words of which were, " that all men are created equal, that they are endowed by their Creator with certain inalienable rights, that among these are Life, Liberty, and the Pursuit of Happiness." The Constitution adopted later was based upon these principles, yet in spite of a constitution which stressed the equal rights of mankind, the negroes were still kept in slavery.

Certain scholarly advocates of Liberty and Equality saw that this condition of affairs was seriously out of harmony with the spirit which founded the nation, and opposed the existence of large numbers of slaves in a free and equal republic. How did the Americans of that time treat the negroes ? They abused them cruelly and made them work like cows and horses. They had to toil as slaves at hard labor, wearing themselves out each day at heavy tasks and in the end receiving not wages but only their food. When the people of the nation saw these pitiful

conditions, they realized how unjust and unequal
and inconsistent with the principles of the Constitution they were.   So they began to plead for
humanity and to attack the unequal system of
slavery.   As the idea spread more and more
widely, it gained larger numbers of adherents.
Then there were many earnest people who made
investigations into the sufferings of the negro
slaves and published reports of what they saw.
The most famous of these described many actual
tragic facts of slave life in the form of a novel,
which was read by everybody with intense interest.   This book was called "The Black Slave's
Cry to Heaven,"[1] and when it came out, people
realized what the slaves were enduring and were
indignant on their behalf.   Then all the Northern
States which did not use slave labor advocated
the freeing of the slaves.   The Southern States
owned a vast number of slaves ; each southern
state had numerous vast plantations which depended solely upon slave labor for cultivation.
If they should free the slaves, they would have
no hard labor and could not plant their fields.
The Southerners, from selfish motives, opposed
emancipation, saying that the slave system was
not started by one man only.   Americans had
brought over negroes from Africa to be slaves just

[1] Chinese title of *Uncle Tom's Cabin.*

as several decades ago Westerners transported
Chinese to the American continent and to Malaysia to be "swine"; the black slaves were the
African "swine." The Southern States fought
emancipation on the ground that the slaves were
their capital and they demanded reimbursement
if the slaves were freed. At that time a negro
slave brought about five or six thousand dollars
in the market; and as there were several million
slaves in the South, their total value ran into billions of dollars. The nation had no way to pay
such a large sum to the slave owners.

Therefore, although agitation for the freeing of
the slaves had begun long before, there was still a
period of ferment, and it is only sixty years since
the final explosion took place, precipitating the
war between the North and the South. This
war lasted five years, and was one of the world's
great wars; the fighting was terrific on both sides,
and North and South each lost several hundred
thousand men. It was a war against the inequality
of the black slave, a war against human inequality,
a war for equality. Hitherto, Europeans and
Americans had fought for equality as a result of
their own awakening and to alleviate their own
distress. But the American Civil War was waged
for the equality of the black slave and not because
the negro himself knew how to struggle. The
negroes had been slaves so long that they did not

understand anything except to be perfectly content as long as their owners gave them food, clothing, and shelter. There were probably some masters who were very generous to their slaves; and so long as a slave knew that he had a good master who would not treat him with special severity, he would not think of resisting, of demanding emancipation, or of becoming his own master. So in the American Civil War, it was the whites who fought for equality on behalf of the blacks. The war was carried on by men outside the oppressed group and did not begin with an awakening within the group.

The war resulted in defeat for the South and victory for the North, and the government of the United States immediately issued a proclamation freeing the slaves throughout the country. The defeated Southern States had no choice but to obey, but they thereupon gave up all responsibility for the slaves. From the day of emancipation they ceased giving them food to eat, clothes to wear, and houses to live in. Then the negroes, although they had been liberated by the white men, had become citizens of the Republic, and faced a great future with their new political equality and liberty, yet because they were no longer working for masters and could not get food, clothing, and shelter, because "the green did not immediately succeed the

yellow," [1] felt that they had "lost the support of
T'ai Shan" [2] and were in great distress. They
began to harbor resentment against the states
which had freed them and all the more against the
great president in the North who had advocated
emancipation. Who was that president? You
all know that the United States has had two very
famous presidents. One was the first president,
Washington, who is always mentioned whenever
people speak of the father-statesmen of nations;
he occupies a place of glory in the history of man's
struggle for equality. The other president is Lincoln, who advocated the liberation of the slaves
more earnestly than any other man of his day,
and who, because he emancipated the slaves and
secured equality for all mankind, reached a position of eminent glory. The people of the whole
world still do him honor. But the newly freed
slaves, because for the moment they suffered the
lack of food, clothing, and shelter, were bitter
against him. There is a lampoon verse which
reviles Lincoln and calls him a deluge of water
and a savage beast. The writers of such things
are like the counter-revolutionists to-day who
revile the Revolutionary Party. The intelligent
negroes of to-day, who realize that emancipation

[1] Said of the time just before the new harvest when the old stock of
grain is nearly exhausted.
[2] The sacred mountain of Shantung, highest mountain in east China.

was a blessing, naturally laud Lincoln. But there
are ignorant negroes even yet who hate Lincoln
as their forefathers did.

The freeing of the slaves was one of the struggles
for equality in American history. The two
finest periods in American history were: first,
when the people, suffering under the unequal
treatment of the British, waged the War of Independence and, after eight years of fighting, broke
away from Britain and established an independent
state; second, when sixty years later the war between the North and the South was fought, for a
cause similar to that of the War for Independence.
The Civil War lasted five years, while the Revolutionary War lasted eight years; but the sacrifice
and shedding of blood was much greater in the
later war. Briefly, then, the first American war
was a war of the people for their own independence
and equality; the second war was for the equality
of negroes, not of themselves, and more sacrifice
was made and more blood was spilled in the second
war than in the first. American history is a story
of struggle for equality and makes a shining page
in the history of the world.

After the war for equality in America, a revolutionary struggle for equality broke out in France
also. The conflict experienced vicissitudes over
a period of eighty years before it could be counted
a success. But after equality had been secured,

the people pushed the word "equality" to an
extreme and wanted to put everyone on the
same level. It was the kind of equality which
Diagram II represents: the line of equality
was not placed underfoot but overhead — false
equality.

China's tide of revolutionary ideas came from
Europe and America, and the theory of equality
has also been introduced from the West. But
our Revolutionary Party advocates a struggle,
not for liberty and equality, but for the Three
Principles of the People. If we can put these
Three Principles into practice, we will have liberty
and equality. Although Western nations warred
for liberty and equality, they have since been
constantly led astray by them. If we put the
Three Principles into operation and achieve true
liberty and equality, how can we be sure to keep
on the right track? If, as in Diagram II, we
put the line of equality at the top, we will not
be following the right course. But if, as in Diagram III, we make the line of equality the base
upon which to stand, we will be on the right track
of equality. So if we want to know whether the
principles we are using in our revolution are
desirable or not and whether they are following
the right line, we must first study carefully the
history of European revolutions from their very
beginnings. And if people want to understand

thoroughly our Three Principles and to know whether they are really a good thing, suitable to the needs of our country, if they want to be able to believe in our Three Principles and never waver in their faith, they, too, must study carefully the history of Western revolutions from their inception.

The United States passed through two wars for " Liberty and Equality " — the first one lasting eight years, the second one five years — before they reached their objective. China has never before had a war for liberty and equality. All the wars in China's millenniums of history have been struggles for the throne ; every one who took part in them cherished the hope of becoming king. The recent revolution in which we overthrew the Manchus can be said to be the first time that we have not struggled for royal power. Yet this freedom from royal ambitions was true only of those within the Revolutionary Party. Those outside the Party, like Tsao Kun and Wu Pei-fu in the North, were nominal supporters of the Republic, but really advocates of unification by force and coveters of autocratic power. If their scheme for unification by force had succeeded and no one had opposed them, each would certainly have wanted to be emperor. For instance, when the Manchus were overthrown in 1911, did Yüan Shih-kai not support the Republic ?

Had he ever advocated a monarchy ?   The people
of the whole nation believed then that monarchy
would never rear its head again in China.   And
yet, when in the second year of the Republic
Yüan Shih-kai had used military force to defeat
the Revolutionary Party and to drive its members
out of the country, he at once changed the system
of government and made himself emperor.   And
this military caste in China now is full of insuf-
ferably corrupt ideas just like Yüan Shih-kai's.
No one can prophesy that the same danger will
not arise again.   So the reason why China's revolution is not yet accomplished is because we have
not entirely cut off, we have not completely suppressed, these ambitions for kingship.   If we
want to uproot entirely and suppress these
ambitions completely, we must fight against
them once more and start another revolution.

Many of the ardent young intellectuals in
China are still proposing that we fight for liberty
and equality.   Europe fought for these things
over a hundred years ago, but the result was
really democracy ; only when the people won
their rights did liberty and equality have a
chance to survive.   Without democracy, liberty
and equality would have been but empty terms.
The origin of democracy lies far back in history ;
two thousand or more years ago Rome and Greece
already had ideas of people's rights and were

democratic states. South of the Mediterranean, at the same time was another republic called Carthage, and several small states which sprang up in succession afterwards were also republics. Although Rome and Greece of that day were democracies in name, in reality they had not attained to true liberty and equality. The people's sovereignty had not been applied. Greece had the slave system; the nobility all owned many slaves; in fact, two thirds of all the population were slaves. The warriors of Sparta were each given five slave attendants by the state. So in Greece the people with sovereign rights were a small minority; the large majority had no rights. The same thing was true in Rome. So Greece and Rome two thousand years ago were republics only in name; still having their slave system, they could not realize the ideal of liberty and equality. Not until the United States, sixty years ago, freed her slaves, smashed the slave system, and made the equality of mankind a reality did the hope of true liberty and equality begin to appear in modern democracy. True liberty and equality stand upon democracy and are dependent upon democracy. Only where democracy flourishes can liberty and equality permanently survive; there is no way to preserve them if the sovereignty of the people is lost. So the Revolutionary Party of China, in its inception, took liberty and equality as aims in its struggle but made Democracy — the Sovereignty of the People — its principle and watchword. Only if we achieve democracy can our people have the reality and enjoy the blessings of freedom and liberty. They are embraced in our principle of the People's Sovereignty, hence we are discussing them in connection with our main theme.

After struggling so hard and pouring out so much blood for liberty and equality, how highly should we expect Europe and America to value these principles! How careful they should be to weigh them and not recklessly to abuse them! But the truth is, as I have said before, that many evil practices have flowed from the newly acquired liberty of the West. It is more than one hundred years since the American and French revolutions secured equality. Has equality, too, been abused? I think it has. We cannot afford, after the experience of Western nations, to follow in their tracks and fight only for equality. We must fight for democracy; if democracy prevails, we shall have true equality; if democracy languishes, we can never have equality. Why has equality been so abused in the West? Because the principle was too foolishly conceived and because democracy was not fully developed, therefore equality has not kept in the right road. This is the reason why European peoples are still

struggling for democracy. In order to struggle
more effectively, the people have naturally organized themselves and, realizing the value of
organization, have achieved freedom of assembly
and of association. This freedom has resulted
in various groups, such as political parties and
labor unions.

The largest organized bodies in the world to-day
are the labor unions which have grown up after
the revolutions when liberty was won. The
story of their development is something like this:
in the old days workers were ignorant and had
no group consciousness; they did not realize that
their position was unequal or that they were being
harshly oppressed by the capitalists. They were
like the American negroes, who only knew that
they and their forefathers had been slaves; they
did not feel that they were in a bad way or see
anything like liberty and equality beyond their
own horizon of slavery. Workers in all countries had no conception of their own positions
until from without came to them men of good will,
who were dissatisfied with labor conditions and
who proclaimed among the workers the inequality
of capital and labor, the need for organization,
and the duty of resistance against nobles and
capitalists. Only then did labor begin to organize.
What has been labor's weapon in its struggle
against capital? Only the negative weapon of

noncoöperation through strikes, but it has been more deadly than any military weapon. If the workers make requests to the state or to the capitalists which are not granted, they can unite and strike as one man. Such a strike affects the people of the whole country no less than does a real war. Because the workers had these friendly intellectuals from outside as leaders to guide them and to show them how to organize strongly and how to strike, they were able to display great power as soon as they rose up in society. With their great, newly acquired power the workers began to be self-conscious and to talk of equality. The British and French workers then noticed that the leaders and teachers within their organization were all men of different occupations from themselves, either nobles or scholars all from outside, so they expelled them. This movement in the West against outside leaders of the labor organizations has been on the increase during the last few decades, all because the workers have gone astray in the pursuit of equality. So the unions, although they themselves did not possess the necessary intelligence for leadership, gave up their wise guides. Then, in spite of their large organization, they not only failed to advance and demonstrate great power but even disintegrated within and lost their united strength because of the lack of promoters.

Within the last decade or so, many labor organizations have been formed in China also. Since the Revolution, workers in each trade have begun to unite and form unions. Among the union leaders have also been many who were not workers. Of course, we cannot say that all these leaders were acting for the best interests of the workmen; many have taken advantage of the name of the organization and have used the laborers as tools for their own selfish profit. Yet there have been quite a number who have served the workers out of a genuine sense of justice. The workers, therefore, should understand this and should distinguish the colors of their leaders.

Chinese workers are also abusing the idea of equality. For instance, a few days ago I received a labor paper from Hankow in which were printed two big slogans: "We workers do not want long-gowned leaders" and "We workers are fighting only for bread; we don't care about politics." Such slogans are similar to the denunciations which nonlaboring leaders received in the West. But Western workers, in spite of the fact that they denounced the nonlaboring leaders, still aimed to concern themselves with politics, so the second slogan is not exactly like the Western labor talk. The happiness and the welfare of a people depend entirely upon the question of government and the state's greatest problem is government. If the government is corrupt no problem of state can be solved. China, for example, is now bound by the shackles of foreign economic control and is losing $1,200,000,000 annually. This is simply because the Chinese government is bad, her finances cannot prosper, and she loses a large sum every year. The greatest part of this loss is in the excess of imports over exports amounting annually to $500,000,000. This half billion dollars' worth of goods is the product of human labor, and we are losing it because our industries are languishing. Let us study this loss a moment. Chinese laborers can work for less wages and toil and drudge harder than any other laborers in the world — ten hours a day steadily — which should make them win out in competition with foreign industry. But why are Chinese-manufactured exports no match for foreign-manufactured imports? Why do we have to lose half a billion dollars a year in the field of industry alone? The chief reason is the corruption of the Chinese government. It has no power; if it had, it might prevent this loss to industry. The saving would mean half a billion dollars' worth of bread for the country. How could a strong government prevent this loss? — By increasing the tariff. Foreign goods would then naturally find it difficult to enter our ports, and Chinese native goods could find a wide market.

Then the workers of the whole country would have
$500,000,000 more income. But according to
the slogans in the Hankow labor publication, the
workers do not care about politics and therefore
would not demand that the government increase
the tariff against foreign goods and support
native industry. But unless that is done, China
will stop manufacturing native goods and the
workers will not have employment. Then where
will the worker get his bread? This shows that
without good leadership the workers open their
mouths only to blunder. Such labor organizations
cannot prosper and will soon break up. They are
too stupid if they do not know that bread is an
economic problem and that politics and economics
are closely related. If they are not going to concern themselves about government, how can they
settle the economic question of bread and make a
living? The Hankow workers' slogans are the evil
effects of a misunderstanding of equality. Therefore, in our revolution we must not talk only about
getting equality; we must hold up the people's
rights. Unless democracy is fully developed, the
equality which we fight for will be only temporary
and will soon disappear. But although our revolution does not make Equality its slogan, still we
do include equality in the Sovereignty of the
People. When equality is a good thing we will
apply it; when it is an evil, we will do away

with it. Only thus can we make democracy develop and use equality to advantage.

I once suggested that the people of the world might be divided, according to their natural endowments, into three groups : those who know and perceive beforehand, those who know and perceive afterward, and those who do not know and perceive — the discoverers, the promoters, and the practical men. If these three groups could use each other and heartily coöperate, human civilization would advance "a thousand miles a day."

Although Nature produces men with varying intelligence and ability, yet the human heart has continued to hope that all men might be equal. This is the highest of moral ideals and mankind should earnestly strive towards it. But how shall we begin? We will better understand by contrasting two philosophies of life — the selfish which benefits self and the altruistic which benefits others. Those who are out for themselves are continually injuring others with no pang of conscience. When this philosophy prevailed, intelligent and able men used all their powers to seize others' rights and privileges, gradually formed an autocratic caste, and created political inequalities — that was the world before the revolutions for democracy. Those who are concerned with benefiting others are glad to sacrifice themselves. Where this philosophy prevails, intelligent and

able men are ever ready to use all their powers
for the welfare of others, and religions of love and
philanthropic enterprises grow up. But religious power alone is insufficient and philanthropy
alone cannot remedy all evil. So we must seek
a fundamental solution, effect a revolution,
overthrow autocracy, lift up democracy, and level
inequalities. Hereafter we should harmonize the
three types which I have described and give them
all equal standing. Everyone should make service,
not exploitation, his aim. Those with greater
intelligence and ability should serve thousands
and ten thousands to the limit of their power
and make thousands and ten thousands happy.
Those with less intelligence and ability should
serve tens and hundreds to the limit of their
power and make tens and hundreds happy. The
saying, "The skillful the slaves of the stupid"
is just this principle. Those who have neither
intelligence nor ability should still, to the limit
of their individual power, each serve one another
and make one another happy. In this way,
although men now may vary in natural intelligence
and ability, yet as moral ideals and the spirit of
service prevail, they will certainly become more
and more equal. This is the essence of equality.

LECTURE 4

Western democracy has not brought its peoples a full measure of political rights — Difficulties in administration of a democratic government — Struggle between Jefferson and Hamilton in the early days of the American Republic — The victory for the Federalists and policy of centralization — The United States Constitution — Why China does not need a federal union like the United States — China has already been a united country under a single government — False arguments for federation advanced by ambitious Chinese — Balance between federal and states' rights in the United States — Development of the suffrage in Western democracies — Woman suffrage a recent achievement — Mob rule during the French Revolution and the resulting setback to democracy — The democratic movement in Great Britain, British concessions to democracy — Bismarck's powerful hand in uniting and building up the German state — His skillful opposition to the democratic and socialistic movements in Germany — Advance of democracy in spite of setbacks — New political rights and direct democracy in Switzerland — Representative government in the West; its failure to date in China.

In the preceding lectures we saw that Europeans and Americans have been engaged for two or three centuries in their struggle for democracy. To-day I want to speak about the measure of people's rights which they have won and the progress which they have made in democracy during this period. Democratic ideas have already spread to China and are making their impression upon the Chinese people through current books and newspapers. The books and the newspapers which advocate democracy are, of course, very strong supporters of democracy; they speak of the "roar of the democratic tide" and of the "phenomenal growth of democratic ideas" in a way that naturally inspires all of us who read; and those who are making a study of democracy are naturally inclined to read only these books and newspapers. We begin to cherish thoughts of democracy and suppose that since the Western peoples have achieved such great victories in their fight for political rights, democracy is surely coming to full bloom in every nation of the world. China, we say, is standing in the world current of to-day and must also promote and further the cause of democracy. Moreover, there are many who feel that if Chinese democracy can reach the standard of Western democracy, it will have realized its aim and China will be considered a very civilized and progressive state. But there is a wide divergence between the Western democracy which we find in books and that which we see in actual practice. Look at the so-called pioneers of democratic government in the West, like the United States and France, whose revolutions took place over a century ago — how many

political rights have the people really won ? To
the believer in democracy, it seems that the people
have gained but very little power. Those who
fought for the people's rights thought that they
would reach the democratic ideal at once, so they
sacrificed everything and pooled all their resources
of strength in a life and death struggle. But
after they had conquered in battle, they found
that they had gained much less power than they
had hoped for during the revolution. They had
not yet attained to perfect democracy.

Take once more the American War of Independence against Great Britain. It took eight
years for the colonies to win the war and to achieve
their ideals of popular sovereignty. According
to the Declaration of Independence, liberty and
equality are natural and inalienable rights.
The American revolutionists had hoped to win
complete freedom and equality, yet after their
eight years of struggle they still did not enjoy
many popular rights. Why ? The great enemy
to the people's sovereignty in the American
colonies was the British king ; his oppressions
gave rise to the independence movement and to
war against Great Britain — a war of democracy
against autocracy. Since the war resulted in
victory for democracy, it seems that the people
should have gained all their rights. But why was
the democratic ideal not realized ? Because, after

independence had been won and autocracy had
been overthrown, problems as to the administration of democratic government arose among its
supporters. How far could popular sovereignty
be actually applied? Here the fellow disciples of
democracy began to differ in their opinions. As
a result there was a division into two great parties.
You have all heard of the illustrious leader of
the American Revolution, the father-statesman
of the United States — Washington. But there
were other heroes also who helped him in his
struggle against Great Britain. Among these were
Washington's secretary of the treasury, Hamilton,
and his secretary of state, Jefferson. As these
two men differed radically over methods of administration and as both had large followings,
they became the founders of two absolutely
different political parties. Jefferson's party
believed that the people were endowed with
natural rights and that if the people were given
complete democratic power, they would be discriminating in the use of their freedom, would
direct their power to the accomplishment of
great tasks, and would make all the affairs of the
nation progress to the fullest extent. Jefferson's
theory assumed that human nature is naturally good, and that if the people under complete
democratic rule sometimes do not express their
natural virtue and do good but abuse their power

and do evil, it is because they have met some obstacle and are for the time being forced to act that way. In short, every man is naturally endowed with freedom and equality and hence should have political power; every man is intelligent and if given political power to govern would do great things for the nation; if all the citizens would shoulder the responsibility for good government, the state would prosper long in peace. Such was the Jeffersonian party's faith in the rights of the people.

The policy proposed by Hamilton's party was directly opposed to Jefferson's ideas. Hamilton did not think that human nature was always perfect; and he felt that, if democratic power were given equally to all men, bad men would direct their political power to bad ends. And if corrupt individuals should get much of the power of the state into their hands, they would use the rights and privileges of the state for the selfish benefit and profit of their own party; they would not care a rap for any morality, law, justice, or order in the nation, and the final result would be either a "state with three rulers"— divided authority and want of unity — or mob rule, that is, liberty and equality pushed to excess and anarchy. Such an application of democracy would not advance the nation but would only throw it into disorder and make it lose ground. So Hamilton proposed

that the political power of the state should not
be given entirely to the people, but should be
centralized in the government, in a central
authority ; the common people should have only
a limited degree of democracy. If the people
should all have unlimited power and should use
it for evil, the effect upon the nation would be
far more serious than the evil deeds of one king.
A wicked king still has many people to oversee
him and restrain him, but a people who get
unlimited power into their hands and use it for
wicked purposes have none to oversee and restrain them. Therefore Hamilton declared that,
as autocracy had to be restricted, so democracy
must also be limited, and he founded the Federal-
ist Party which advocated the centralization and
not the diffusion of sovereign power.

Before the War of Independence the thirteen
original colonies were governed by Great Britain
and were unable to unite. Later, when they
found that they could not endure the extreme
despotism of the British government, they resisted,
and out of their common aim a common spirit
was born. But after the war, the colonies again
divided and found themselves unable to agree.
At the time of the Revolution the total population
of the thirteen colonies was not over three million, of which only two million opposed Great
Britain. The other one million were still loyal

to the British king; that is, one third of the people in the states were still "Loyalists." Only two thirds of the people were true Revolutionists, and the disturbances created by the one-third Loyalists in their midst made the war stretch out to eight years before victory was finally assured. After the victory over England, the Loyalists had no place to hide, and so fled northward, crossed the St. Lawrence River, and helped to found the great colony of Canada, which is even yet British territory, loyal to the mother country.

After the states had secured their independence, they were no longer troubled by enemies within, but their three million people were scattered throughout thirteen states with not over two hundred thousand in any one state, and the states did not get along well together. Since they would not unite, the nation's power was weak; it might easily be swallowed up by another European power. The future was full of dangers. Then the farseeing statesmen of the different states saw that they must increase their national strength tremendously if they wanted to avert the dangers ahead and establish a permanent nation. So they proposed that all the states unite and form one great state. Some advocated purely popular sovereignty and others purely national sovereignty as a means of bringing about union. The former group advocated local authority, the

latter group advocated centralized authority and
the limitation of the people's power. They
wanted the states all to pool their own rights
and powers in a strong central government, and
so were called the Federalists. The fight waged
between these two opposing groups by mouth and
pen was long and bitter. Finally the Federalists
who advocated the limitation of popular sovereignty won out, the states got together, formed
a federal union, and promulgated the Constitution
of the United States. From the beginning of the
Republic until now the United States has used this
Constitution, which divides clearly the legislative,
judicial, and executive powers of the government
so that they do not encroach upon each other.
It was the first complete constitution in human
history and the United States was the first
nation to adopt a written constitution separating
the three branches of government. The United
States " broke through the barren heavens " —
set the precedent — in written constitutions of
nations. This constitution is what we call the
Federal Constitution of the United States. Since
the United States formed a federal union and
adopted the Constitution, it has become the
wealthiest and, since the European War, the
most powerful nation in the world.

Because the United States started on the road
to its present position of wealth and power from

a federal constitution which yet leaves the local
affairs of the people to state control, a group of
Chinese intellectuals and scholars during the last
decade have been proposing that China, in order
to be wealthy and strong, must also form a federal
union. They have thought to solve China's
present problems, but they have not made a fundamental comparison of the conditions in the United
States and in China ; their only argument is that
since a federal union made the United States
wealthy and strong, and since China's great hope
is to be wealthy and strong, therefore we should
have a federal union of the provinces. The
fundamental advantage of the American federal
system came from the fact that each state already
had a constitution and a government of its own.
If we want to follow the United States' federal
plan and form a union of provinces, all the
provinces should first adopt constitutions and
establish their own governments, then unite and
decide upon a national constitution. In a word,
we would have to take our already united China,
divide it into twenty-odd independent units to
correspond with the dozen or so independent
American states over a century ago, and then weld
them together again. Such views and ideas are
utterly fallacious. We become mere parrots, re-
peating with our eyes shut what others tell us.
Because the United States, with its federal system,

has become the world's wealthiest and greatest
power, we think that we must copy her system
in order that China may be wealthy and strong.
This is similar to what I have said before : while
Westerners fought for democracy, they did not
talk about democracy but about liberty and
equality ; so we Chinese in our revolution must
take the Western slogans and cry that we are
struggling for liberty and equality! All this is
but blind following and foolish incomprehension.
Those who propose self-government in the provinces of this Union argue superficially that the
United States was built upon the foundation
of several small self-governing states and that
China has a foundation of many provinces which
could also become self-governing, wealthy, and
strong. They have no idea of the conditions
that existed when American independence was
declared.   When the states had achieved freedom
from Great Britain, why did they talk of union ?
Because the thirteen states had been entirely
separate, were not under one control, and therefore had to unite in order to form a single
nation.

But what is the situation in China ?   China
Proper has apparently been divided into eighteen
provinces ; add the three provinces of Manchuria
and Sinkiang province and we have twenty-two
provinces.   Then   there   are   Jehol,   Suiyüan,

Kokonor, and many other special areas, besides Mongolia, Tibet, and the other dependencies. During the two hundred sixty years of the Manchu dynasty, all these places were under the central Manchu government. During the Ming dynasty the provinces were united; during the Yüan dynasty not only was all territory within China's boundaries united, but Europe and Asia were almost united under one government. Going back to the Sung dynasty we find the provinces closely tied together and after the crossing of the Yangtze the southern provinces were also a united country. Even as long ago as the T'ang and Han dynasties, the provinces of China were all united under a single government. From this we see that the provinces in past history have been united, not separate, parts of China and have not been incapable of unified rule. Moreover, the periods of unity have been the periods of good government; the periods of disunity, the periods of disorder. The United States' wealth and power have not come only from the independence and self-government of the original states, but rather from the progress in unified government which followed the federation of the states. Her wealth and power were the result of the union of the states, not of the division into states. Since China was originally unified, we should not divide her again into separate provinces.

The present want of unity in China is but a
temporary phenomenon of disorder, the result
of the grasping of domains by militarists. We
must do away with this sort of thing. On no
account can we again allow the misleading
principle of federation to serve as a charm to
protect the militarists in their seizures of territory.
If the militarists have an excuse to divide China
into domains, China will never again be wealthy
and powerful. If we say that the American
federal system is the key to wealth and power, we
are putting effect before cause. Why do foreign
nations now want to impose international control
upon China? Whence do they perceive our
weakness? They see the intellectual class in
China expressing opinions and making proposals
which are all against the trend of the times, and
consequently they look down upon China. They
say that we Chinese cannot manage our own affairs so the Powers must manage them for us.

If we of the Far East who stand in the current
of modern world movements want to make an
exact use of the phrase " federation of states,"
we should talk about a union of China and Japan,
or of China, Annam, Burma, India, Persia, and
Afghanistan. For these states never have been
united, and a union of them in order to make Asia
wealthy and powerful and to oppose Europe would
be the only consistent use of the idea of federation.

As for the eighteen provinces of China Proper, the three provinces of Manchuria, and all the other special divisions of China, they were already unified under one rule during the Manchu dynasty. It was only when we overthrew the Manchu dynasty and inherited its territory that we were able to set up the present Republic; why should we again split up the country which has always been unified ? Those who advocate the division of China are votaries of ambition who want the provinces for their own special domains. T'ang Chi-yao has seized Yünnan; Chao Heng-t'ang has seized Hunan; Lu Yung-t'ing has seized Kwangsi; Ch'en Ch'iung-ming has seized Kwangtung — such a type of federation would be a military federation, not a federation of self-governing peoples. Such a federation would not profit China, it would only profit individuals. We must make a clear distinction here.

When the thirteen American states secured their independence from England, they had absolutely no political unity, and the formation of a unified nation was a tremendously difficult task. So the debates between the parties of Hamilton and Jefferson were very fierce. When the Constitution was drawn up, each state was given freedom in casting votes. Finally, Hamilton's party won out and the Jeffersonian policy began to lose ground. Because the people of the

country at the time when the Constitution was
framed were divided into these two great parties
with different political theories, the Constitution
which was finally promulgated was a document
of compromise between the two parties. The
important political powers which belonged to
the central government were clearly defined in
the Constitution ; matters not regulated by the
Constitution were left to local governments. The
coinage of money, for example, was put under
control of the central government, and local
governments were not allowed to transgress upon
this right. Foreign relations were delegated to
the central government and no state could make
a private treaty with a foreign country. Other
matters, like national defense, the training of
troops upon land and sea, the right to move and
dispatch state militia, were all intrusted to the
central government. Matters of detail which
were not delegated by the Constitution to the
central government were left to the individual
states to regulate. This division of power was
a compromise measure between the central
government and the state governments. What
rights did the people obtain out of this compromise ? — Only a limited suffrage. The suffrage
at that time was limited to the election of
congressmen and of various state and local
officials. The president and the senators were

still elected indirectly by electors chosen by the people. Later the powers of the people were gradually enlarged until to-day the president, the senators, and all state and local officials who have any direct, important relation with the people are elected by direct popular vote. This is what we call universal suffrage.

Therefore, the evolution in the United States from limited to universal suffrage was very gradual. At first suffrage was enjoyed only by men. Only a decade or two ago women still did not have the right to vote. Twenty years ago the movement for woman suffrage became very strong in Europe and America. You all know that at that time many people felt that the women would not succeed in their struggle on the ground that they were inferior in intellect and ability to men and could not do all the things that men could do. So there were many opponents of woman suffrage not only among men but even among the women themselves. Even if all the women of the nation had fought violently for the right to vote, they could hardly have hoped to succeed. But seven or eight years ago the women of Great Britain, and not long afterward the women of the United States, were successful in their struggle. The cause was the European War. During the war, the men went into the army and spent their strength upon the battlefields. Consequently,

much of the nation's business was left without
men to care for it; there were not enough men
to be officers and day laborers in the arsenals, to
be engineers and conductors on the street cars, and
to assume responsibility for the various kinds of
business which required energetic attention at
the home base. Women were called upon to
fill men's jobs, and then those who had opposed
woman suffrage, saying that women could not
do the work of men, were stripped of their arguments and no longer dared to thwart the movement. The advocates of woman suffrage then
won a complete victory and after the war the
question was finally settled. From this we can
see that the objective of the Western revolutions
was originally democracy. The American War
of Independence was a war for democracy; after
the war, however, comrades in the cause divided
into two groups — one group advocating complete
democracy, the other group advocating limited
powers for the people but large powers for the
state. Many later events went to prove that
the common people did not possess the necessary
intelligence and power to wield complete sovereignty. That Jefferson and his disciples tried
to obtain more rights for the people, but failed,
shows that the common people did not know
how to exercise political sovereignty. So, although the Western revolutions of these two or

three hundred years have been fought under the standard of democracy, the actual result has only been the attainment of suffrage for men and women.

The French Revolution also set up democracy as its goal. Scholarly advocates of democracy like Rousseau declared that all men had natural rights which kings and princes could not take away, and such theories gave birth to the revolution. When democracy began to be applied after the revolution, nobles and members of the royal house received so many injuries that they were unable to remain in France and had to flee to other countries. The French people were now making their first experiment in complete democracy; no one in the country dared to say that the people did not have intelligence and power; if one did, he would be accused of being a counter-revolutionist and would immediately be brought to the guillotine. The result was that a mob tyranny was instituted. Anarchy followed, society was panic-stricken, no one was sure of his life from morning till evening. Even a regular member of the revolutionary party might, because of a careless word which offended the multitude, be sentenced to death. In this experiment at pure democracy, not only were many princes, lords, and nobles killed, but not a few ardent revolutionists of the time, like Danton, were put to death by the populace because of some word that did not please them. When the French people afterwards came to realize that such a state of affairs was too oppressive, many who had been eager supporters of democracy grew despondent and cold, turned against democratic government, and supported Napoleon for emperor. Democracy now met a great obstacle. Not from autocracy: the democratic movement had already become powerful and, as I have been saying, the world had reached the age of democracy. It stood to reason that democracy would steadily advance. Why, then, after democracy had overthrown autocracy, did such barriers to the progress of democracy arise? What created them? One cause was the attitude of the conservative supporters of democracy who advocated definite limitation of the people's sovereignty and the centralization of the state's power, rather than complete democracy. But this group was not powerful and did not impede the progress of democracy very seriously. The real obstructionists were the believers in absolute democracy. When, during the French Revolution, the people secured complete power, they no longer wanted leaders and they put to death many of the wise and able ones. The groups of violent followers who were left were devoid of clear perception and were easily made tools of by others. Without

their " good ears and eyes " the people of the
nation were unable to distinguish who was right
and who was wrong in any issue that arose ;
only let someone incite them and everyone would
blindly follow. Such a state of affairs was
extremely perilous. So when the people awoke
to it in the course of time, they did not dare to
advocate democracy again. Out of this reaction
against democracy developed a great obstacle to
the progress of democracy, an obstacle created by
the very people who advocated people's rights.

Since the French Revolution, small countries
of Europe, like Denmark, Holland, Spain, and
Portugal, have almost unconsciously developed
democratic movements. The democratic movement in Europe met many obstacles and encountered the opposition of autocracy, but could not
be destroyed. When it met obstacles within the
movement itself, it still could not be stopped,
and went on with its natural progress. Why
was this ? Because there is no way of checking
a great current or tendency from flowing in its
natural direction. Because of this principle,
many autocratic states have been following the
tide and trimming their sails to the wind. England, for instance, once staged a revolution and
put her king to death, but after ten years the
monarchy was again restored. The British nobility, however, have been opportunists ; they saw

that democracy was too great a force for them
to resist, so they have not fought it but have compromised with it. The beginnings of modern
democracy were originally found in England.
After the restoration of the monarchy and the
overthrow of democracy in England, the government was controlled by the nobility ; only nobles
were allowed a hand in government affairs and
all other classes had to keep quiet. After 1832,
the common people were given the right to vote,
and after the European War women were granted
the suffrage. In the treatment of her colonies,
Great Britain has also used well the method of
gradual concession as the democratic tide advanced. Take Ireland, which is one of the three
islands of Great Britain. At first England used
military force to suppress Ireland, but when she
saw the growth of the democratic movement in
Ireland she gave up the policy of suppression,
advocated yielding to the Irish, and granted them
independence. The British government has also
given way not only within the British Isles, but
also without. It has yielded to Egypt : during
the European War, Egypt worked hard for Great
Britain and in order to encourage the Egyptians
in their fighting, the British government promised
them many rights after the war and ultimate
independence. After the war Great Britain went
back on her word and did not grant any of the

rights which she had promised to Egypt   Egypt
demanded independence and the fulfillment of
the pledges ; a tremendous agitation followed,
Great Britain yielded, and Egypt secured independence. India is now demanding an extension
of the suffrage and Great Britain is promising
everything that is asked for. That England has
a labor party and gives workers representation
in the formation of its cabinets is enough to show
that the nobility are making concessions and that
democracy is advancing. The British nobility
have realized the great power of democracy and
have followed the trend of the times instead of
opposing it ; consequently they can still maintain
their old form of government and the state does
not face any serious danger.

Since the American and the French Revolution,
democratic ideals have been spreading steadily
throughout the world. The newest theories of
democracy owe their real origin, however, to
Germany. The German mind has always been rich
in democratic ideas ; labor unions are numerous
in Germany, and the largest labor party in the
world is still to be found in Germany. Democratic
philosophy developed early in Germany, but up
to the time of the European War it had not
produced as much fruit as in France or Great
Britain. The reason was that the methods used
by the German government in dealing with

democracy were different from those used by
the British government; therefore, the results
attained were also different. What were the
methods used by the German government?
Who hindered the growth of democracy in Germany? Many students say that the setback
began with Bismarck, the renowned and talented
statesman of Germany who thirty or forty years
ago was determining all the important policies
of the world. The statesmen of the world could
not escape his influence, so the Germany of his
day was the most powerful state in the world.
Germany's power was built up entirely by
Bismarck's hand. Before he took the reins of
government, Germany was composed of twenty
or more small states with homogeneous peoples,
but under separate rule and even more disunited
than the thirteen American colonies. Under the
subjection of Napoleon the people suffered intolerable distress. Then Bismarck came forth and
used his wisdom and ability, together with a strong
political arm, to fuse the twenty neighboring
states with their homogeneous peoples into a
great confederation, and started Germany on
the road to wealth and power.

Ten years ago Germany was the mightiest
nation in the world, while the United States was
the wealthiest. Because Germany and the United
States are federations of states, many people

think that China, to be wealthy and powerful, must follow their example. They do not realize that Germany thirty or forty years ago had only Prussia to start with ; it was after Bismarck took political control, made Prussia a foundation, organized the army, prepared for war, cleaned up the government, and united the twenty or more other states, that modern Germany was built up. When Bismarck was forming the Confederation, France and Austria opposed him with all their might. The reason why Austria opposed the federal union of Germany is this : although Austria and Germany were of the same Teutonic race, the Austrian emperor was also struggling for supreme power in Europe and so did not want Germany to unite and become stronger than Austria. But no man was more skillful than Bismarck ; he determined to scheme for power and in 1866, with a lightning move, made war upon Austria. Austria was at once defeated. Germany after her victory could have wiped Austria off the map, but Bismarck felt that, although the Austrian government had opposed Germany, yet the Austrian people were of the same blood as hers and would not make much trouble for her in the future. Bismarck was very farsighted, knowing fully that the great trouble makers for Germany in the future would be England and France. So immediately after his victory over Austria, Bismarck proposed the most magnanimous terms of peace to her, and Austria, with defeat fresh in her mind, was of course extremely grateful. Only six years after this, in 1870, Germany declared war on France, defeated Napoleon III, and captured Paris. When peace was made, France had to cede Alsace-Lorraine to Germany. As a result of these two wars the twenty or more small German states were bound powerfully together and became a unified nation. From the establishment of the German Confederation until before the European War, Germany was the strongest state in the world. She was the master of Europe and the nations of Europe followed her as a leading horse. Germany was raised to her eminent position entirely by the creative arm of Bismarck. Within twenty years after he had taken charge of the government, Bismarck transformed a weak Germany into a powerful state. After such an achievement, democracy while it flourished in Germany did not have sufficient strength to challenge the government.

While Bismarck was in power, he not only dominated the world in political and military affairs and in all kinds of diplomacy, but he also used consummate skill in dealing with the democratic movement and in winning victories over his own people. In the latter part of the nineteenth century, after the Franco-Prussian War,

economic wars as well as wars for democracy
began to break out. The hot passion for
democracy was gradually cooling, but something
else was being born — socialism. Socialism is
similar to the Principle of the People's Livelihood,
which I have been advocating. When the people
got hold of the theory of socialism they began to
give up their eager fight for democratic rights and
to struggle instead for economic rights. This war
was a class struggle between the workers and
the wealthy class. Labor organizations had been
formed first in Germany, so socialism also developed first in that country. The greatest socialist
thinkers in the world have been Germans. You
all know of the great Socialist, Marx, who was a
German. The veteran revolutionary party in
Russia which tried to practice Marxian socialism
was composed of Marx's disciples. At that time
German socialism had a very wide influence.

Socialism was originally closely related to
democracy and the two should have developed
simultaneously. But why did democratic ideas
in Europe give rise to democratic revolutions,
while the spread of socialist theories failed to
give rise to economic revolutions?—Because the
birth of socialism in Germany coincided with
Bismarck's régime. Other men would certainly
have used political force to crush socialism, but
Bismarck chose to employ other methods. He

knew that the German people were enlightened
and that the labor organizations were firmly
established; if he attempted the suppression of
socialism by political force, he would only labor
in vain. Bismarck had already been in favor of
absolute control by a centralized authority.
What methods did he use to deal with the
socialists? The Socialist Party advocated social
reforms and economic revolution. Bismarck knew
that they could not be suppressed by political
power, so he put into effect a kind of state socialism as an antidote against the Marxian socialists'
program. Railroads, for example, are a vital
means of communication and a fundamental
industry in any nation, essential to the development of all other industries. Before the Tientsin-
Pukow Railway was built, Chihli, Shantung, and
northern Kiangsu were extremely poor sections
of country; after the railway came, the regions
along the route became very productive. Before
the construction of the Peking-Hankow Railway,
Chihli, Hupeh, and Honan were barren country,
but after the railway had brought convenient
transportation, the provinces through which it
passed became quite prosperous. At the time
when Bismarck was seizing the reins of government in Germany, most of the railways in Great
Britain and France were privately owned. Because the capital industries were owned by the

wealthy, all the industries of the nation became
monopolies of the wealthy class, and the many
evils of an unequal distribution of wealth began
to appear. Bismarck did not want such conditions in Germany, so he put into effect a state
socialism ; he brought all the railways of the country under state ownership and control and put all
the essential industries under state management.
He determined upon hours of labor and arranged
for old-age pensions and accident insurance for
the workers. These measures were items in
the program of reform which the Socialist Party
was trying to carry out ; the farseeing Bismarck
took the lead and used the state's power to accomplish them. Moreover, he used the profits from
the state-managed railways, banks, and other
businesses for the protection of workers, which of
course made the workers very contented. Before
this, several hundred thousand workers had been
leaving Germany for other countries every year,
but after Bismarck's economic policy was put into
effect, not only did no more German workers
leave but many came from other countries to
work in Germany. Bismarck met socialism by
anticipating it and by taking precautions against
it, rather than by a head-on attack upon it ; by
invisible means he caused the very issues for which
the people were struggling to dissolve. When
there was nothing left for the people to fight for

revolutions naturally did not break out. This was the artful method by which Bismarck resisted democracy.

Looking now at the whole history of democratic progress, we see that the first setback occurred after the American Revolution when the supporters of democracy split into two camps, Jefferson's group advocating absolute democracy and Hamilton's group centralization of power in the government, and when the policy of centralization won out. The second setback occurred during the French Revolution when the people secured complete sovereignty but abused it and changed it into mob rule. The third setback occurred when Bismarck checked the people's power with his clever scheming. Democratic thought in the West has passed through these phases and has met these setbacks, yet, contrary to all expectation, it has of its own accord still moved forward and no human power has been able to thwart it or to hasten it. To-day democracy has become the great world problem, and the scholars of the world, whether conservative or progressive, all realize that the democratic idea cannot be suppressed. But as democracy develops, it will be inevitably abused in the same way as liberty and equality have been abused.

To sum up: the European and American struggles for liberty and equality bore fruit in democracy: after democracy prevailed, it was much abused. Before the development of democracy, the Western nations tried to suppress it and to destroy it with autocratic power. When autocracy had been overthrown, the followers of democracy became the obstructionists of democracy. When democracy was realized, it produced many evils, and a greater obstacle thus resulted. Finally Bismarck saw that the people could not be downed in their desire for democracy, so he employed the power of the state as a substitute for the people's power and put into effect a state socialism; this policy also obstructed the march of democracy. Since the European War, the despotic governments of Germany and Russia have been overthrown and women in several countries have won the right to vote, so democracy to-day becomes a greater problem, not easy of solution.

Tracing the beginnings of applied democracy, we see the American people after their revolution winning first the right to vote. At that time Westerners thought that democracy meant suffrage and that was all. If all the people without regard to social status, wealth, or intellectual capacity had the right to vote, democracy had reached its final goal. But what has been happening in the three or four years since the European War? In spite of many setbacks, democracy is

still moving forward and cannot be checked.
Recently the people of Switzerland have won, in
addition to the right to vote, the rights of
initiative and referendum. If the people have
the right to choose their officials, they should also
have the right to initiate and amend the làws.
The rights of initiative and referendum are related
to the enactment of laws. If a majority of the
people think that a certain law will be beneficial,
they can then propose it — this is the right of
initiative ; if they feel that a certain law is disadvantageous to them they can amend it — this is
the right of referendum. The Swiss people have
thus two more popular rights than other peoples,
altogether three. Some of the newly developed
states in the northwestern part of the United
States have, in recent years, gained another right
besides those of the Swiss people — the right of
recall of officials. Although the enjoyment of
this right is not universal throughout the United
States, yet several states have practiced it, so
many Americans enjoy the four popular rights —
suffrage, recall, initiative, and referendum. In
some of the northwestern states they have been
applied with great success, and some day they
may be applied throughout the United States
and perhaps throughout the world. In the future, any nation which wants complete democracy must certainly follow the example of these

American states which have given four rights to
the people. Do these four rights, when applied,
fully solve the problems of democracy ? World
scholars, seeing that, although people have these
four ideals of popular rights, yet the problem of
democracy is not fully solved, say that it is only
a matter of time. Ideas of direct popular rule,
they consider, have developed but recently. The
old theocracy lasted for tens of thousands of
years; the old autocracy has lasted for thousands
of years. Autocracy to-day in Great Britain,
Japan, and Italy is still faced with serious problems
and will certainly not last much longer. This
direct democracy is a very new thing; it has come
only within the last few decades. No wonder it
is still a great, unsettled issue!

What is the share of the people in the government in those nations which have the highest
type of democracy ? How much power do they
possess ? About the only achievement within
the past century has been the right to elect and
to be elected. After being elected as the representatives of the people, citizens can sit in Congress
or Parliament to manage the affairs of state.
All measures of national importance must be
passed upon by Parliament before they can be
put into effect; without Parliament's approval
they cannot be carried out. This is called representative or parliamentary government. But

does this form of government insure the perfect
development of democracy ?   Before a representative system of government had been secured,
the European and American peoples struggled
for democracy, thinking that it would certainly
be the highest type of popular sovereignty, just
as the Chinese Revolutionary Party thinks that
reaching the standard of Japan or of the West
will be the highest success we can achieve.   If
you believe that becoming like Japan or Western nations will be the limit of perfection, listen
to my next remarks.

Europeans and Americans once thought that if
they could attain to representative government,
they would be absolutely satisfied.   After our
revolution in 1911 did we not attain to representative government ?   What benefits of democracy
did the people really obtain ?   You all know that
our representatives have all become mere "swine";
if there is money to be had they will sell
themselves, divide the booty, and covet more
gain.   They are despised by the whole nation.
No nation which uses a representative system of
government can avoid some of its abuses, but in
China representative government has led to
intolerable evils.   If all the people ignore their
representative government and do not try to
remedy it, but put the affairs of the nation in
the hands of "swine" representatives and let

them misbehave, the future of the nation is in
awful danger. So the hope of foreigners that
representative government will insure the sta-
bility and peace of the state is not to be trusted.
Democracy as soon as it was born met with many
difficulties; after it was applied it experienced
many humiliations, but still it steadily grows.
Yet the fruit of democracy has been only representative government; when this is achieved the
nations think that the limit is reached. Recently
Russia has developed a new type of government,
not a representative government but an absolute government of the people. We do not
have much data with which to appraise this new
form of government, but one would think that
a government absolutely of the people had
many advantages over a representative government.

But the democracy advocated in the Three
Principles upon which the Kuomintang Party
proposes to reconstruct China is different from
Western democracy. When we use Western history
as material for study, we are not copying the
West entirely or following in its path. We will
use our Principle of the People's Sovereignty
and remake China into a nation under complete
popular rule, ahead of Europe and America. To
realize this aim we must first study democracy
until we understand it with perfect clearness.

The main purpose of my lecture to-day has been to make you see that the advanced nations of the West which have practiced democracy for the past hundred years have attained only to some kind of representative government. This system brought over to China has produced many abuses, so that democracy is still a knotty problem for us. I shall give two more lectures upon the People's Sovereignty and try to discover a fundamental solution of our difficulty in China. If we cannot solve our difficulty, China will still trail behind the Western nations ; if we can find a solution, China will be able to outstrip Europe and America.

April 13, 1924.

LECTURE 5

The Boxers' fearless opposition to Westerners and their confidence in ancient Chinese weapons of warfare — Defeat of the Boxers showed China the superiority of Western material civilization and was followed by extreme faith in and imitation of the West — Western material sciences have progressed far beyond Western science of government — Rapid advance in Western military science ; battleships, guns — Slow advance in methods of applying political democracy — Western political systems cannot be applied wholesale in China — Need for careful study and thought in adapting democracy to China — The Western fear of a too powerful government and its influence on the Chinese mind— Decreasing reverence for China's ancient sage emperors — A new theory proposed : distinction between sovereignty and ability — The three types, discoverers, promoters, operators, compared with engineers, foremen, and workmen — Democracy cannot wait for intelligence and foresight of all the people — New attitude towards government needed — Illustration from the "Three Kingdoms," Ah Tou and Chu Ko-liang — The able emperors of olden days — The people as shareholders should choose able managers— Use of specialists applied to government — The government as expert chauffeur or mechanic — Lesson from an automobile ride in Shanghai.

The Chinese people's ideas of political democracy have all come in from the West, so in carrying forward our Revolution and in reforming our government we are imitating Western methods.

Why ?   Because we see that Western civilization
has been "flying like a cock, crashing its way, a
thousand miles in a single day," and that it is
in every way more advanced than Chinese civilization.   In the matter of military weapons alone
the West is making daily improvements and is
far ahead of China.   For thousands of years the
Chinese weapons have been the bow and arrow, the
sword, and the lance, and twenty or thirty years
ago these were still in use.   In 1900 the Boxers,
whose original aim it was to drive all Western
influence out of China, engaged in war with allied
forces of eight nations and the weapons they used
were big swords !   Big swords against the machine
guns and cannon of the Allies !   This was the
reaction of the Chinese to the new culture of the
Europeans and the Americans, a kind of opposition
to their material progress.   The Boxers did not
believe that Western civilization was superior to
Chinese civilization, and in order to demonstrate
the greatness of Chinese civilization they went to
the length of doubting the superiority of Western
rifles and cannon, those deadly and accurate
weapons, to Chinese swords.   The Boxer trouble
was thus brought about.

The valor of the Boxers, when they first rose
up against the Westerners, was almost irresistible.
Take the battle of Yangtsun.   When the British
admiral, Seymour, with three thousand allied

troops, tried to go from Tientsin to Peking to lift
the siege of the legations, he was surrounded by
the Boxers at Yangtsun. The Boxers had no
foreign rifles or cannon, only swords, while the
besieged allied forces had sharp rifles and cannon.
For the Boxers the battle was one of hand-to-
hand fighting. When Seymour found that he was
surrounded he ordered the machine guns to mow
down the Boxers, but although large numbers of
them were killed by the machine gun fire and
flesh and blood were flying in all directions, the
Boxers did not fear or falter. As the ones in
front fell, others took their places, determined,
even if they died, to encircle the Allies. As a
result, Seymour's three thousand soldiers did not
dare to march direct on Peking by way of Yangtsun but retreated to Tientsin to wait. Only
after securing heavy reënforcements were they
able to reach Peking and to lift the siege of the
legations. Seymour's comment on the battle of
Yangtsun was that if the Boxers had had Western
rifles and cannon in addition to their marvelous
bravery, they would certainly have annihilated
the allied forces. But the Boxers from first
to last had no faith in foreign arms and used
only their swords and bodies in fighting the
Allies. Although tens of thousands were killed
and the wounded were lying upon each other,
soldiers from behind still filled the gaps in the

front line. Their courage was dauntless and made
everyone fear and respect them. Only after the
bloody war with the Boxers did foreigners realize
that the Chinese still had a nationalistic spirit
which could not be crushed.

But the Boxers of 1900 were the last Chinese
to believe that their own ideas and strength could
resist the new civilization from the West. After
the defeat of the Boxers, the Chinese saw that
their old bows and arrows, swords, and lances
could not compete with foreign rifles and cannon.
They perceived that the new civilization from
abroad was really much superior to the ancient
civilization of China. In the matter of military
weapons the contrast between the new in the
West and the old in China is naturally very
marked. But let us look at other things. In
communication, railways and telegraphs are
much superior to the old coolie and post-courier
system of China. Trains naturally can transport
goods more quickly and easily than coolies;
telegraphs naturally carry news faster and better
than post-couriers. Take other machinery which
serves the needs of daily life and methods which
are used in agriculture, industry, and business —
the West has advanced far beyond China.

So, ever since the Boxer defeat, Chinese
thinkers have felt that, to make China strong and
able to avenge the shame of the Peking Protocol,

they must imitate foreign countries in everything.
Not only must they learn material science from
the West, but also political and social science.
Thus, since the Boxer uprising Chinese have lost
all confidence in their own power, and a higher
and higher respect has been paid to foreign countries.   As a result of this imitation of and respect
for foreign nations, China has taken in a lot of
foreign ideas. Ideas which foreigners have simply
considered but have not carried out we have tried
to put into practice.   In our revolution thirteen
years ago, we copied after Western revolutions
and established a democratic form of government.
We wanted to take after the best pattern, so
we tried to apply in China the highest political
philosophy and the newest political theories of
the West.   This was a great change in China's
political thinking.   Before the Boxer uprising
China had engaged in foreign trade and knew
many of the advantages of other countries, but
the people as a whole did not believe that foreign
nations really had a civilization, and at the time
of the Boxers they destroyed the railroads and
telegraphs modeled after the West.   Even foreign
rifles and cannon were not trusted and the old
Chinese bows and swords were used instead as
weapons.   But when China was defeated, the
people turned about and began to believe in the
West.   Everything which China used then had

to be copied from the West. From this we can
see that old China was extremely conservative,
resisted foreign influence, and was absolutely
convinced that China excelled every other nation.
After China was defeated by the West, she became
extremely liberal, swung about to an absolute
reverence for foreign nations and was convinced
that every other nation was better than China.
Hence Chinese wanted nothing from old China;
everything must be modeled after the West. If
we heard of anything foreign, we ran to copy it
and tried to ·use it in China. Democracy also
met with this abuse. After the Revolution of
1911, the whole country went mad and insisted
upon applying in China the political democracy
which Westerners talked about, without any study
of its real meaning. In the last few lectures I
described in detail the history of the democratic
struggle in the West and the results which
followed the victory of democracy. From these
studies we saw that democratic rule had not been
fully carried out in the West and that democracy
had met with many obstacles in its onward march.
Now China is proposing to practice democracy.
If we imitate the West, we will have to imitate
Western methods. But there is no fundamental
solution as yet in Western politics of the problem
of democracy; it is still a serious issue. Westerners who are using the newest scholarship to

aid them in finding a solution have not made
any worth-while discoveries in democratic theory,
nor have they found any satisfactory answer to
the difficulties of democracy.　So the methods of
Western democracy cannot be our model or guide.

Since the Boxers' time, the Chinese generally
have thought only of imitating foreign countries — every moment of the day and in regard
to every possible thing.　Should we imitate foreign
things ?　If we are speaking of military weapons,
there is no comparison between the machine gun
and the bow or sword ; certainly the foreign
machine gun is more effective and deadly.　All
sorts of other foreign articles are also better than
ours.　That the West has advanced far beyond
China in the physical sciences cannot be denied.
But how about government ?　Has political
philosophy or physical science made the greater
progress in the West ?　The science of government has lagged far behind the other sciences.

Take military science : the Western art of warfare is constantly being developed and improved ;
it is "new every day and different every month,"
so that no one to-day follows the military manuals
of a century ago.　Even the military manuals
of ten years ago are now out of date.　Every
decade sees great changes in Western armaments
and methods of warfare ; in other words, a revolution in military science takes place every ten years.

The largest and most expensive weapon of war
in the West is the battleship ; every battleship
costs from fifty to a hundred million dollars;
anything less expensive can hardly be called a
battleship. Weapons of war have been developed
more rapidly than anything else in the material
line and among weapons of war the battleship
has seen the highest development. In ten years
at most a battleship is out of date. Battleships
built before the European War have now been
scrapped. Great changes are also being made in
land armaments and weapons ; every day sees
some improvements and every decade great
changes, a practical revolution and a renovation.
The kind of rifle which we are now using has
been discarded in other countries. The big
guns which were used in the European War are
now considered old style. Not only in military
equipment are advances being made, however.
All articles of manufacture are undergoing continual improvement and new inventions are
constantly appearing. Western material civilization is indeed " new every day and strange every
month"—never the same from one day to another.

But how much has the West advanced beyond
China in the matter of government ? In the
last two or three centuries, Europe and America
have passed through many revolutions and their
political progress has been much more rapid than

China's, yet the Western political treatises do
not show much advance upon the past. For
instance, there lived in Greece two thousand years
ago a great political philosopher named Plato ;
his *Republic* is still studied by scholars who
say that it has much to contribute towards the
political systems of to-day. It is not like battleships and drill manuals, which are discarded
as worthless after ten years. From this we see
that the physical sciences of the West undergo
marked transformations from one decade to
another ; they are making rapid strides forward.
But in the field of political theory, we find
Plato's *Republic* written two millenniums ago still
worthy of study and of great value in modern
times. So the advance of Western political
philosophy has not kept pace with the advance
of Western material science. There has been no
radical change in political thinking for two
thousand years. If we copy Western government
as we are copying Western material science, we
shall be making a great mistake. The material
civilization of the West is changing daily, and to
keep up with it will be exceedingly difficult. But
political thought in the West has advanced much
more slowly than material civilization. The
United States, for example, has been applying
democracy for one hundred fifty years, but
there is not much difference between the present

democracy and that of a century ago. Modern French democracy has not progressed as far as the democracy of the Revolution, which was so broadly conceived that even the people felt it did not suit, and opposed it; consequently French democracy has made practically no gains within the past century. If we want to follow other countries, we must first analyze such conditions very carefully. The reason why Western democracy has not made more progress is because Western nations have not fundamentally solved the problem of administering democracy.

We saw in the preceding lectures that the West has not yet found any proper method of carrying out democracy and that the truths of democracy have not yet been fully manifested. The democratic spirit has swollen like a noisy torrent within the last two or three centuries; in issues which men could not think through, the masses of the people have simply followed nature and have drifted with the tide. The recent growth of democracy is not an achievement of thoughtful scholarship but the result of a popular following of natural tendencies. For this reason, no fundamental method of directing democracy was worked out beforehand, the problem was not considered from beginning to end, and so the Western peoples have met innumerable disappointments and difficulties halfway on the road of democracy.

Since the Revolution, China has wanted to follow the example of Europe and America and to apply political democracy. Since Western political democracy has developed to the point of representative government, China, too, must have a representative government! But the fine points of Western representative government China has not learned; the bad points she has copied tenfold, a hundredfold! The members of Parliament have become mere "swine," filthy and corrupt, worse than anything the world has ever seen before — an amazing phenomenon in representative government. China has not only failed to learn well from Western democratic government but has been corrupted by it.

From what I have already said, you must realize that Western democratic government does not have any fundamentally good method of application. So in our espousal of democracy, we should not entirely copy the West. Then what road shall we follow? China still has many conservatives, powerful reactionaries, who are advocating the overthrow of the republic, the restoration of autocracy, and the reëstablishment of the throne, as the only means of saving China. We who understand world tendencies naturally know that such a way is wrong. We must oppose it, follow world tendencies, apply democracy, and take the right road of government. If we want to take the right road of government, we must first understand the true meaning of government. You remember the definition in the first lecture : government is the control of the affairs of all the people. For thousands of years Chinese social sentiments, customs, and habits have differed widely from those of Western society. Hence methods of social control in China are different from those used in the West, and we should not merely copy the West as we copy the use of their machinery. As soon as we learn Western machinery we can use it anytime, anywhere ; electric lights, for example, can be installed and used in any kind of Chinese house. But Western social customs and sentiments are different from ours in innumerable points ; if, without regard to customs and popular feelings in China, we try to apply Western methods of social control as we would Western machinery — in a hard and fast way — we shall be making a serious mistake. Although the government (laws and systems by which society is controlled) is also a kind of invisible machine, as evidenced by the fact that we speak of organized administration as an organ, yet visible machinery is built upon the laws of physics, while the invisible machinery of government is built upon the laws of psychology. Discoveries have been made in the field of physics for several hundred years, but the science of psychology began only twenty or thirty years ago and is not yet very far advanced. Hence this difference: in ways of controlling physical objects and forces we should learn from the West, but in ways of controlling men, we should not learn only from the West. The West long ago thought through the principles and worked out the methods of physical control, so we can wholly follow Western material civilization — we could even follow it blindly as we introduce it into China, and not go astray. But the West has not yet thought through its principles of government, and its methods of government have not been fundamentally worked out; so China to-day, when putting democracy into operation and reforming its government, cannot simply follow the West. We must think out a radically new method; if we only blindly follow others, we shall work serious injury to our national welfare and to the people's living. The West has its society; we have our society, and the sentiments and customs of the two are not the same. Only as we adapt ourselves, according to our own social conditions, to modern world tendencies, can we hope to reform our society and to advance our nation. If we pay no attention to our own social conditions and try simply to follow world tendencies, our nation will decline and our people will be in peril. If we want China to progress and our race to be

safe, we must put democracy into effect ourselves
and do some radical thinking upon the best way
to realize its ideals.

Can we find a real way to carry out democratic
government ?   Although we cannot wholly copy
Europe and America, yet we can observe them
and study their experience in democracy very
carefully.   For although Western democracy has
not reached a perfect stage of development or
found fundamental solutions, yet many Western
scholars are putting much time upon the study of
democracy and are constantly bringing forth new
theories. Western nations, moreover, have gained
not a little experience in the past century, and
this experience, along with their various new
theories, should be used as data in our study.
Otherwise, we shall waste time to our own injury
or simply follow in the tracks of the West.

Foreign scholars, in studying the historical
facts of democracy, have deduced many new
theories.   One of the newest has been proposed
by an American scholar, who says that the greatest
fear of modern democratic states is an all-
powerful government which the people have no
way of checking, but yet the finest thing would
be an all-powerful government in the employ of
all the people and working for the welfare of all
the people.   This is a very new theory: what
is both feared and desired is an all-powerful

government. First the theory declares that the people dread an all-powerful government which they cannot control, then it asks how an all-powerful government which will work for the welfare of the people can be secured, and how it can be made responsive to the will of the people. In many nations where democracy is developing, the governments are becoming powerless, while in the nations where democracy is weak, the governments are all strong. As I said before, the strongest government in Europe within the past few decades was Bismarck's government in Germany. That was certainly an all-powerful government; it did not advocate democracy, for at first it opposed democracy, but yet it became all-powerful. Of the governments which have supported democracy not one could be called all-powerful. A certain Swiss scholar has said that since various nations have put democracy into practice, the power of government has declined, and the reason has been the fear on the part of the people that the government might secure a power which they could not control. Hence the people have always guarded their governments and have not allowed them power, lest they become all-powerful. Therefore democratic countries must find a solution for this difficulty, but the solution will not come until the people change their attitude towards government.

The reason why the people have always been opposing government is because, after the revolutions, the liberty and equality thus obtained were overdeveloped, and certain groups abused them, setting no limits upon them and going into all sorts of excess, with the result that the government became impotent, and the state, although it had a government, became no different from a state without a government. The Swiss scholar whom I mentioned saw this evil train of events, and as a remedy proposed that the people should change their attitude to government. What did he mean? What has the attitude of the people to do with government?

In China's long history, what has been the attitude of the people to the government? As we study Chinese history, we find that the governments of Yao, Shun, Yü, T'ang, Wen Wang, and Wu Wang [1] are always lauded and held in admiration by the Chinese people; Chinese of every period hoped that they might have a government like those, which would seek the welfare of the people. Before Western democratic ideas penetrated China, the deepest desire of the Chinese people was for emperors like Yao, Shun, Yü, T'ang, Wen Wang, and Wu Wang, that the people might enjoy peace and happiness. This was the old Chinese attitude towards government.

[1] Emperors of ancient China.

But since our recent revolution, the people have absorbed democratic ideas and are no longer satisfied with those ancient emperors. They were all autocratic rulers, the people say, and do not deserve to be extolled even though they were splendid. This shows that the rise of democracy has developed an attitude of opposition to government among the people; no matter how good the government is, they are not content with it. If we let this attitude of mind continue without any attempt to change it, it will be exceedingly difficult for government to make any progress. How are we to change the attitude? Western scholars only know that the attitude ought to be changed, but so far they have not yet thought of the way to change it.

When we launched our revolution, we advocated the practice of democracy; and I have thought of a method to solve the problem. The method which I have thought of is a new discovery in political theory and is a fundamental solution of the whole problem. My proposition is similar to the thesis of the Swiss scholar that the attitude of people to government must be changed, and the recent appearance of such theories in the West proves that the principle which I have advocated is right; namely, that a distinction should be made between sovereignty and ability.[1] Western scholars

1 See note at end of chapter.

have not yet discovered this principle. To make clear what I mean, I must first review my theory as to the classes of human society.

Upon what did I base my division of human society ? — Upon ¦the individual's natural intelligence and ability. I classified mankind into three groups. The first group are those who see and perceive first : they are the people of superior wisdom who take one look at a thing and see numerous principles involved, who hear one word and immediately perform great deeds, whose insight into the future and whose many achievements make the world advance and give mankind its civilization. These men of vision and foresight are the creators, the discoverers of mankind. The second group includes those who see and perceive later : their intelligence and ability are below the standard of the first group ; they cannot create or discover but can only follow and imitate, learning from what the first group have already done. The third group are those who do not see or perceive : they have a still lower grade of intelligence and ability and do not understand even though one tries to teach them ; they simply act. In the language of political movements, the first group are the discoverers; the second group, the promoters; the third group, the operators. Progress in everything depends upon action, so the responsibility for the world's progress rests upon the third group.

For example, the construction of a large foreign-style building is not something which can be undertaken by the ordinary person. First there must be a construction engineer, who makes a complete estimate of the work and materials necessary for the desired building, and then draws a detailed plan for the contractor or foreman. The foreman first studies the plan carefully, then hires workmen to move materials and to work according to the plan. The workmen cannot read the plan ; they merely work according to the foreman's directions and take his orders to put a brick here or to lay a tile there — simple tasks. The foreman, in turn, is unable to make complete estimates on the building or to draw a plan ; he can only follow the plan made by the construction engineer and give orders to the workmen as to the laying of the brick and covering with tile. The construction engineer who designs the plan is the one who sees and perceives first; the foreman who reads the plan is the one who sees and perceives afterward, the workman who lays brick and tile is the one who does not see or perceive. The foreign buildings in every city depend upon these groups — engineers, foremen, and workmen — and upon their coöperative effort. All the great achievements of the world also depend upon these three groups, but the largest group is the one of practical operators who do not know

or perceive. A smaller group are those who
know and perceive afterward; the smallest group
are those who know and perceive first. Without
men who see and perceive ahead, the world would
have no originators; without men who see and
perceive later, the world would have no supporters;
without men who do not see or perceive, the
world would have no practical workers. The
business of the world certainly requires first,
initiators; next, many promoters; and lastly, a
large number of operators, in order to be successfully accomplished. The progress of the world
depends on these three types, and not one type
must be lacking. The nations of the world, as
they begin to apply democracy and to reform
the government, should give a part to every man—
to the man who sees first, to the man who sees
later, to the man who does not see. We must
realize that political democracy is not given to
us by nature; it is created by human effort. We
must create democracy and then give it to the
people, not wait to give it until the people fight
for it.

A few days ago I had a visit from a Japanese
official in Korea. After we had chatted for some
time, I took occasion to ask him about the revolution in Korea and whether he thought it could
succeed. As he had no ready answer to this
question, I asked him again what was the attitude

of the Japanese officials in Korea towards the political rights of the Korean people. He replied: " We can only wait and see what sort of democratic ideas the Koreans will have; if they know enough to struggle for their rights, we shall certainly have to give political sovereignty back to them. But at present they do not know much about fighting for their rights, so we Japanese cannot but administer Korea for them." Such talk always sounds very fine, but we revolutionists must not treat the people of our nation as Japan is treating Korea, and wait for the people to fight for democracy before we give democracy to them. For in China those who neither see nor perceive are in the majority, and thousands of years from now I doubt whether all the people will know that they ought to struggle for their rights. So those who pride themselves upon being men of prevision or men of later vision should not, like the Japanese, calculate only for their own interests; they should first calculate for the interests of the people and give the political sovereignty of the whole state into the hands of the people.

Since the West has not solved the difficulties of democracy, we cannot find a solution to-day by merely copying the West. We must look for a new way, and that new way depends, as the Swiss scholar said, upon a change of attitude

towards government. But to secure this change
of attitude we must distinguish clearly between
sovereignty and ability. To help us in studying
this distinction, let us review a few of the points
mentioned in a former lecture. The first point
is our definition of the people's sovereignty;
briefly, it means the control of the government
by the people. To explain this further: Who
controlled the government in former times?
Two ancient Chinese sayings, "One who does not
hold a position under the government does not
concern himself with the government" and "The
common people are not in the councils," show
that political sovereignty used to be entirely in
the hands of the emperor and had nothing to do
with the people. To-day we who advocate democracy want to put the political sovereignty into
the hands of the people. What, then, will the
people become? Since China has had a revolution
and has adopted a democratic form of government, the people should rule in all matters. The
government now may be called popular government; in other words, under a republic we make
the people king.

Looking back through the millenniums of
Chinese history, the only emperors who shouldered
the responsibility of government for the welfare
and happiness of the people were Yao, Shun,
Yü, T'ang, Wen Wang, and Wu Wang; no others

were able to use their office for the blessing of the people. Of all China's emperors, only Yao, Shun, Yü, T'ang, Wen Wang, and Wu Wang so fulfilled their duties of government that they could stand "unabashed before Heaven above and unashamed before men below." They were able to reach this high ideal and to elicit pæans of praise from succeeding generations because of two special qualities which they possessed — fine native ability, which enabled them to establish good government and to seek the welfare of the people; and noble character, "mercy to the people and kindness to all creatures, regard for the people as for the wounded and suffering, love for the people as for their own children." Because they possessed these two fine qualities, they were able to shoulder the full responsibility of the government and to reach their goal. These are the only emperors who have called forth reverence from posterity. Other emperors there have been — we do not know how many — and most of them, with their names, have been forgotten by posterity. Only Yao, Shun, Yü, T'ang, Wen Wang, and Wu Wang possessed great natural ability and noble character. Most of the others lacked ability and character, yet they wielded sovereign power.

You have all read a good deal of Chinese history; I am sure almost everyone here has read particularly

The Story of the Three Kingdoms. [1] We can find
an illustration of our point in this book. Chu-
Ko Liang, you remember, was a very scholarly
and able statesman. The first chief that he
served was Liu Pei ; later he supported Ah Tou.
Ah Tou was exceedingly stupid and did not have
a bit of ability, which was the reason why Liu Pei
just before his death said to Chu-Ko Liang, "If he
is deserving of your support, support him;
otherwise you may displace him." After Liu
Pei's death, Chu-Ko Liang still showed his splendid
character; although Ah Tou was worthless, Chu-
Ko Liang aided him as loyally as ever, "wearing
himself out with the duties of his office until he
died." Thus, in the age of autocracy the ruler
might have no ability but great power. Ah
Tou and Chu-Ko Liang, in the period of the Three
Kingdoms, make this very clear to us: Chu-
Ko Liang had ability but not power; Ah Tou had
power but not ability. Ah Tou was incompetent,
but he turned the affairs of state over to Chu-
Ko Liang to administer. Chu-Ko Liang was exceedingly capable and so was able to build up a fine
government in Western Shu (modern Szechwan);
moreover, he was able to lead his troops six
times across the Ch'i Mountains in a punitive

[1] The period of the Three Kingdoms, A. D. 122–265, was rich in
military heroes and deeds of valor and has been immortalized by this
well-known voluminous novel.

expedition against the North and to establish a tripod of power along with the Wei and Wu kingdoms. The comparison between Chu-Ko Liang and Ah Tou helps us to understand the distinction between sovereignty and ability.

In the age of autocracy fathers and elder brothers were kings, sons and younger brothers were heirs. Although they might have no ability at all, yet they could become kings some day. So incompetent men still had great sovereign power. Now that we have established a republic and acknowledge the people as ruler, will you look about to see to what groups our four hundred millions belong? Of course they cannot all be seers; most of them are not even followers of seers; the great majority are those who have no vision or foresight. Now democratic government depends upon the rulership of the people, hence our tour hundred millions are very powerful. The people of the nation with sovereign power to control the government are these very four hundred millions. To whom can you compare all these political sovereigns? I think that they are very much like Ah Tou. In fact, each one of them is an Ah Tou with great sovereign power. Ah Tou had no ability, but Chu-Ko Liang did; so after Liu Pei's death, Western Shu was still well governed. Westerners now are opposing a powerful government; the Swiss scholar, to remedy this defect, proposes

that the people's attitude to government should
be changed — they should no longer be hostile
to strong government. But what the next step
is, after the popular attitude to government is
changed, they have not made clear. The principle
which I am bringing out is that sovereignty must
be distinguished from ability; without this clear
distinction we cannot hope to change the people's
attitude to government. Ah Tou knew that he
was incompetent, so he turned over all the political
authority of the kingdom to Chu-Ko Liang and
asked Chu-Ko Liang to govern for him. So when
Chu-Ko Liang handed in his memorandum upon
the expedition to Ah Tou, he advised him to
separate clearly the affairs of the palace and the
affairs of the court. Ah Tou could execute the
duties of the palace, but the duties of the court he
could not perform alone, for they were duties of
government. Chu-Ko Liang's distinction between
palace and court was a distinction between
sovereignty and ability. In governing the state,
we must make the same distinction. How shall
we do it? We shall succeed only as we take a
long and dispassionate view of world affairs.
Everybody now has a peculiar idea of government
which has grown up out of millenniums of autocracy. In this long period of autocratic government, incompetent men have sat upon the throne
while the four hundred millions have been their

slaves; now, although autocracy is overthrown, a republic is established, and we are apparently free, yet the people have not gotten rid of their idea of autocracy and are still afraid that the government will oppress them as the emperors did. The fear of an imperial, despotic government makes them want to destroy the government, and the attitude of hostility to government develops. This present hostility is still the reaction from the old reverence for the emperor. In other words, from an attitude of extreme veneration for the emperor the people have swung to an attitude of opposition to all government. The old worship of the emperor was wrong, of course, but the present hostility to all government is also wrong.

We must go back thousands of years in political history in order to understand how this wrong conception to-day can be broken down. Before the day of despotic emperors, China had the splendid rulers Yao and Shun; they both opened the throne to the people and did not attempt to keep it in their own family. Autocracy did not flower until after Yao and Shun; before their time there was no autocracy to speak of, and men of ability who could work for the welfare of all and organize good government were appointed emperors. In the wild age of conflict between men and beasts, which we formerly described, there was no complete state organization; the people

lived by clans and depended upon some skillful
and strong man to provide for their protection.
At that time people were afraid of the attack of
venomous serpents and wild beasts, so they had
to get an able man to assume the responsibility
for protection. Responsibility for protection
required ability to fight; the man who could
overcome venomous serpents and savage beasts
was considered the ablest, and, as men of that day
had no weapons but bare hands and empty fists
with which to fight, the one with the strongest
body was raised by the people to the position of
chief. China, however, had examples of others
besides fighters who were made kings. Sui-jen
Shih[1] bored wood for fire and taught the people
to cook with fire; thus the dangers of eating raw
vegetables and meat were avoided and many fine
flavors to satisfy the palate were discovered. So
the people made Sui-jen Shih king. Boring wood
for fire and teaching people to cook with fire were
the work of a cook, so we may say that a cook
became king. Shen Nung[1] tasted a hundred herbs
and discovered many medicinal properties to heal
diseases and to raise the dead to life — a wonderful and meritorious work — so they made him
king. Tasting herbs is the work of a physician,
and thus we may say that a physician became
king. Hsien Yüan[1] taught the people to make

Legendary figures in ancient Chinese history.

clothes, so it was the tailor who became king;
Yu Ch'ao Shih taught the people how to build
houses, and so the carpenter became king.   So in
Chinese history we find not only those who could
fight becoming king; anyone with marked ability,
who had made new discoveries or who had achieved
great things for mankind, could become king and
organize the government.   Cooks, physicians, tailors, carpenters, and all others who had special
ability had become king.   An American professor
named William P. Martin once went to the Western
Hills outside of Peking on a pleasure trip.   On the
way he met a farmer and began to chat with him.
The farmer asked Professor Martin, " Why does not
a foreigner come to China and be emperor ? "   Martin
replied, "Might a foreigner be emperor of China ? "
The farmer pointed to the telegraph line that ran
along the edge of the field, and said, "The man who
made that thing might be emperor of China."   The
farmer thought that the person who could make a
steel wire carry news and messages was of course
a man of great ability and could certainly become
China's emperor.   From all this we can see that
the general psychology of the Chinese is that a
man possessing marked ability should become king.

Since the time of Yao and Shun China's emperors have gradually become despots, wanting to
monopolize the empire and refusing to let the people
freely choose able men for the throne.   If now

our four hundred million people should be asked
to elect an emperor by ballot, if they had complete power and freedom of choice without any
outside interference, and if, at the same time,
Yao and Shun should come to life again,
whom do you think they would elect? I think
they would undoubtedly elect Yao or Shun.
Chinese have not the painful and bitter feelings
towards their emperors which Westerners have
had, because despotism in China was never as
severe as despotism in the West. In Europe
two or three centuries ago the tyranny of kings
had reached its limits: the people looked upon
their rulers as they would upon an overwhelming
deluge or a savage beast — with mortal terror.
So the people wanted to reject not only their
kings but everything closely connected with
kings, such as government. Now that democracy
prevails in the West and the people are in power,
the rejection of government is truly easy. Would
it not have been easy for Ah Tou of Western Shu
to throw Chu-Ko Liang overboard? But if he had
dismissed Chu, could the government of Western
Shu have lasted very long, could the troops
have been dispatched six times across the Ch'i
Mountains to punish the North? Ah Tou realized all this, so he gave complete authority to
Chu-Ko Liang; the setting in order of the government, the suppression of the South, the punitive

expedition against the North, were all carried out by Chu-Ko Liang. We are now putting democracy into practice: the four hundred millions of China are the kings; they are the Ah Tous, and as Ah Tous they should naturally welcome Chu-Ko Liangs to administer the government for them and to perform the great tasks of state. As Western nations have applied democracy, the people have developed an attitude of hostility to government, and the fundamental reason is their failure to distinguish between sovereignty and ability. Unless we act upon this principle which I have set forth, we will simply follow in the ruts of the West. Only as the people, in accordance with the theory that I have set forth, see the clear difference between sovereignty and ability will hostility to government cease and will government have a chance to develop. It should be very easy for China to make the distinction, for we can cite the precedent of Ah Tou and Chu-Ko Liang. If the government is a good one, we four hundred millions will let it be our Chu-Ko Liang and give all the authority of the state to it; if the government is bad, we four hundred millions can exercise the privileges of kingship, dismiss it and take back the sovereignty into our own hands. Westerners have not drawn a clear line between sovereignty and ability, so they have not yet solved the problems which have arisen out of democracy these two or three hundred years.

Let us make another comparison between the past and the present. In olden times those who could fight well were crowned king by all; now wealthy families engage fighters to protect them. The military officials, for example, who, after they have robbed the land in the provinces and have made their pile, move into the foreign settlements at Shanghai, are afraid that people will attack them and take their money, so they engage several Sikh policemen to stand as guards at their gates. If the old principle, that one who could protect others might become their king, were followed, these Sikh policemen who protect the military officials should rule over them as kings; but, as it is, they can have nothing to do with the private affairs of the officials. Barehanded warriors in the days of old became king; modern Sikh policemen with their long rifles should all the more be king! But the military officials treat them not as their kings but as mere slaves and, although the slaves with their rifles are very powerful, they are rewarded by the officials not with the glory of kingship but with only some material money. If we follow this line, the ancient kings might be likened to these modern Sikh guards or the Sikh guards to the ancient kings. And to push the analogy further, since protecting kings are like Sikh guards at the gate, why should anybody want to reject them!

To-day, when wealthy men organize a company or open a factory, they have to engage a man with natural capability to be general manager and to control the concern. This general manager is an expert who has the ability ; the shareholders hold the authority or sovereignty. Within the factory, only the general manager gives orders ; the shareholders simply keep a supervision over him. The people of a republic are shareholders, the president is general manager, and the people should look upon the government as an expert. With such an attitude, the shareholders can make use of the manager to improve the factory, turn out a large quantity of goods with a small capital, and make large profits for the company. But in none of the democratic states of the West do the people have such an attitude towards government, hence they cannot make use of gifted men to direct the government. As a result, the men in political life are generally incompetent, and democratic government is developing very haltingly. Democratic states have progressed less rapidly than autocratic states like Germany and Japan. Japan has been modernized for only a few decades and is now wealthy and powerful. Germany used to be an exceedingly poor and weak state, but when William I and Bismarck took the reins of government, united the states into a confederation, and laid bold political plans, Germany within

a few score years was able to dominate Europe.
But the other nations which support democracy
have not been able to advance, like Japan and
Germany, with tremendous strides each day, and
the reason lies in their failure to solve some of the
basic problems of democracy. To solve them
they must put the important affairs of the nation
in the hands of capable men.

Westerners to-day are constantly making use of
experts: in training soldiers they use experienced
military men, in running their factories they use
engineers, and in the administration of government they know that they ought to use specialists.
They have not succeeded in doing so because they
are not able to change the old, deep-rooted habits
of the people. But in this new age a distinction
must surely be made between sovereignty and
ability. In many things we have to trust to experts
and we should not set limitations upon them. Take
that very recent invention, now in such common
use and so convenient — the automobile. When
automobiles were first introduced twenty or thirty
years ago, there were no expert chauffeurs to
drive them or expert mechanics to repair them.
I had a friend who bought an automobile and
had to be both chauffeur and mechanic himself,
which was a lot of trouble, as one could not be
expected to do all these things well. But now
there are many chauffeurs and mechanics, and

the owner of an automobile has only to pay out
money and engage someone to drive or to repair
his car for him. The chauffeurs and the mechanics
are specialists in driving and in repair work, and
they are essential if we use automobiles. The
nation is a great automobile and the government
officers are the great chauffeurs. When Westerners first won political sovereignty, they were
like the wealthy owners of automobiles twenty
years ago, who did not have suitable experts to
help them and so had to do all the repairing and
driving themselves. But now that there are so
many gifted specialists, the sovereign people
should engage their services; to drive and repair
for themselves is only "seeking worry and trouble."
In this illustration we can make a distinction,
also, between the chauffeur who has skill but not
sovereignty over the car, and the owner of the
car who has sovereignty but not skill. The
sovereign owner should depend upon the skillful
expert to drive his car, and the same principle
should apply in the vital affairs of the nation.
The people are the owners; they must be sovereign.
The government are specialists; they must be men
of ability and skill. We are therefore to look
upon all the officers of the government, from
president and premier down to heads of departments, as specially trained chauffeurs; if they are
able men and loyal to the nation, we should be

willing to give the sovereignty of the state into
their hands. We must not limit their movements
but give them freedom of action; then the state
can progress and progress with rapid strides.
If, on the contrary, we attempt to take everything
into our own hands, or to hamper our experts at
every turn and not allow them freedom of action,
the state can hardly hope to progress much and
will move forward very slowly.

I can give you a very good illustration of this
principle out of my own experience. Once, when
I was living in Shanghai, I made an appointment
for a conference with a friend in Hongkew. But
when the day came, I forgot the appointment
until just fifteen minutes before the set time.
I was then living in the French concession, which
is a long distance from Hongkew. It would be
almost impossible to get there in fifteen minutes.
In hot haste I called a chauffeur and asked him
excitedly whether he could drive to Hongkew
in fifteen minutes. He replied that he certainly
could. So I took my seat in the automobile and
we started for the appointed place. I was very
familiar with the streets of Shanghai; the trip
from the French concession to Hongkew is somewhat like that from Shakee to Tungshan (in
Canton) which you can cut short by going through
the Bund and Ch'uan Lung K'ou. But my chauffeur did not go, let us say, by the Bund and Ch'uan

Lung K'ou; he first went down Fungning Road,
turned through Taoteksun Road, and drove
through the small North Gate before he reached
the Great East Gate and then Tungshan. The
automobile was flying along and making such a
noise that I could not speak to the chauffeur; I
was much puzzled, however, and angry at the
chauffeur, because I thought he was playing a
trick on me and deliberately going out of the way
to extend the time. The situation was similar to
that in a nation when the government, for a
special reason, does something extraordinary which
the people do not understand, and the people mis-
interpret it and find fault. But that chauffeur,
going by the route he had chosen, reached Hongkew in not over fifteen minutes. My indignation
cooled and I asked the chauffeur why he had come
by such a circuitous route. He replied, "If we
had taken the direct route, we would have driven
along the Nanking Road where traffic is heavy with
street cars, automobiles, jinrickshas, pedestrians,
and moving vans, and where it is difficult to get
through." This cleared up my misunderstanding;
I realized that the way I had planned through
Nanking Road and over the Garden Bridge at the
Bund was conceived only in terms of distance, but
the chauffeur had experience. He knew that an
automobile could travel very fast, thirty or forty

miles an hour, and that a few more turns and a few more miles with the chance, however, of increasing the speed, would still put us at our destination within the appointed time. He calculated directly from the time ; he was not a philosopher and did not understand the formal relations of time and space, but he was a specialist in his line. He knew that an automobile has the power of shortening distance, and that if he could increase the speed of the car a few more turns would not prevent him from reaching Hongkew within fifteen minutes. If I had not given the chauffeur complete authority and allowed him freedom of movement, but had insisted that he take my route, I certainly could not have kept my engagement. Because I trusted him as an expert and did not bind his arm, he was able to take that route which he thought was best, and arrived at the appointed time. But since I was not an expert, I misunderstood why he should go out of the direct way. The people are masters of the nation and should act towards the government as I did towards the chauffeur on that ride to Hongkew, that is, let it drive and choose the way. Only such a conception of government will change the attitude of people towards government.

The hostility of Western peoples to their governments is due to their failure to separate sovereignty from ability, and consequently they have not yet cleared up the difficulties of democracy. Let us not, as we pursue democracy, copy the West; let us make a clear distinction between sovereignty and ability. Although the democratic ideas came to us from Europe and America, yet the administration of democracy has not been successfully worked out there. We know a way now to make use of democracy and we know how to change the attitude of people towards government, but yet the majority of the people are without vision. We who have prevision must lead them and guide them into the right way if we want to escape the confusions of Western democracy and not follow in the tracks of the West. Western scholars to-day have only gotten to the point of realizing that the attitude of the people towards government is wrong and ought to be changed, but they do not yet see how to change it. I have now discovered the way — we must distinguish between sovereignty and ability. The foundation of the government of a nation must be built upon the rights of the people, but the administration of government must be intrusted to experts. We must not look upon these experts as stately and grand presidents and ministers, but simply as our chauffeurs, as guards at the gate, as cooks, physicians, carpenters, or tailors. It does not matter what sort of workmen the people consider them. As long as they have this general attitude towards them, the state can be governed and the nation can go forward.

March 16, 1924.

_____

Note to page 294. *Ch'üan* and *nen* are difficult to translate by one phrase because of the various shades of meaning in different contexts. They convey the idea of "rights" and "power" as well as "sovereignty" and "ability" and might be so rendered.

LECTURE 6

Government as machinery — Rapid development of manufacturing machinery in the West compared with slow development of political machinery — Difficulty of experiment in government — The steam engine — Evolution of the piston from single-action to double-action — Modern political machinery largely " single-acting "— Methods of perfect control over powerful machinery, e. g., the steamship engine— Defects in methods of control over political machinery — Fear of high-powered government — Sovereignty and ability in the machine — Disadvantages in modeling after old political machinery of the West — A new machinery must be created — Western superiority in material science does not necessarily mean superiority in political science — Anecdote about Newton — The plan for China's new government machinery — High-powered government and effective control — Easy and safe methods of control over material machinery, e. g., electric light, flying machines, must be applied to political machinery — The four controlling powers of the people : suffrage, recall, initiative, and referendum — The five administrative powers of government : legislative, judicial, executive, civil service examination, and censorship — Precedents in Chinese political history of the last two powers — A quintuple-power constitution — Balance of power in the new system.

Western statesmen and students of jurisprudence now speak of government as machinery and of law as an instrument. A great many Chinese books on government and law are translations from the Japanese; the Japanese have given government organization the designation of *chi-kuan* (organ, or bureau). *Chi-kuan* means the same thing as the common word " machinery " in China; Chinese once used *chi-kuan* in the sense of "opportunity," but since the Japanese have made the word serve as a translation for government organization, it has come to have a meaning in China similar to " machinery." We used to speak of the government *yamên*, now we speak of the administrative *chi-kuan*, the financial *chi-kuan*, the military *chi-kuan*, the educational *chi-kuan*. These *chi-kuan*, or bureaus, correspond to the Japanese term for government organ; there is no difference between them. When we say *chi-kuan* we mean the same thing as machinery; a *chi-kuan* gun is a machine gun. And an administrative organ, or bureau, may, therefore, be called administrative machinery. But what is the difference between political machinery and manufacturing machinery? Manufacturing machinery is made entirely of material things — wood, steel, leather belts, and such — fitted together; political machinery is constructed of human beings and depends upon human beings, not material things, for its action. So there are great differences between political and manufacturing machinery, but the one that stands out is the fact that political machinery is moved by human forces, while manufacturing machinery is moved by material forces.

From the preceding lectures, we have seen
that Western civilization and culture have been
developing and progressing with great rapidity.
But when we analyze this progress we find that
material civilization, as represented by manufacturing machinery, has been advancing very
rapidly, while human machinery, as seen in political
organization, has made very slow advance. What
is the reason for this? When material machinery
is constructed, it can be easily tried out, the bad
features can be discarded, and the imperfect parts
can be improved. But after human machinery
has been set up, it is not easily experimented with
and improvements are not at all easily made,
except through revolution. The only other way
would be to treat it as scrap iron, as we do old
material machinery, but this is manifestly impossible. Hence manufacturing machinery in the
West has progressed by leaps and bounds, while
political machinery has just stumbled along.
When the democratic tide began to rise in the
West, all the nations wanted to put democracy
into practice; the pioneer nation was the United
States. It has been one hundred forty years
since the birth of the American Republic, yet the
measure of sovereignty exercised by the people
in the beginning has come down to the present
time without any marked difference, and the
Constitution in present use is the same as that

adopted by the first United States, with no great
fundamental changes for more than one hundred
years. Most manufacturing machinery was invented more than a hundred years ago, yet
who would now use machinery a century old?
It has long since become scrap iron. There is
nothing over ten years old among the machines
used in modern agriculture, industry, and business;
for every decade brings numerous inventions and
improvements and every year marks some advance. Yet the political machinery of a hundred
years ago is still in use to-day. The individual
human beings in this machinery of human forces
can change at will, but the whole organization
is not easily reconstructed from the bottom up
because of deep-seated habits and the close sequence of life activities. Without some sort of
revolution, it is impossible in ordinary times to discard entirely the old organization. This explains
the rapid advance of material machinery in the
West, while political machinery advanced so slowly
and with such difficulty.

In two former lectures, I said that Westerners
had not yet found a fundamental method of
procedure in carrying out democratic government.
This is because they have not experimented carefully and skillfully with their political machinery.
Between the first inventions of material machinery
and the machinery we see to-day there have been

we know not how many thousands of experiments and improvements. Look back at the early days of mechanical invention and what do you see? Those of you who have studied the history of machinery know the interesting story of its development. Take the story of the engine, for instance. The first engines could drive only in one direction; they were single-acting and not double-acting like modern engines. All machines to-day, as in locomotives and steamers, are double-acting. Power is generated in this way: water is placed in a boiler and heated by coal in the furnace underneath until it boils and turns into steam; the steam with its tremendous power of expansion is led through pipes to a chest or cylinder in which there is what we call a "live stop" and what foreigners call a "piston"; the piston is what makes the engine move and is the most important part of the whole machine. The piston at one end of the cylinder receives steam and is driven by the steam's power to the other end; when that steam is exhausted, new steam enters the other end of the cylinder and drives the piston back again. The uninterrupted driving of the piston to and fro gives a continuous movement to the machine. Water used to be the only material used to generate movement, but now oil, called "gas oil," is also used; it is highly volatile and as it vaporizes, drives the piston. But

whether water or oil is used as motive power, the
principle is the same; the uninterrupted movement of the piston makes the machine revolve
and do whatever work we want it to do.

Machinery drives steamers and pulls trains,
travels thousands of miles a day or transports all
the freight we want moved.   It seems a wonderful
thing to-day, yet the beginnings of the piston were
exceedingly simple.   When the piston was first
invented, it could take steam on only one side
and move forward; it would not take steam on
the other side and move back; that is, it was
single-acting.   This fact caused much inconven-
ience in the use of machinery.   When the earliest
machinery, for example, was used to bow cotton,
every machine had to have a child standing by
it to pull the piston rod back after its forward
movement ; otherwise the steam could not drive
the piston forward again.   Children were employed
to assist in this to-and-fro movement.   What a
contrast in efficiency with the unassisted double
action of the modern piston !   What were the
steps in the development of our modern convenient piston ?   The engineer who built that cotton-
bowing machine had no idea how to make the
piston drive back of its own accord.   The cotton
mill of that time was not large, and although it
contained only between ten and twenty of the
one-way machines, yet each machine needed a

child to assist it. These children, employed to pull the machines day after day and to go through the same motion over and over again, found their task most uninteresting and irksome. A foreman had to supervise them and prevent them from shirking their work; if the foreman left for a moment, the children would stop pulling the machines and would begin to play. One of the children was very bright and also very lazy; he did not want to pull the machine continually with his hand, so he tried to find a substitute method. He fixed a piece of string and a stick above the machine in such a way as to make the piston, after its forward movement, come back of its own accord; without the pull of the child's hand the piston would naturally return and continue its movement without interruption. This child's invention immediately communicated to the other children and soon the whole group were making their machines work automatically with the aid of a string and a stick, and were playing around without having to give attention to the machines. When the foreman returned that day to the mill and saw all the children playing and not standing at their machines to pull the piston rod, he was astonished, and said: "How is it that these children are playing, and yet the machines are moving back and forth of their own accord and are continuing their work? What sort of tricks are the children

up to ? This is certainly strange." The foreman
then investigated the cause of the automatic
movement and reported the results of his investigation to the engineer. The engineer perceived
that the child's method was quite remarkable, and,
following it up, he made several improvements
in the invention. This led to our modern automatic machines.

The machinery of democratic government has
not been altered in one hundred years. If we
study this machinery, we find that the democracy
in practice in various countries is simply the
right to vote. This means that the people have
the power of only one motion, not two; they
can only advance their sovereignty but cannot
take it back. This is like the early engines. But
once a little child found that a piece of string
and a stick with the aid of the machine's own
power could make the machine move backward
and forward automatically. Modern democratic
government, however, has not had a lazy child
to find some way of recalling the people's sovereignty. Therefore the machinery of democratic
government, after more than a hundred years,
is limited to the power of voting ; there has been
no advance beyond this stage for a long time.
There is no other way of controlling the men who
are elected to office, whether they turn out to be
worthy or incompetent. Such a condition is due

to imperfections in the machinery of democracy, and consequently democratic government has not yet found a good mode of procedure and has made but little progress. If we want to improve the machinery, what shall we do? As I said in my previous lecture, we must make a clear distinction between sovereignty and ability.

To use again the illustration of machinery: control and power are clearly separated in the machine, one part does the work, another initiates the motion, and each has its limits of activity. Take the machinery on a steamship. The largest steamships now have a displacement of fifty or sixty thousand tons and the machinery which drives them has more than 100,000 horse power, yet one man can control it perfectly. If this man wants the steamer to start, it immediately starts; if he wants it to stop, it immediately stops. The development of machinery has reached this marvelous stage. When machinery was first invented, men did not dare to use a machine with more than a few hundred or a thousand horse power, for if the horse power were too great, no one could control it. We commonly measure the size of machines by their horse power; one horse power is the equivalent of the power of eight men taken together. Ten thousand horse power means 80,000 man power. The motive power on the big modern commercial liners and battleships has a

strength of 100,000 to 200,000 horse power. If
the control is not perfect, the whole machinery,
once set forward, cannot be turned back; "it
can be started but not stopped." The lack of
control has caused many inventors to be killed
while experimenting with their machines; human
history is full of stories of such tragedies. Foreigners have a name, Frankenstein, for a machine
that can be started but not stopped. But as the
construction of machinery steadily improved,
machines of even 100,000 or 200,000 horse power
could be quietly controlled by one man, without
a particle of danger. One hundred thousand horse
power is 800,000 man power; 200,000 horse power
is 1,600,000 man power. It would not be easy to
control 1,600,000 men in this way; it is difficult
for one man to direct an army over 10,000 or 20,000
strong. Yet one man can quietly direct more
than 1,600,000 man power in a machine. From
this we see that modern machinery has made great
advances and methods of control have been
wonderfully improved.

Statesmen and students of jurisprudence are
now speaking of government as a machine and of
law as an instrument, and our modern democratic
age looks upon the people as the motive power
in government. In the old autocratic age the
king was the motive power and all the activities
of the state were initiated by him. The greater

the power of the government, the greater the majesty of the throne. A strong government was essential for the effective carrying out of the imperial edicts. Since the king was the power behind the machinery, a strong government organization made it possible for the king, in his exalted position, to do whatever he pleased — initiate political reforms, carry on " long-range aggressions," prepare for war, or anything else. So in the age of autocracy, increased power in the government brought advantage but no injury to the king. But in the age of democracy, people are the motive power in government. Then why are they loath to have too strong a government? Because if the government is too powerful they cannot control it and will be oppressed by it. Because they were once excessively oppressed by their government and suffered so much from it, they are trying to prevent oppression in the future by limiting the power of government. In the early days of machinery, a small child could pull back a machine after it had been driven forward, which shows that the machine had very little strength—not over a few horse power. A machine of 10,000 horse power could not, of course, be pulled back by a child. Since methods of controlling machinery were defective, people did not dare to use any but low-powered machinery. These are the early days of democracy and our methods of controlling government are also defective. The people are naturally the motive power in a democracy, but the people must also be able at any time to recall the power they set loose. Therefore the people will use only a low-powered government, for they cannot control a government of several hundred thousand horse power and will not dare to use it. The fear of powerful government among Western peoples to-day is just like the fear of powerful machinery in the old factories. If the small machines in the beginning had not been improved, machinery would never have made progress and would always have required people to pull it back. But because of the continual improvements up to to-day, machinery no longer needs people to pull it back and can automatically move to and fro. As for their political machinery, however, the people are not thinking of ways to improve it and are fearful of giving it too much power lest they be unable to call the power back. Instead, they are constantly thinking of ways to limit the government until it has no chance to develop and democracy has no chance to advance. Looking at present tendencies in the world, we may say that there is steady progress in democratic ideas but no progress at all in the control of democratic government. This is the reason why Western democratic nations have not found as yet a fundamental method of procedure.

As I have said in my preceding lecture, we must
make a distinction between sovereignty and
ability. When we apply this distinction to the
illustration of the machine, where do we place the
ability or power? The machine itself is what
possesses the ability or power. A 100,000 horse
power machine, fed with the proper amount of
coal and water, will generate the proper ability
and power. Where is the sovereignty? The
engineer in control of the machine possesses the
sovereignty. No matter what the horse power of
the machine, the engineer has only to move his
hand and the machine will start and start immediately, or stop and stop immediately. The engineer can control the machine and make it do as
he wishes; as soon as the machine starts he can
make the steamship or the train go very fast, and
by stopping the machine he can make the steamer
or the train cease moving. The machine, then, is
an able and powerful thing, while the engineer is a
man with a large degree of sovereignty. If the
people in their control of government will make
a distinction between sovereignty and ability or
power, they will be like the engineer who controls
the great machinery. When democracy is highly
developed and methods of controlling government
are perfected, the government will have great
power, but the people will only have to make
their opinions known in their national congress;

if they attack the government, they may overthrow it, or if they laud the government they may
strengthen it.   But as it is, if the government
carries on with a high hand, the people have no
way to control it; no matter how much the people
may criticize or praise the government, their
words are ineffective and the government pays no
attention to them.   To-day government is making
no progress, while the democratic spirit flourishes.
The people of all countries are finding that the
present political machinery does not suit their
ideas or needs.

China now is in a period of revolution.   We
are advocating a democratic form of government.
Our ideas of democracy have come from the West.
We have recently been thinking how we might
copy these ideas and build up a nation under popular government.   When we were first considering
this kind of state, one group of revolutionary
enthusiasts believed that if we would imitate the
West exactly, follow right in the tracks of the
West, and copy everything from the West, then
Chinese democracy would develop to the limit
of perfection.   At first such ideas were not entirely
wrong, for China's old autocratic government was
so corrupt that if we could, after effecting a revolution and overthrowing the autocracy, begin our
constructive effort by learning from the West, we
should certainly be better off than under the old

régime. But are the peoples of the West thoroughly
satisfied with the present situation in their national
and social life ?   If we will make a careful study
of Western government and society we shall find
that in the so-called pioneer revolutionary states,
like the United States and France, people are still
proposing improvements in government and are
still thinking of revolution.   Why, when they had
revolutions a century ago, are they thinking of
other revolutions ?   This proves that we were
wrong when we thought that following the West
would lead us to the heights of perfection; and if
we should fully copy the United States and France,
which   are   still   contemplating   revolution,   we
could not escape another revolution a hundred
years hence.   For the governmental machinery
of the United States and France still has many
defects, and does not satisfy the desires of the
people nor give them a complete measure of
happiness.   So we in our proposed reconstruction
must not think that if we imitate the West of
to-day we shall reach the last stage of progress and
be perfectly contented.   If we follow the dust of
the West, will not each generation be more dissatisfied than the one previous, and will we not
finally have to stage another revolution ?   If
another revolution is going to be necessary, then
is not this one a vain effort ?   What shall we do
to keep this revolution from being a futile waste

of energy? What plans shall we lay in order to secure a permanent government and a lasting peace — "enduring repose after one supreme effort" — and prevent calamities in the future?

Can we bring over the methods of the West and apply them wholesale in China? Take the newest features of Western material civilization. The most important means of communication are the railways. The first Oriental nation to model its railways after the Western railways was Japan. Only recently has China come to realize the value of railways and the need of constructing them, so she was much later than Japan in adopting a foreign railway system. But compare the railroads at present in China and Japan. If you have ridden on both Chinese and Japanese trains, you know that the Japanese track is quite narrow and the coaches are quite small, while Chinese tracks, as on the Shanghai-Nanking or the Peking-Hankow Railway, are very wide and the coaches are very large. Why is it that on the Chinese railroads, which were built later than the Japanese railroads, the tracks are wider and the coaches are larger? Because China modeled after the newest inventions in the West, while Japan modeled after old styles. If China had modeled after the old styles of Japan, instead of after the latest inventions of the West, would we be satisfied? Europe and America formerly used only the narrow-gauge railway and

small coaches ; Japan at the beginning modeled
after these and unknowingly fell into a bad trap.
Should we also in building railroads copy these
inconvenient old models ? In fact, China has
not been copying Japan s antiquated model, but
has copied from the most efficient and recent
models in the West, and consequently our railroads
are better than Japan's. " The last has become
first." For this same reason we, in our political
reformation, should not copy the antiquated
features of the West ; but we should make a
careful study of political conditions in the West,
see how far Western nations have really progressed
in government, and learn from their newest discoveries. Only then can we hope to outstrip
other nations.

As I said in a former lecture, Europe and America have not gone to the bottom in their study of
the problems of democracy, and consequently the
people are in daily conflict with their governments.
The force of democracy is new, but the machinery
of democracy is old. If we want to solve the
difficulties of democracy we must build another
machinery, a new machinery, upon the principle
that sovereignty and ability are different things.
The people must have sovereignty, the machinery
must have ability and power. Modern efficient
and powerful machinery is operated by men who
can start and stop it at will. The West has made

the most complete inventions in the field of
machinery but very imperfect discoveries in the
field of government.   If we want to make a complete change in government, we have no model to
follow but must discover a new way for ourselves.
Are we able to do such a thing ?   Since the Boxer
year, Chinese have completely lost their self-
confidence.   The attitude of the people is one of
absolute faith in foreign countries and of distrust
of themselves.   That they should accomplish
anything of themselves or make any original discovery seems to them impossible.   No, they must
run after the West and copy Western ways.   Before
the Boxer year we were full of self-confidence ;
the people believed that China's ancient civilization was superior to Western civilization, that
Chinese were superior in mental capacity to
Westerners, and that we could make any sort
of new inventions or discoveries.   Now we think
that such a thing is out of the question. We do
not see that Western civilization is strong only
in its material aspects and not in its various political aspects.   From the standpoint of scientific
theories of a material civilization, Europe and
America have developed remarkably in recent
years.   But because a man is outstanding in one
field of knowledge does not necessarily signify
that he is equally proficient in all fields of knowledge ; in many of them he may even be blind.

Their physical sciences have developed to the highest point in the past century and their many new inventions have "usurped the powers of Nature" beyond our wildest dreams. But to say that what they have not thought of in political science we cannot think of or discover is unreasonable. Western machinery has indeed made much progress in recent times, but this does not prove that Western political systems have progressed. also. For two or more centuries the specialty of the West has been only science. The great scientists are naturally well advanced in their own branches of knowledge, but this does not necessarily make them equally advanced in all branches of knowledge. There is a very good story to illustrate this.

There was a great English scientist, named Newton, who has not been excelled by any modern scholar. Newton was a man of great wisdom and learning, who made many epochal discoveries in the field of physics, the most famous of which was the universal law of gravitation. This was first stated by Newton and has since become a foundation principle in science, more important than any other principle since discovered. Newton had this extraordinary aptitude for science, but let us see whether he was equally intelligent in other matters. As I study his life, I do not think he was wise in all matters, and there is one

very interesting anecdote to prove my point.
Newton had from his birth, apart from his passion
for study and experiment, a great fondness for
cats. He once owned two cats of different sizes,
that followed him everywhere in and out of the
house. Because of his love for the cats he always
waited on their wishes; if he were studying or
experimenting in his room and the cats wanted to
go out, he would stop all his work and open the
door for them himself; if the cats wanted to enter,
he would stop all his work and let them in. But
the cats went out and came in so much that they
became exceedingly troublesome; and so one day
Newton thought that he would invent a way by
which the cats could come and go freely without
disturbing his work. What was his way ? He
made two holes in the door, a large one and a
small one, the large one for the large cat and the
small one for the small cat ! This plan was the
wisdom of a great scientist ! Common sense
tells us that if the big cat could go through the
big hole, the small cat could of course do the
same, and one big hole would suffice. Why, then,
waste time on making a small hole ? But the
great scholar Newton insisted on making two
holes. How ludicrous ! Is the scientist wise in
all matters ? This story shows that he is not;
because he is strong in one line does not mean that
he is equally strong in all lines.

Western science has progressed to the point of making material machinery automatically double-acting, but the people's sovereignty over the government is still single-acting; it can only be advanced and not taken back.   While we are advocating democracy for the reconstruction of our republic, let us have a thoroughgoing new democracy and a thoroughgoing new republic.   If we should not wholly follow the advanced states of the West, we should think out a new and better procedure ourselves.   Are we capable of doing this ?   If we want to answer this question, we must not continually despise ourselves and " disparage ourselves as small and mean."   The stream of democracy has flowed into China and we welcome it for the reconstruction of our nation, but can we ourselves find a new and better way to make use of it ?   For thousands of years China has been an independent country.   In our former political development, we never borrowed materials from other countries.   China had one of the earliest civilizations in the world and never needed to copy wholly from others.   Only in recent times has Western culture advanced beyond ours, and the passion for this new civilization has stimulated our revolution.   Now that the revolution is a reality, we naturally desire to see China excel the West and build up the newest and most progressive state in the world.   We certainly possess the qualifications necessary to reach this ideal, but we must not merely imitate the democratic systems of the West. These systems have become old-style machinery.

To reach our ideal we must construct a new machinery. Is there any material in the world for such a new machinery? Yes, there is much material scattered in various countries, but we must first decide upon a fundamental line of procedure. And this line of procedure is the separation of sovereignty and ability which I have already discussed. Then, as we put democracy into operation, we must separate the organization of the state and the administration of democracy. Western nations have not thought through these basic principles and have not distinguished between sovereignty and power or ability, consequently their government's power does not expand. Now that we have thought through our basic principle, we must go a step further and divide the machinery of government. In order to do this, we must understand well the idea of government. In Lecture I, I gave a definition for government — a thing of and by all the people and control of the affairs of all the people. The government machinery which is constructed according to the principle of sovereignty being distinct from ability and power is just like material machinery which has power in itself and is

controlled by a power outside. In building the
new state according to the newest discoveries, we
should separate clearly these two kinds of power.
But how ? We must start from the meaning of
government. Government or politics is a concern
of all the people, and its centralizing force is
political sovereignty. Political sovereignty, then,
means popular sovereignty, and government which
centralizes the forces controlling the life of the
people is called government power or government
authority.

There are, then, two forces in politics, the political power of the people and the administrative
power of the government. One is the power of
control, the other is the power of the government
itself. What does this mean ? A steamship has
a 100,000 horse power engine : the generation of
100,000 horse power and the moving of the vessel
are in the power of the machinery itself, and
this power may be compared to the power of the
government. But the movement of the great steam
vessel forward and backward, to the right or left,
its stopping, and its rate of speed, all depend upon
the control of a good engineer. He is essential to
the direction and control of a perfect machine; by
perfect control the powerful vessel can be made to
start and to stop at will. This power of control
may be compared to the control over government,
which is political sovereignty. Building a new

state is like building a new steamship. If we put
in low-powered machinery, the speed of the vessel
will naturally be low, its freight capacity will be
small, and profits from its running meager. But
if we install high-powered machinery, the vessel
will have a high rate of speed, will be able to
carry heavy freight, and will bring in large profits.
Suppose a steamship with a mechanical horse
power of 100,000 and a speed of 20 knots could
make a profit of $100,000 in a two-week round
trip between Canton and Shanghai. Then suppose we should build a very large steamship and
put in it machinery with 1,000,000 horse power,
so that it could make a speed of 50 knots; a
round trip between Canton and Shanghai would
take only one week and each trip would bring a
profit of $1,000,000. The fastest steamships now
in the world cannot make a speed of over twenty
or thirty knots. But if we could build a steamship
with a speed of 50 knots, then no other steamship
could compete with it, and we would have the
fastest an largest new steamship in the world.
The same principle applies in the building of a
state. If we construct a low-powered, weak
government, its activities will be limited and its
accomplishments will be meager. But if we put
in a high-powered, strong government, its activities
will be broad in scope and it will accomplish
great things. If a powerful government should

be installed in the largest state in the world, would not that state outstrip all others ? Would not that government be unequaled under heaven ?

Why have the nations of the West steamships with high-powered machinery but not states with high-powered strong governments ? Because they can only control high-powered machinery, but have not found a way to control high-powered government. To discard a low-powered old vessel and build a high-powered new one is an easy task; but the state has very deep roots and the construction of a new powerful government in place of an old weak government is a very difficult thing. China with her four hundred million people is the most populous state in the world ; her territory is broad and her products are rich and abundant, exceeding those of the United States. The United States has now become the wealthiest and most powerful nation in the world, and no other nation can compare with her. When we compare our natural resources, it seems that China should outstrip the United States, but as a matter of fact, not only is this impossible now but the two countries cannot even be mentioned in the same breath. The reason is that the Chinese have the necessary qualifications but want human effort. We have never had a real good government. But if we add human effort to our natural qualifications, build up a complete, strong government

which will display great power and move the
whole nation, then China can immediately begin
to advance in line with the United States.

After China secures a powerful government,
we must not be afra:d, as Western peoples are,
that the government will become too strong and
get from under our control. Because our plan
for the reconstructed state includes the division
of the political power of the whole state into two
parts. The political power will be given into the
hands of the people, who will have a full degree
of sovereignty and will be able to control directly
the affairs of state; this political power is popular
sovereignty. The other power is government,
and we will put that entirely in the government
organs, which will be powerful and will manage
all the nation's business; this political power is
the power of government. If the people have a
full measure of political sovereignty and the
methods for exercising popular control over the
government are well worked out, we need not fear
that the government will become too powerful
and uncontrollable. Westerners formerly did not
dare to build machines with over 100,000 horse
power ; because machines were not perfectly
constructed and the means of control were not
compact, they were afraid of their power and would
not risk the control of them. But now such
wonderful improvements have been made in

machinery, the machines themselves are so well constructed and the control mechanism is so compact, that Westerners are building machines with tremendous horse power. If we want to build a much-improved political machinery, we must follow the same line : we must have a complete and powerful government organ, and at the same time have a compact method of popular sovereignty to exercise control over the government organ. Western governments lack this compact and effective control, so they are not yet making much progress. Let us not follow in their tracks. Let the people in thinking about government distinguish between sovereignty and power. Let the great political force of the state be divided ; first let there be the power of the government and then the power of the people. Such a division will make the government the machinery and the people the engineer. The attitude of the people towards their government will then be like the attitude of the engineer towards his machinery.

Such advances have been made in the construction of machinery that not only men with mechanical knowledge, but even children without any knowledge of machinery can control it. Take, for example, the electric light in common use to-day. When electricity was first discovered, it was a very dangerous thing, like lightning, and without

good means of control would kill people. As a
result there were numberless victims among the
scientists who first studied electricity. The danger was so great that for a long time after the
discovery of electric light people did not dare use
it in lamps. Then a compact and effective method
of control was invented, and with one turn of a
switch a person could turn the light on or off.
This little movement of the hand is very convenient and very safe; a person without any knowledge of electricity, a child of the city or the most
ignorant man in the country, can turn the electric
switch with the hand. Thus that most dangerous
force, electric light, has now been made to serve
as a lamp.

The development of other machinery is a similar
story. The most recently invented machines,
the flying machines, are extremely dangerous
things. When they were first used, countless
numbers of people were killed by them. Do you
remember Feng Ju, of Kwangtung? He was a
builder of flying machines, and while piloting one
fell to the ground and was killed. In the early
days of the invention, people did not know how
to use it, and so the builder of the aëroplane had
to be the aviator also. The early aviators, because
they did not have compact and effective control
mechanisms on their machines and because they
lacked experience in flying, were not able to

manipulate the machines well, and many fell to their death. This made ordinary folks unwilling to ride in aëroplanes. But now the control mechanism is delicate and compact, and many people have had the experience of flying through the air like a bird, back and forth, up and down, and know how extremely convenient and safe such travel is; so ordinary folks dare to ride in aëroplanes. As a result, aëroplanes are now used regularly as a means of communication. The road from Kwangtung to Szechwan is very long and there are enemies on the way. Travel by land or water is exceedingly difficult and tedious. But in an aëroplane we could fly quickly and directly to Szechwan.

China has now the idea of democracy, but no perfect machinery has yet been invented in the world to express this idea. The people do not know how to use it. We who have vision and foresight must first build the machine. We must construct a very serviceable kind of faucet, a very safe kind of electric button which ordinary people can learn how to use by a single turn of the hand; then the idea of democracy will become a reality. China was later than the West in getting the idea of democracy, just as she was later than Japan in building railroads. Although Japan began to build railroads before China, yet her railroads are an old style and are not suited

to modern use. Our newly finished railroads
are well adapted to modern requirements. What
methods shall we use in applying the democracy
which we have adopted from the West? Only
after we have thought through these methods will
democracy be adapted to our use. If we insist on
using democracy without careful preparation
beforehand, we will find it extremely dangerous
and liable to kill us. Have such methods of
applying democracy yet been found? Switzerland in Europe has some partial methods which
she has already tried out; they are radical and
give the people direct sovereignty, but are not
very complete. The larger nations of Europe have
not even experimented with these incomplete
methods. The fact that only the small state of
Switzerland has tried a partial form of direct
sovereignty makes many people question whether
it is applicable in large states also. Why are not
the large states using Switzerland's methods?
They are like Japan who already has narrow-
gauge railroads and who would find the change to
broad-gauge railroads now exceedingly costly in
time and money and a poor policy from the economic point of view. Because they " fear difficulties and seek ease," because they set store by
finance, these advanced people are familiar with
the newly invented models but do not make use
of them. But we in China never had any old

machinery of democracy, so we ought to be able to choose and use the newest and best discoveries.

What are the newest discoveries in the way of applying democracy ? First, there is the suffrage, and it is the only method in operation throughout the so-called modern democracies. Is this one form of popular sovereignty enough in government ? This one power by itself may be compared to the early machines which could move forward only but not back. The second of the newly discovered methods is the power of recall. With this power, the people can pull the machine back. These two rights, the right to elect and the right to recall, give the people control over their officials and enable them to put all government officials in their positions or to move them out of their positions. The coming and going of officials follows the free will of the people just as modern machines move to and fro by the free action of the engine. Another important thing in a state, in addition to officials, is law; "with men to govern there must also be ways of governing." What power must the people possess in order to control the laws ? If all the people think that a certain law would be of great advantage to them, they should have the power to decide upon this law and turn it over to the government for execution. This third kind of popular power is called the initiative. If everybody thinks that an old

law is not beneficial to the people, they should
have the power to amend it and to ask the government to administer the revised law and do away
with the old law. This is called the referendum
and is a fourth form of popular sovereignty.
Only when the people have these four powers can
we say that there is a full measure of democracy,
and only where these four powers are effectively
applied can we say that there is thoroughgoing,
direct, popular sovereignty. Before there was
any complete democracy, people elected their
officials and representatives and then could not
hold them responsible. This was only indirect
democracy or a representative system of government. The people could not control the government directly but only through their representatives. For direct control of the government it is
necessary that the people practice these four forms
of popular sovereignty. Only then can we speak
of government by all the people. This means that
our four hundred millions shall be king, exerting
their kingly authority and controlling the great
affairs of state by means of the four powers of
the people. These four powers are like four
faucets or four electric switches. With the faucet
we can control directly the running of water, with
the electric switch we can control directly the
electric light, with the four powers of the people
we can control directly the government of the state.

These four powers are also called political powers and are powers for control of the government.

The government's own power to transact business may be called the power to work, to work on behalf of the people. If the people are very powerful, whether the government can work or not and what kind of work it does will depend entirely upon the will of the people. If the government is very powerful, as soon as it starts work it can display great strength, and whenever the people want it to stop, it will have to stop. In a nutshell, if the people are really to have direct control over the power of government, they must be able to command at any time the actions of the government. An illustration may be drawn from the battleship. If a foreign battleship of the old style had twelve guns, they were mounted on six different turrets and many gunmen had to work separately to find the range in order to fire upon an enemy. The control officer could not control the firing directly. But in the new modern battleships, there is an instrument for finding the range in the conning tower aloft and the calculations for the gunsights are made in the control officer's room, from which the guns are aimed by direct electric control. So when a battleship meets the enemy now, it is not necessary for many different gunmen to work the gunsights and fire the guns; the control officer sits

in his room and after hearing the reports of the
range finders and calculating the distance manip-
ulates the electric mechanism by which one gun
is fired in one direction or all twelve guns are
sighted and fired together. The guns all fire as
he directs and all hit the mark. Only an arrangement like this can be called direct control, but
direct control does not mean that the control
officer does all the work himself. A machine only
becomes serviceable as it does the work for the
person using it.

With the people exerting these four great powers
to control the government, what methods will the
government use in performing its work? In
order that the government may have a complete
organ through which to do its best work, there
must be a quintuple-power constitution. A government is not complete and cannot do its best work
for the people unless it is based upon a quintuple-
power constitution. I spoke before of an American scholar who advanced the new theory that
what a nation fears most is an all-powerful,
uncontrollable government, yet what it most
desires is an all-powerful government which the
people can use and which will seek the people's
welfare. Popular rule cannot really prevail until
there is the latter kind of government. We are
now making a distinction between sovereignty
and ability; we are saying that the people are like

the engineer and the government like the machinery.   On the one hand, we want the government machinery to be all-powerful so that it can do any sort of work; on the other hand, we want the engineer-people to be very strong so that they can control the all-powerful machinery.   Now what great powers are the people and the government each to have in order that they may balance each other?   I have already discussed the four powers on the people's side — suffrage, recall, initiative, and referendum.   On the side of the government there must be five powers — executive, legislative, judicial, civil service examination, and censoring.   When the four political powers of the people control the five governing powers of the government, then we will have a completely democratic government organ, and the strength of the people and of the government will be well balanced. This diagram will help us to understand more clearly the relation between these powers:

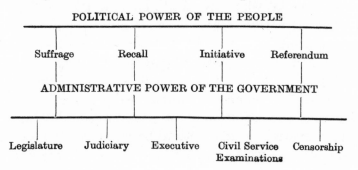

POLITICAL POWER OF THE PEOPLE

Suffrage   Recall   Initiative   Referendum

ADMINISTRATIVE POWER OF THE GOVERNMENT

Legislature   Judiciary   Executive   Civil Service   Censorship
Examinations

The political power above is in the hands of the people, the administrative power below is in the hands of the government. The people control the government through the suffrage, the recall, the initiative, and the referendum; the government works for the people through its legislative, judicial, executive, civil examination, and censoring departments. With these nine powers in operation and preserving a balance, the problem of democracy will truly be solved and the government will have a definite course to follow. The materials for this new plan have been discovered before now. Switzerland has already applied three of the political powers but does not have the recall. Some of the northwestern states in the United States have taken over the three political rights from Switzerland and have added the right of recall. Suffrage is the people's power most widely exercised in the world to-day. Switzerland is already exercising three of the popular powers and a fourth part of the United States is exercising all four. Where the four powers have been exercised in a careful, compact way the results have been excellent. They are facts of experience, not mere hypothetical ideals. We will be safe in using these methods and will not run into any danger.

All governmental powers were formerly monopolized by kings and emperors, but after the

revolutions they were divided into three groups :
thus the United States, after securing its independence, established a government with three
coördinate departments, with splendid results.
Other nations followed the example of the United
States. But foreign governments have never
exercised more than these three powers — legislative, executive, and judicial. What is the source
of the two new features in our quintuple-power
constitution? They come from old China. China
long ago had the independent systems of civil
service examination and censorship and they
were very effective. The imperial censors or
historiographers of the Manchu dynasty and the
official advisers of the T'ang dynasty made a fine
censoring system. The power of censorship includes the power to impeach, which other governments have but which is placed in the legislative
body and is not a separate governmental power.
The selection of real talent and ability through
examinations has been characteristic of China for
thousands of years. Modern foreign scholars who
have studied Chinese institutions give high praise
to China's old independent examination system,
and there have been imitations of the system for
the selection of able men in the West. Great
Britain's civil service examinations are modeled
after the old Chinese system, but only ordinary
officials are examined. The British system does

not yet possess the spirit of the independent examination system of old China. In Chinese political history, the three governmental powers— judicial, legislative, and executive — were vested in the emperor. The other powers of civil service examination and censorship were separate from the throne. The old autocratic government of China can also be said to have had three departments and so was very different from the autocratic governments of the West in which all power was monopolized by the king or emperor himself. During the period of autocratic government in China, the emperor still did not have sole authority over the power of examination and censorship. So China in a way had three coördinate departments of government, just as the modern democracies of the West have their three departments, with this difference — the Chinese government has exercised the powers of autocracy, censorship, and civil examination for many thousands of years, while Western governments have exercised legislative, judicial, and executive powers for only a little over a century. However, the three governmental powers in the West have been imperfectly applied and the three coördinate powers of ancient China led to many abuses. If we now want to combine the best from China and the best from other countries and guard against all kinds of abuse in the future, we must take the three

Western governmental powers — the executive, legislative, and judicial — add to them the old Chinese powers of examination and censorship and make a finished wall, a quintuple-power government. Such a government will be the most complete and the finest in the world, and a state with such a government will indeed be of the people, by the people, and for the people.

Each of these four popular powers and five governmental powers has its own focus and function; we must separate them clearly and not confuse them. There are many people to-day who cannot distinguish between these various powers — not only ordinary folks but even specialists blunder. Recently I met a comrade who had just graduated in America. I asked him, " What do you think of the revolutionary principles ? " He said, " I am heartily in favor of them." I asked him again, " What did you study abroad ? " He replied, " Political science and law." " What is your opinion of the people's sovereignty which I am advocating ? " I questioned him once more. " The quintuple-power constitution is a splendid thing ! " he answered. " Everybody welcomes it." The reply of this specialist in political science and law missed entirely the point of my question, which showed that he had not clearly understood the difference between the four powers and the five powers and was still muddled as to the relationship between people and government; he did not know that the five powers are governmental powers.

From the standpoint of function, the governmental powers are mechanical powers. In order to make this large machinery, which can develop tremendous horse power, function most effectively, we make it work in five directions. The popular powers are the powers of control which the people exercise directly over this high-powered machinery. The four powers of the people we may say are four controls which the people manipulate in order to make the machinery move and stop. The government works for the people and its five powers are five forms of work or five directions of work. The people control the government and their four powers are four methods of control. Only as the government is given such power and the opportunity to work in these different directions can it manifest great dignity and authority and become an all-powerful government. Only as the people are given great power and the various checks upon the government will they not be afraid of the government becoming all-powerful and uncontrollable. The people can then at any time command the government to move or to stop. The prestige of the government will grow and the power of the people will increase. With such an administrative power on the part of the government and such political power on the part of the people, we will be able to realize the ideal of the American scholar — an all-powerful government seeking the welfare of the people — and to blaze the way for the building of a new world.

What the actual conditions under a democracy are and how we should administer a democracy we shall understand more clearly and deeply after we have regulated the suffrage, recall, initiative, and referendum. I have not been able to describe all the particulars in these lectures on the People's Sovereignty. Those who wish to make a more detailed study can refer to Mr. Liao Chung-k'ai's translation of the book, *Government by All the People.*

April 26, 1924.

PART III

THE PRINCIPLE OF LIVELIHOOD

THE PRINCIPLE OF LIVELIHOOD

LECTURE 1

Meaning of *Min-sheng*, or the People's Livelihood — New problems of livelihood caused by substitution of machine power for human labor — How the railroads in China are supplanting coolie labor — Relation of the *Min-sheng* Principle to socialism and communism — Factions within Western socialist parties and failure of socialism to solve post-war problems — Marx's contribution to socialism — Utopian socialism and scientific socialism — Marx's materialistic conception of history criticized — The search for livelihood the central force in history — Recent social and economic developments which are disproving Marx's theory of class struggle — Social and economic reform, public ownership of transportation and communication, direct taxation and socialized distribution discussed and appraised — Social evolution through adjustment of economic interests — "Surplus value" created by community, not by labor alone — Marx a social pathologist — Marx's forecasts of capitalist collapse not fulfilled — Gradual improvement of working conditions — Shorter day and workers' benefits have increased production — Marx's conditions for increase of surplus value contradicted by history of Ford factories — Consumers' coöperative societies in England — Importance of the consumer — Reasons for failure of Hanyang Iron and Steel Works — Livelihood must be the center of the economic solar system.

The subject of my lecture to-day is *Min-sheng Chu I*, the Principle of the People's Livelihood. *Min-sheng* is a worn phrase in China.

We talk about *kuo-chi min-sheng*, national welfare and the people's livelihood, but I fear that we pay only lip service to these words and have not really sought to understand them. I cannot see that they have held much meaning for us. But if, in this day of scientific knowledge, we will bring the phrase into the realm of scientific discussion and study its social and economic implications, we shall find that it takes on an immeasurable significance. I propose to-day a definition for *Min-sheng*, the People's Livelihood. It denotes the livelihood of the people, the existence of society, the welfare of the nation, the life of the masses. And now I shall use the phrase *Min-sheng* to describe one of the greatest problems that has emerged in the West during the past century or more — socialism. The Principle of Livelihood is socialism, it is communism, it is Utopianism. But this principle cannot be explained by a few definitions. You must listen to these lectures from beginning to end if you want to understand them thoroughly.

The problem of livelihood is now rising like a tide in every country. Yet the problem is comparatively new, with a history of not much over a century. What has caused the sudden emergence of this question in the last hundred years? Briefly, the rapid progress of material civilization all over the world, the great development of industry and the sudden increase in the productive power of the human race. Candidly speaking, the problem arose with the invention of machinery and with the gradual substitution of natural power for human labor in the most civilized nations. The natural forces of steam, heat, water, and electricity began to be used in place of human strength, and copper and iron in place of human bone and sinew. Since the invention of machinery, one man in charge of one machine has been able to do the work of one hundred or one thousand men. A great discrepancy has arisen between the productive power of the machine and human productive power. The most diligent worker can hardly do more than two or three men's work in one day and can never do more than ten men's work, which means that a most diligent man with the most powerful physique and the greatest strength and energy could not possibly produce more goods than ten ordinary men could. There is not much difference in the productive strength of ordinary men, but there is a vast difference between the productiveness of a machine and the productiveness of simple human labor. When human labor alone is employed, the most powerful and industrious workers cannot accomplish more than ten times the amount of the ordinary worker, but when machinery is employed the most lazy and common worker in charge of it can accomplish hundreds, thousands of times as much as the best worker without machinery. Productiveness is now a very different thing from what it was a few decades ago before the introduction of machinery.

Let us look at some of the verifiable facts before our own eyes. No class is more common on the streets of Canton than the coolies, or carriers. They form a large percentage of the workers of the city. The strongest coolie cannot carry a load of more than two hundred catties or walk more than a few score li in one day. Such carriers are hard to find ; the ordinary one is worn out with a load of less than a hundred catties over a distance of a few score li. Compare these carriers with machine transport. Look at the freight trains at Wongsha station in the city. One locomotive can pull twenty or more freight cars, and each freight car can carry several hundred piculs of goods, which means that a freight train of twenty cars could carry ten thousand piculs. With one or two men in charge of the locomotive and a few others in charge of the freight cars, the train can travel several hundred li in one day. From Canton to Shiukwan (Shiuchow), on the Canton-Hankow Railway, is a distance of about five hundred li. Formerly, when only man power was used to transport goods along this route, it took one man to carry one picul or load, or ten thousand men to carry ten thousand piculs. One man could cover only about fifty li a day, so the trip of five hundred li required ten days. Ten thousand piculs of goods, which formerly demanded the man power of ten thousand laborers for ten days, can now be transported all the way from Canton to Shiukwan in eight hours with the help of, at the most, ten men. Here you see ten men doing the work of ten thousand and eight hours taking the place of ten days. What a tremendous difference between machine power and man power! The railroad not only makes it possible for one man to take the place of a thousand men, and for one hour to take the place of one day, so that transportation becomes exceedingly convenient and rapid, but it also saves money. A carrier has to be paid at the rate of a dollar a day; ten thousand laborers carrying ten thousand piculs for ten days would cost $100,000. Yet railway transportation for the same amount of goods would not cost over a few thousand dollars. In plowing, weaving, building, and all other kinds of work, machine power is also many hundredfold, sometimes many thousandfold, as efficient as man power.

Since the invention of machinery, therefore, the world has undergone a revolution in production. Machinery has usurped the place of human labor, and men who possessed machinery have taken

wealth away from those who did not have machinery. Before the Opium War, Canton was the
only open port of China. Goods from the various
provinces had to be carried overland first to
Canton and thence shipped to foreign countries;
foreign goods were landed at Canton and distributed from that point throughout the provinces.
So all of China's exports had to pass through
Hunan and Kiangsi, by way of Nansiung and
Lochang, before reaching Canton, and imports
took the same route. As a result, the roads
between Nansiung and Shiukwan and between
Lochang and Shiukwan swarmed with carriers,
while tea shops and restaurants along the road-
sides did a thriving business. But later, when
foreign trade opened up, goods from the provinces
were sent either in coast boats to Canton or direct
to foreign countries via Shanghai and Tientsin.
They no longer passed along the roads from
Nansiung and Lochang to Shiukwan, and so the
number of carriers greatly decreased. These
two routes, which were formerly so prosperous,
are now deserted. When trains began to run
along the Canton-Hankow Railway and to take
the place of man power, the carriers between
Canton and Shiukwan simply disappeared. Conditions in other parts of China and in other
countries have been the same. Following the
introduction of machinery, great numbers of men

suddenly lost their occupations and were unable
to get work or to obtain food. Westerners have
called this great change the Industrial Revolution.
On account of this revolution the workers suffered
greatly. This is why, during the last few decades,
a social problem has come into existence, the result
of an effort to relieve this kind of suffering.

It is this social problem that I am discussing
to-day in the Principle of Livelihood. Why not
follow the West and speak directly of socialism?
why use the old Chinese term *min-sheng* in its
stead? There is a very significant reason for
this which we shall consider. Since its first development, and especially since the Industrial Revolution, machinery has become a serious social
problem and has stimulated the rise of socialistic
theories. But although socialism has been a
growing force for several decades, Western nations
have not yet found a solution for the questions
involved in it, and a severe dispute is still raging
over them. Western social theories and ideas
are now pouring into China and are being studied
by certain groups of Chinese seholars. Since
there is a form of socialism called "communism,"
the term "communism" is circulated freely
throughout China along with other theories.
It is very difficult, however, for Chinese students
of socialism and communism to find solutions for
the problems raised by these doctrines when even

Westerners who first advanced the doctrines have not succeeded in interpreting them.

In our study, we must examine carefully into the nature of these doctrines, learn about their origin, and consider their definitions. The terms "socialism" and "communism" are now used synonymously in the West. Although their methods may vary, socialism is often used to describe both theories. There are people in China who look upon socialism and sociology as the same thing, and foreigners are often guilty of the same confusion. One reason is that the first half of the three English words "society," "sociology," and "socialism" are identical. The word "socialism" is derived from a Greek word meaning "comrade," something like our colloquial word for business partner, *huo-chi*. Sociology is the study of the phenomena and development of society and of the phenomena of social groups. Socialism deals with social and economic questions and with the problem of human subsistence, or livelihood. In using the term "Principle of Livelihood" instead of "socialism," my prime purpose is to strike at the root of the social problem and to reveal its real nature, also to make it possible for people to understand the term as soon as they hear it. In the last few decades there have been countless students of socialism and countless books on socialism with so many diverse and clashing

theories of social reconstruction that a foreign
proverb speaks of the "fifty-seven varieties of
socialism," and one cannot tell which variety is
real socialism. As a result, the common people
feel that there is nothing definite to follow in
socialism.

After the European War, social progress was
much accelerated, and it seemed as if the world
had reached a new period when the key to social
questions would be found. Those who before
had paid no attention to socialism now began
to move in that direction. At such an opportune
moment it seems that the Socialist Party should
have accomplished a great deal and should have
found some perfect solutions for the problems of
society. But many struggles broke out within
the socialist movement. "The wind blew and
clouds rolled up" of a sudden in the socialist
parties of all countries. The movement split into
many branches, some of the best known being the
Communists, the State Socialists, and the Social
Democrats. The complex differences between
the various groups now threaten to increase the
"fifty-seven varieties." Observers who, in the
past, criticized the Socialist Party for its many
diverse factions have now "unfortunately hit
the mark." Before the European War, there
were in each country only pro-socialist and anti-
socialist groups. The opponents of socialism

were chiefly capitalists and the main attacks upon
socialism were made by capitalists. After the
war, the enemies of socialism seemed ready to
capitulate and socialism seemed prepared to
take advantage of the opportunity and to reconstruct society. But the supporters of socialism
had not thought out a good method of procedure,
and consequently, at the critical moment, the
Socialist Party was rent with dissensions far more
serious than those in former years between the
advocates and the opponents of socialism. And
so the social question is not yet solved. But we
to-day must set out upon a careful study of it.
Formerly, when capitalists, workmen, and scholars
were opposing socialism, socialists everywhere,
no matter whether of the same or of different
countries, counted each other as comrades. But
now not only are there international conflicts
between socialists — German socialists fighting
Russian socialists and Russian socialists fighting
British and American socialists — but the Socialist Party in each nation is exhibiting internal
differences and the social question is becoming
more confused the more it is discussed, until no
worth-while solution is in sight.

Is the Principle of Livelihood which I am
proposing to-day really different from socialism?
Socialism deals primarily with the economic problems of society; that is, the common problem of

a living. Since the introduction of machinery, a
large number of people have had their work taken
away from them and workers generally have been
unable to maintain their existence. Socialism
arose as an effort to solve the living problem, and
from this standpoint, the social question is also
the economic question, and the principle of
livelihood is the main theme of socialism. But
now every country's socialism has different
theories and different proposals for social reconstruction. Is socialism really a phase of the
Min-sheng Principle, or is the Principle of Livelihood a phase of socialism ?

After the Industrial Revolution, the number of
people studying social questions mounted up
into the thousands. The one man who made
the most profound and rewarding study is known
to you all — Marx. Marx bears somewhat the
same relation to the socialist movement that
Rousseau does to the democratic movement.
A century ago Westerners who were studying the
problems of popular sovereignty all worshiped
Rousseau as a sage of democracy just as Chinese
have worshiped Confucius. Students of socialism to-day all worship Marx in the same way as
a sage of the socialist movement. Before Marx
set forth his theories, socialism had been highly
speculative and too far removed from actual
facts. Marx, however, began with facts and with

history, and made a radical and thorough exposition of the changes in the economic phase of the social question. As a result, later scholars have divided socialists into two groups: Utopian socialists, whose ideal is similar to Lieh-tze's [1] dream of the Land of the Hwa-hsü people; and the scientific socialists, who use only scientific methods in the study of social problems. The Utopian socialists would reform society and make a peaceful and happy state simply out of their imagination. This idea of a vain and unreal refuge originated with certain virtuous and compassionate folks who could not bear to see suffering about them, but who had no power to eliminate it. All they could offer was empty ideals. A Chinese proverb well describes this sort of ideal refuge place: " Heaven brings forth a worm and Earth brings forth a leaf, Heaven brings forth a bird and Earth brings forth a worm," meaning that there will always be a leaf to nourish the worm and a worm to nourish the bird. But man has not been given a perfect body by nature; he is not born with hair or feathers, but needs clothes for protection against cold and food to sustain his life.

In primitive times, when man ate fruits, when the earth was wide and people were few, it was a very simple matter for everybody to find food.

---

[1] A Chinese philosopher of the fifth century before Christ.

Men could get a living without much effort. In the hunting age men had to fish and to hunt in order to secure food and keep alive; only those who worked could find anything to eat. In the pastoral age, men had to tend flocks in order to make a living; everybody lived near water and grass and was constantly moving from one place to another. Work was arduous and wearisome. When the agricultural age arrived, men had to plant the " five grains " [1] in order to live, living conditions became increasingly complex, and work demanded yet more wearisome effort. But when the industrial and commercial age dawned and everything began to be done by machinery, man found that although he had strength yet he could not utilize it. He was willing to sell his labor but could not find a buyer. It was then that large numbers of people could hardly find food and almost starved. Their sufferings cannot be described in a single sentence.

Then certain moralists, seeing that the birds and the beasts in the world of nature found food and clothing without pain and trouble, while man toiled and suffered, procuring with great difficulty a little to eat and to wear, were moved with pity. In the hope of reducing the suffering of mankind and of making it possible for all to eat and to be

[1] Hemp, millet, rice, wheat, pulse.

clothed, they set forth the doctrine of socialism
as a panacea. The first exponents of socialism
were mostly moralists and their followers were
also men of fine conscience and character. The
only people who fought socialism or who showed
indifference to social questions were the capitalists, who had become hopelessly selfish with their
money and did not care about the living conditions
of the masses. Since the social question had to
do with procuring livelihood for the majority of
mankind, the seers and the prophets who proposed
the doctrine of socialism naturally won the sympathy and support of large numbers of people.
As soon as the doctrine appeared, socialist parties
began to be organized. The socialist movement
grew steadily in unity and in magnitude and
spread to every country. But the first socialists
were all Utopians ; they hoped to build an ideally
peaceful and happy world in which there would
be no more human suffering, but they did not
think at all of any concrete methods by which
suffering was to be removed. Then Marx came.
He devoted his wisdom and intellect, his learning
and his experience, to a thoroughgoing study of
these questions. Problems which men before
him had not understood clearly or could not
fathom he made plain. He based his new theories entirely upon economic principles. He criticized the previous socialists for depending upon

the individual moral sense and the feelings of the masses when economic questions could not be solved by morality and emotion. The first essential, he declared, was a careful examination of social conditions and of social progress. The principle upon which he proceeded was absolute respect for facts rather than for ideals. His books and theories may be said to have crystallized the best thinking of mankind for thousands of years upon social questions.

Soon after Marx set forth his doctrines, the whole world began to follow after him, while scholars of all lands declared their faith in him and became his disciples, just as students of democracy put their trust in Rousseau when he proposed his democratic theories. After Marx, the socialist movement divided into two groups — the Utopian socialists and the scientific socialists. The Utopian socialists I have already described to you. Scientific socialists advocated the use of scientific methods in solving social problems. In this epoch, when material civilization is advancing so rapidly and science is becoming so powerful, all study must be based upon scientific principles in order to achieve satisfactory results, and we cannot expect a solution of the social question until careful scientific research has been made.

Here let me return to my theory that understanding is difficult, action easy. Anything in the world can be done if it is first understood.

For example : it is very hot to-day in this lecture
hall, and yet without man power, simply by
the use of electric fans, we can allay the heat.
If ancient man or a contemporary countryman
without any intelligence should see such a thing,
he would certainly think it was being moved by
spirits within, that "the powers of Heaven were
being usurped," and would fall down in prayer
before it. But all of you, while you do not understand the detailed construction of the electric fan,
are familiar with the principle of electric magnet-
ism which causes the fan to revolve, and you
certainly do not believe that it is a supernatural
object. Was the wisdom of the ancients inferior
to ours ? No; but they did not know anything
about science and so they could not invent an
electric fan. They were not without natural
intelligence and the power to use an electric fan.
It is due to the modern knowledge of science and
to the scientific inventors of the electric fan that
we can all use such an instrument and enjoy the
cool air. If ancient man, with his natural intelligence and ability, had understood science, he
might have been more ingenious than modern man.

Before Marx, social reconstruction saw only a
vague hope, an unattainable ideal. Marx saw that
if he followed socialistic ideals in his study, he,
too, would create only a dream; even if the whole
world believed in it, it could not become a reality.

He must base his study upon hard facts and use
scientific methods of careful research if he
wanted to accomplish anything. So he devoted
his whole life to a scientific study of socialism and
wore himself out at the task. At the time that
he was exiled to England, England was the most
cultured nation of the modern world ; no other
nation could surpass her. Consequently she was
well supplied with all the means for the advance-
ment of culture. She had a great library of
several million volumes covering fully every
possible subject. In this library Marx studied
daily. He worked thus for twenty or thirty years
and used up the best energies of his life ; he brought
together all the writings on socialism by ancient as
well as by contemporary authors, compared them
in detail and then tried to deduce a conclusion.
This was the scientific method of studying social
problems, and so Marx's proposal for social reconstruction was called scientific socialism.

From his painstaking and profound study, Marx
worked out the theory that all human activity
upon the globe which has been preserved in written
records for succeeding generations can be called
history; and all human history, viewed in this
way, gravitates about material forces. This latter
point was the new emphasis which Marx gave to
history. If the material basis of life changes, the
world also changes ; human behavior, moreover,

is determined by the material environment, and so the history of human civilization is the story of adaptation to material environment. This discovery of Marx has been likened by some to Newton's discovery of the astronomical law of gravitation. Marx's materialistic conception of history was based upon such thorough study and such perfect reasoning that many who had opposed socialism now indorsed it. Those who made a minute study of Marx's theories believed all the more in him. After the European War there were hardly any people who opposed socialism. The socialist parties had a clear field and might have solved the problem of social reconstruction in each nation. The strongest branch of the Socialist Party was now the Marxian group of scientific socialists ; hitherto the Utopian socialists had predominated. In the period of social disorganization following the war, the scientific and Utopian factions in the socialistic parties of the different countries inevitably conflicted, and dissensions took place also among the scientific socialists themselves. As a result, the socialists have not yet been able to find the way to social reconstruction.

What about the economic theory of history enunciated by the sage of the socialist movement, Marx ? In 1848 Marx's disciples held a world congress of socialists at Brussels and decided upon several policies which are still adhered to

by large numbers of Marxian socialists everywhere.
After the European War broke out, Russia began
to put Marx's theories into practice, but of late she
has made great changes in the interpretation of his
theories. For what reason? We have not made a
very careful investigation of conditions in Russia
and hardly dare to judge of them, but according to
what Russians themselves say, Russia's policy,
during her revolution, was not Marxism but a war
policy. This war policy was not adopted by
Russia alone. Great Britain, Germany, and even
the United States, during the war brought all the
great industries of the nation — railroads, steamship transportation, and all the important manufacturing enterprises — under state control in
the same way that Russia did. Why were such
actions on the part of the government called war
measures in Great Britain and the United States,
but Marxism in Russia ? The reason is to be
found in the Russian Revolutionary Party's faith
in Marx's social and political philosophy and in
their ambition to put this philosophy into practice.
But according to what Russians now say, the
industrial and economic system of the country
at present is not developed highly enough for the
application of Marx's theories ; an industrial and
economic standard like that of Great Britain or
of the United States is necessary before Marxism
can be carried out. So after the European War

the disciples of Marx all began to quarrel over matters of theory. The socialist parties of Germany, France, and Russia had formerly been common followers of Marx and had been branches of the Internationale, but after the differences of opinion arose, they began to attack and to vilify each other and to accuse each other of disloyalty to Marxism. As a result of the attacks of this branch upon that and of this National Socialist Party upon that, Marx's theories began to be seriously questioned.

Have material forces really been the center of gravity in history? Newton found that the sun is the center of gravity in our solar system and astronomers and other scientists have corroborated this principle. Marx discovered that history gravitated about material forces; was his principle correct or not? After a few years of experiment with it following the European War, many people are saying that the principle is wrong. What, then, is the central force in history? Our Kuomintang has been advocating the Principle of Livelihood for over twenty years now; we have not championed socialism but the *Min-sheng* Principle. Are the spheres of these two doctrines in any way related? Recently an American disciple of Marx, named William,[1] after making a deep study of Marx's philosophy, came to the

---

[1] Referring to Maurice Williams, author of " Social Interpretation of History."

conclusion that the disagreement between fellow
socialists is due to defects in the Marxism doctrines. He sets forth the view that the materialistic conception of history is wrong; that the
social problem, not material forces, is the center
which determines the course of history, and that
subsistence is the heart of the social problem.
This social interpretation of history he believes
is the only reasonable one. The problem of
livelihood is the problem of subsistence. The
new theory of this American scholar tallies exactly
with the third principle of our party. Williams's
theory means that livelihood is the central force
in social progress, and that social progress is the
central force in history; hence the struggle for a
living and not material forces determines history.
We have held forth the Principle of Livelihood
for twenty years; when we first studied and
pondered upon this question we felt that the term
Min-sheng defined the field of social problems better than the terms "socialism" or "communism,"
so we chose to use it. We little foresaw at that
time how the clarifying of principles and development of knowledge following a European war
would lead students of the Marx school to discover
the same point. This shows that our *Min-sheng*
Principle is consistent with the law of progress
and is not a mere parroting of what contemporary
scholars are saying.

According to this American scholar, the energies of mankind, both in ancient and modern times, have been spent largely in trying to solve the problem of subsistence. The struggle for existence is one of the laws of social progress and is the central force in history. Marx's materialistic theory did not set forth any law of social progress and cannot be a determining factor in history. If we want to understand clearly the positions of these two social philosophers and to know which one is right, we must make a detailed study of their doctrines and see whether these doctrines harmonize with the facts of modern social progress. Marx, in his investigation of the social problem, emphasized the material side. In dealing with material forces you inevitably come first to the question of production. Where there is no overproduction, there would naturally be no industrial revolution, and so production holds a place of prime importance in modern economics. . If you want to understand modern economic conditions, you must know the facts about production. The large-scale production in modern times is made possible by labor and machinery, by the coöperation of capital and machinery together with the employment of labor. The benefits of this large-scale production are reaped largely by the capitalists themselves; the workers enjoy but a small fraction of the benefits.

Consequently the interests of capitalists and of
workers are constantly clashing and when no solution of the difficulty is found, a class war breaks
out. Marx held the view that class war was not
something which had only followed the industrial
revolution ; all past history is a story of class
struggle — between masters and slaves, between
landlords and serfs, between nobles and common
people; in a word, between all kinds of oppressors
and oppressed. Only when the social revolution
was completely successful, would these warring
classes be no more. It is evident from this that
Marx considered class war essential to social
progress, the driving force, in fact, of social progress. He made class war the cause and social
progress the effect. Let us look at recent facts
in the development of society to see whether this
principle of cause and effect is really a law of social
progress. Society has made tremendous progress
in the last few decades and the details of this
social progress would make a complicated story.
The facts on the economic side alone cannot be
described in a few words. But to summarize
briefly : recent economic progress in the West
may be said to have taken four forms — social
and industrial reform, public ownership of trans-
nortation and communications, direct taxation,
and socialized distribution. These four socionomic practices have all evolved through the

method of reform, and we should see more reforms and increasing improvements as time goes on.

I shall explain these four practices a little more in detail. The first one — socionomic reform — means the use of government power to better the workingman's education and to protect his health, to improve factories and machinery so that working conditions may be perfectly safe and comfortable. Such reforms give the worker more strength for his work and make him quite willing to work; they also greatly increase the rate of production. Germany was the first country to put these socially progressive policies into operation and she obtained the best results; in recent years Great Britain and the United States have imitated her with equally good results.

The second new practice means putting electric and steam railways, steamship lines, and all the big business of the postal and telegraph service entirely under government management. When the government's great power is employed in the direction of all these great enterprises, rapid transport and convenient communication are assured. Then materials can be moved easily from all parts of the country to the factories and manufactured articles from the factories can be easily distributed to the markets for sale, without loss of time and the stoppage in transit which causes so much damage to both raw materials and manufactured goods. If private individuals, rather than the government, are intrusted with these enterprises, they either do not have enough financial resources to carry on the enterprise or they develop, through monopoly, too much obstructive power. Transportation is then certain to slow down and communications become less effective. All economic activities throughout the country suffer intangible and serious losses. Germany was the first nation to see the advantages and the disadvantages of private business and long ago put all her means of transportation and communication under the direct management of the state. During the European War, all the private transport and communication companies in the United States were brought under government direction.

The third feature of modern economic reform, direct taxation, is also a very recent development in the socionomic method. It is applied by means of a graduated tax scale which levies a heavy income tax and inheritance tax upon capitalists and secures financial resources for the state directly from capitalists. Because of the large income of capitalists, direct taxation by the state "gets much without seeming oppressive." The old system of taxation depended entirely upon the tax on money and grain and upon the customs tariff. These methods laid the burden of national income entirely upon the poor people and let the capitalists enjoy all the privileges of the state without shouldering any financial responsibility, which was exceedingly unjust. Germany and Great Britain long ago became aware of this injustice and put into effect a plan of direct taxation. In Germany the receipts from the income and inheritance taxes amount to from sixty to eighty per cent of the annual revenue. Great Britain's receipts from the same sources were, at the beginning of the European War, fifty-eight per cent of the annual income. The United States was much later in adopting this method of taxation. The income tax law was passed only ten years ago, and since then the national income has shown a tremendous increase annually. In 1918 income tax receipts alone totaled about $4,000,000,000 gold. All the nations of the West which have recently adopted direct taxation have greatly increased their financial resources and have thus secured the financial power necessary to undertake various social reforms.

The fourth new economic activity, socialized distribution, is a most recent development in Western society. Since the invention of money and the development of the trade system all

commodities for ordinary consumption have been
bought indirectly through tradesmen or merchants.
The merchant buys the commodities at the lowest
possible price from the producer and then sells
them to the consumer; by this one transaction
he earns a large commission. Such a system of
distribution may be called the trade system or
merchant distribution. Under such a system of
distribution the consumer unconsciously suffers
heavy losses. Recent studies have shown that the
trade system can be improved upon, that goods
do not have to be distributed by merchants but
can be distributed through social organizations
or by the government. England, for example, has
introduced consumers' coöperative societies which
are social organizations for the distribution of
commodities.

The most modern municipal governments in
Europe and America themselves undertake the
distribution of water, electricity, and gas, bread,
milk, butter, and other foods for the community.
This saves the merchants' profit and reduces the
loss which the consumers suffer. The principle
in this new system is that of socialized distribution,
of socialism applied to distribution. These four
forms of social and economic development —
social and economic reform, public ownership of
transportation and communications, direct taxation and socialized distribution—are overthrowing

old systems and giving rise to new systems. It
is the constant emergence of new systems that
makes constant progress possible.

What is the cause of social evolution ?   Why does
society have to undergo these transformations ?
Judging by Marx's theory, we would have to say
that social change is caused by class struggle and
class struggle is caused by the capitalist oppression of workers.   Since the interests of capitalists
and workers inevitably conflict and cannot be
reconciled, struggle ensues and this struggle within
society is what makes for progress.   Look, however,
at the actual facts of social progress in the West
during the last few decades.   Best of all has been
the development of socialized distribution which
destroys the monopoly of the tradesman.   Heavier
taxes upon the incomes and the inheritances of the
capitalists increases the wealth of the state and
enables the state to take over means of transportation and communication, to improve the education and the health of workers and equipment within
the factories, and to increase the productiveness
of society.   When production is large and products
are rich, the capitalists naturally make fortunes
and the workers receive high wages.   From this
point of view, when the capitalists improve the
living conditions of the workers and increase their
productivity, the workers can produce more
for the capitalists.   On the capitalists' side, this

means greater production; on the workers' side,
higher wages. Here is a reconciliation of the
interests of capitalists and workers, rather than
a conflict between them. Society progresses,
then, through the adjustment of major economic
interests rather than through the clash of interests.
If most of the economic interests of society can
be harmonized, the majority of people will benefit
and society will progress. The reason why we
want to make these adjustments is simply because
of the living problem. From ancient times until
now man has exerted his energies in order to
maintain his existence. And mankind's struggle
for continuous existence has been the reason
for society's unceasing development, the law of
social progress. Class war is not the cause of
social progress, it is a disease developed in the
course of social progress. The cause of the
disease is the inability to subsist, and the result
of the disease is war. What Marx gained through
his studies of social problems was a knowledge of
diseases in the course of social progress. Therefore, Marx can only be called a social pathologist;
we cannot say that he is a social physiologist.

According to Marx's theory of class struggle,
the "surplus value" which the capitalist enjoys
is taken entirely out of the workingman's labor.
Marx gave all the credit for production to the
labor of the industrial worker and overlooked the

labor of other useful social factors. For example, China's newest industry, the spinning and textile mills in Shanghai, Nantungchow, Tientsin, Hankow, and other places, made enormous sums of money during the period of the European War; each factory created an annual surplus value of at least several hundred thousand dollars; in some cases the surplus value ran into millions. To whose labor was this immense surplus value due? Simply to the labor at the spindles and looms within the mills? When we think about the raw material of yarn and cloth, our minds turn to cotton; when we think about the source of the cotton, our minds turn to questions of agriculture. If we want to discuss in detail the cultivation of cotton, we shall have to refer to the scientific agriculturalists who study the selection of good cotton seed and the best methods of planting and raising cotton. Many implements and machines must be used to plow the soil before the planting of the seed and to weed the soil after the planting; fertilizers must be applied to nourish the plants. When we consider the machines and the fertilizers, we have to give credit to the discoverers and manufacturers of these things. After the cotton is picked, it must be transported to the mills to be spun and woven; after the yarn and piece goods are manufactured they must be transported to the markets for sale. This leads

our minds naturally to steamships and trains and
if we think why they are able to transport goods,
we shall have to give credit to the inventors of
steam and electric engines ; if we think about the
materials of which they are made, we shall have to
give credit to miners and manufacturers of metals
and to foresters and lumbermen.   If, after the
manufacture of the thread and the cloth is complete,
no classes in society except industrial workers
use the thread or wear the cloth, these things will
not have a wide market ; and then, how can the
capitalists make large profits and create a large
surplus value ?   When you put these facts before
you, to whom do you think the surplus value belongs ?   How can the workers in the factories say
that it is created entirely by their own labor ?   The
circumstances under which the surplus value is
created is the same in all industries : it is the fruit
not only of labor within the factories but of many
useful and powerful factors in society working directly or indirectly and making a large or a small
contribution towards the production or consumption of the manufactured commodities.   These
useful and powerful factors occupy a large place
in society.

As for the industrial workers, even in such an
industrially prosperous nation like the United
States, they do not number more than twenty
millions, one fifth of the total population; while

in other countries, such as China, they represent a
very small proportion of the people. If we look
at the question from this standpoint, then if there
is a lack of adjustment of economic interests in
a highly industrialized nation, leading to conflict
and war, we shall not see one working class in a
struggle against one capitalist class but most of
the useful and able factors in all society lined up
against the capitalists. And it is because these
numerous social factors want to find a living and
to eliminate economic strife that they are intro-
ducing public distribution of goods, heavy taxes
upon capitalist incomes and inheritances for the
development of national transportation and communication, reform of living conditions among
workers and of working conditions in the factories,
and all sorts of practices which will help to harmonize the larger number of economic interests
within the nation. Since these various methods
of economic adjustment have developed in the
West, society has made much progress and the
majority of the people have come to enjoy happiness. Marx, in his study of social problems, found
only one of the diseases of society ; he did not
discover the law of social progress and the central
force in history. As stated by the American
scholar, the struggle for subsistence is the law of
social progress and is the central force of history.
The struggle for existence is the same thing as the

problem of livelihood, and therefore the problem of livelihood can be said to be the driving force in social progress. When we fully understand this principle, it will be easy for us to find another solution for the social problem.

Marx's assumption that class struggle is a cause of social progress puts effect before cause. Because of this confusion in source ideas, Marx's theory has not been borne out and has sometimes been directly contradicted by subsequent facts in social history. For instance, Marx's disciples in 1848 held an international congress of communists and made various declarations. The International Communist League organized at this time was dissolved at the time of the Franco-Prussian War. Later the Second International was organized, differing from the First International in several particulars. The First International stood wholly upon the theory of class struggle, advocated revolutionary methods for the reconstruction of society and no compromise with the capitalists, absolute noncoöperation. Political activity of members in the national assemblies was forbidden by the party as an unscientific method. But later the German communists all began to agitate in the Reichstag, while in Great Britain the Labor Party has recently, under a constitutional monarchy, been able to organize a cabinet. These facts indicate that many of the political and economic changes which have occurred have not followed the procedure outlined by the First International. The wide difference in policy between the First and the Second International aggravated the strife among the disciples of Marx, a thing unlooked for by Marx in his day. Truly, as my theory states, action is easy but understanding difficult. Marx wanted to use science in the solution of the social problem. He spent his greatest energy in the period before the founding of the First International, devoting an enormous amount of time to a discriminating study of history and current events. He came, as the result of his research, to the conclusion that the capitalist system would certainly collapse in the future; as capitalism flourished, competition within the system would become severer, the larger capitalists would be sure to swallow up the smaller capitalists, and finally only two classes would be left in society — the extremely wealthy capitalists and the extremely poor workers. When capitalism had reached its peak, it would break up rapidly of its own accord and a capitalist state would follow. Then socialism in the course of nature would come into force and a free socialist state would be established. In Marx's judgment, the highly capitalistic states had already reached the period of dissolution, and so a revolution would rise immediately. But the facts of Western history, in the seventy-odd years since Marx, have directly contradicted his theory. In Marx's time, the workers in England were demanding an eight-hour day and were using the strike weapon to force capitalists to yield to them. Marx criticized the British workers, saying that their demand was an idle dream which the capitalists would certainly not grant; in order to secure the eight-hour day they would have to use revolutionary weapons. Yet, later, the eight-hour day not only became a reality where workers had demanded it, but it was enforced by state law throughout the country so that all workers in factories, banks, and railway companies needed to work only eight hours a day. Many other events which Marx did not foresee are inconsistent with his theory. Marx even had to acknowledge that some things had happened contrary to his expectations. Take the matter of capitalism: Marx held the view that as capitalism developed capitalists would tend to swallow each other up and so would hasten their own destruction, but to-day not only have capitalists everywhere not been destroyed, but they are multiplying faster than ever before without any sign of an end. This throws more light on Marx's theory.

Let us take up again the social situation in Germany. During Bismarck's régime, the power of the state was used to relieve the distress of

workers. The labor day was limited by law to
eight hours and various restrictions were put upon
the age and working time of employed boys and
girls. The state also made certain provisions
for workers' old-age pensions and insurance and
put the burden upon all the capitalists in the
country. Although many capitalists objected,
yet Bismarck was a "blood and iron" minister
and forced the execution of his plan by a mailed
fist. At the same time, many people declared
that these new national policies for the protection
of workers and the reduction of working hours
would of course benefit the workers but would
bring loss to the capitalists. Theoretically, sixteen hours of labor should mean more production
than eight hours of labor. But what was the
effect of the eight-hour day? As a matter of
fact, the eight-hour day proved to be much more
productive than a sixteen-hour day. The reason
is that in an eight-hour system the workers do
not exhaust their strength and energy but keep
in better health; consequently they are always
alert and can take better care of the machinery.
This means that machines are seldom damaged
and factories do not have to stop for repairs.
Production is uninterrupted and is greater in
quantity. When the workers work sixteen hours
a day, their strength and energy is seriously
impaired, they cannot keep their minds on all

parts of the machinery, the machinery is constantly breaking down, and the factory has to close for repairs, production is interrupted, and the productiveness of the factory is inevitably reduced. If you do not believe me, I can furnish you with a comparison that will prove my point. Let each of you try this experiment. Study fifteen or sixteen hours a day until you become fatigued in spirit, and even though you force yourself to study on, you cannot remember clearly what you study. But study only eight hours a day, rest and play the rest of the time, conserve your energy and I believe you will easily remember and easily understand the book which you study. Marx thought that the eight-hour day would diminish productiveness. But when Germany put the shorter working-day into effect, productiveness was increased and exceeded that in other countries. Great Britain and the United States were amazed. They had thought that reduction in working hours and greater expenditure for protection of workmen would decrease production; how, then, had Germany increased production by these policies ? Their amazement led them to study conditions in Germany, and later, when they understood the new economic principles, they began to imitate Germany's methods. Marx in his day did not see these principles, so he came to a false conclusion.

Again, according to Marx's researches, if the capitalists want a larger surplus value, they must fulfill three conditions — reduce wages, lengthen the working-day, and raise the price of the manufactured product. That these three conditions are illogical we can prove from the greatest money-making industry of modern times. You have all heard of the Ford factories in the United States. The factories are immense, and their enormous output of motor cars is distributed all over the world. The profits from these factories run above several score millions of dollars. What are the manufacturing and business conditions in these factories? All the machinery and all the general arrangements, whether in the factories or in the business offices, are complete and beautiful, and admirably designed to protect the health of the workers. The heaviest labor in the factories does not last over eight hours. The most ordinary laborers can earn a daily wage of five dollars gold, or ten dollars in our currency, while more important workers earn higher wages. In addition to high wages, the factories provide playgrounds for the recreation of workers, medical and health offices for the treatment of workers' diseases, and schools for the education of new workers and of workers' children. Insurance against accident and old age is also provided for the workers and after a worker's death his family can draw

insurance money and a pension. All those who
have bought motor cars know the price of the cars
manufactured in these factories. Whereas other
ordinary cars cost five thousand dollars, a Ford
car does not cost more than fifteen hundred.
Although the car is so low-priced, yet its engine
is very strong and is especially suitable for mountain roads; it can also be used a long time without
breaking down. Because the cars produced by
the Ford factories are inexpensive yet of good
quality, they have spread over the world on the
wings of the wind; and because of the wide market
the cars enjoy, the factories are making a
fortune.

Now let us compare the industrial and economic
principles which these great money-making automobile factories maintain with Marx's theory of
surplus value. Marx's three essential conditions
for increasing surplus value are flatly contradicted. Marx said that the capitalist would
have to lengthen the working-day; the Ford factories have shortened the working-day. Marx
said that the capitalist would have to reduce
wages; the Ford factories have raised wages.
Marx said that the capitalist would have to raise
the price of the manufactured product; the
Ford factories have reduced the price of their
product. Marx did not foresee these contra-
dictions, so his conclusion was seriously and

peculiarly false. All that Marx knew from his long study of social problems was facts in past history; he did not at all anticipate what would happen in the future. Consequently his disciples are wanting to make changes in his theories. The fundamental aim of Marx's social philosophy was the overthrow of capitalists. But whether capitalists ought to be overthrown or not is an important question which we must study in detail before we can answer clearly. This shows again that it is very difficult to understand but quite easy to act.

Here is the essence of Marx's theory of surplus value. The capitalists' money is stripped from the surplus value created by labor. The capitalists' production depends upon the workers, the workers' production depends upon materials, and the buying and selling of materials depends upon merchants. In all kinds of production, the capital ists and the merchant class take all the profit and rob the worker of the money he has earned by blood and sweat. Therefore, capitalists and tradesmen are harmful to the workers and to the world and should be destroyed. But Marx's conclusion was that the capitalists would be destroyed first and then the merchant class. The world now is making steady progress and initiating new reforms daily. Take, for example, the new practice of socialized distribution, also called by the name of coöperative societies. These societies

are organized by a union of many workers. If
the workers buy the clothing and food which they
need indirectly through retail merchants, the
merchants will demand a profit and make a lot
of money, while the workers will have to spend
much more upon their purchases. In order to
buy good articles at a low price the workers themselves effect an organization and open their own
store to sell them what they need. In this way
they can buy all goods which they ordinarily use
from their own store. The supplies are handy and
cheap and at the end of every year the surplus
profit which the store makes is divided among the
customers according to the proportion of their
purchases. It is on account of this division of
profits in proportion to the amount of purchase
that the stores are called consumers' coöperative
societies. A large number of banks and productive
factories in Great Britain are now managed by these
coöperative societies. The rise of these societies has
eliminated a great many commercial stores. Those
who once looked upon these stores as unimportant
commercial shops now regard them as powerful
organizations. Due to the rapid spread of such
organizations the big British merchants have now
all become producers. For example, the Standard
Oil Company, although a selling company in
China, is a productive manufacturer of oil in the
United States. Other mercantile companies in

Great Britain are tending to become producing companies. The development of these coöperative societies as a solution for the social problem is a side issue, yet it has disproved Marx's conclusion that capitalists would be destroyed before the merchant class. This inconsistency of Marx's deductions with modern facts is another evidence that my theory — knowledge is difficult, action easy — cannot be effaced.

Again, according to Marx's theory, the great industries of the world depend upon production and production depends upon capitalists, which means that with good production and large capital industry can expand and make profits. What light do industrial conditions in China throw upon this theory? The largest industrial establishment in China is the Han-yeh-ping Company (the Hanyang Iron and Steel Works), whose large factories specialize in the manufacture of steel. Sheng Hsuan-hui used to own the most capital in this company. The annual steel output is usually transported for sale to Seattle, on the American continent, or to Australia; during the European War it was sent to Japan. Yet steel has been one of China's staple imports. Why does China, when she has the Han-yeh-ping Iron Works, still buy steel from abroad? Because the steel wanted on the Chinese market is a fine quality of steel for construction purposes, for rifles, guns, and working tools. The Han-yeh-ping Company makes only steel rails and pig iron, which is not suited to the needs of the Chinese market. So our market buys foreign imported steel rather than the Han-yeh-ping steel. The United States now produces 40,000,000 tons of steel each year and between 40,000,000 and 50,000,000 tons of iron. China, with only the Han-yeh-ping Company, produces 200,000 tons of iron and something over 100,000 tons of steel each year. Why does China, with her small production of steel, still sell to the United States, and why does the United States with its large production of steel, still purchase Chinese steel? Because the Han-yeh-ping Company does not have good smelting factories, and the iron which it produces has to pass through several manufacturing processes before it can be used. It is not suited for use in China so it has to be sold to foreign countries. The United States has very many steel mills which can take cheap iron from anywhere, melt it down, and make good steel at a large profit. Although the United States itself produces much steel, it can still buy the cheap imported iron from China. Because the Han-yeh-ping Company exported its steel to other countries, it was able, during the European War, to shorten working hours, increase wages, and yet make large profits. But now the company is losing money and many workers have been dismissed. Marx would say that since the Han-yeh-ping Company produced a good article like steel and had a large capital, it should make profit and grow rapidly. Why, then, is it failing? If we study conditions in this one company (the Han-yeh-ping Company) we shall see that the heart of industry is a community of consumers. Industry does not depend solely upon capital in production. Although the Han-yeh-ping Company has a large amount of capital, yet the steel which it produces does not find a source of consumption in China and so cannot expand or make profit. Because industry centers about a spending society, all the great modern industries manufacture commodities according to the needs of the consumer. The more intelligent workers now are also coöperating with the consumers. What is consumption but a question of helping all the people to subsist, a question of livelihood? So industry has to rest upon the livelihood of the people.

Livelihood is the center of government, the center of economics, the center of all historical movements. Just as men once misjudged the center of the solar system, so the old socialists mistook material forces for the center of history. The confusions which have resulted may be compared to those which followed the conclusions of the old astronomers that the earth was the center of our solar system. In chronological calculations there was always an error of one month in every three years. Later, when the mistake was corrected and the sun was considered the center of the solar system, there was an error of only one day in every three years. If we want to clear away the confusions from within the social problem, we must correct this mistake in social science. We can no longer say that material issues are the central force in history. We must let the political, social, and economic movements of history gravitate about the problem of livelihood. We must recognize livelihood as the center of social history. When we have made a thorough investigation of this central problem, then we can find a way to a solution of the social problem.

August 3, 1924.

LECTURE 2

Methods of applying the *Min-sheng* Principle in China —
Equalization of landownership and regulation of capital —
Revolutionary versus evolutionary methods of social and economic reform — Class struggle possible only in highly industrialized states — Difference between *Min-sheng* Principle
and Communism in methods rather than in principle —
Absence of extremely wealthy class in China; degrees of
poverty — Effects of Western impact upon land values in
China : Shanghai, Canton — The problem of "unearned
increment" in the West, in China — Present opposition to
communism within the Kuomintang compared with former
opposition to democracy — *Min-sheng* Principle and its
relation to communism not yet understood in the party —
Equalization of landownership — Land values to be declared
by owners and taxed accordingly; if assessed too low, to be
bought back by the government — Future increments to
revert to the community — *Min-sheng* Principle a communism
not of the present, but of the future — Land tax as a source
of government revenue — Marx's methods not applicable to
present situation in China — State capital, state industries
must be developed — Foreign capital necessary at the
beginning.

If we should start upon a detailed discussion
of the livelihood problem from the standpoint of
doctrines, we would not finish in ten or twenty
days; moreover, as there are as yet no settled doctrines in this field, we would only waste much

time, and the more we theorized, the less probably would we understand. So I shall put doctrines
aside for a while and to-day speak only of methods
of procedure.

The Kuomintang some time ago in its party
platform settled upon two methods by which the
Principle of Livelihood is to be carried out.
The first method is equalization of landownership
and the second is regulation of capital. If we
follow these two methods we can solve the livelihood problem in China. The different countries
of the world, because of varying conditions and
varying degrees of capitalistic development, must
necessarily follow different methods in dealing
with the livelihood problem. Many Chinese
scholars who have been absorbing all forms of
Western knowledge have thought that we could
solve our problem by imitating the West, without
realizing how divided are the socialist parties of
the West upon social questions and how far away
they still are from a single course of action. The
Marxians would solve all social questions by a
dictatorship of the proletariat and all political
and economic problems by revolution; they are
the radical group. Another group of socialists
advocates peaceful methods and the use of political action and negotiation. These two factions
are in constant and severe conflict in Europe and
America and each has its own line of action.

Russia in her Revolution employed the revolutionary method for dealing with her political and economic problems. But what we have seen in the six years following the Revolution shows that the revolutionary method was completely successful only so far as the political problem went; it cannot be said to have wholly solved the economic problem. Soviet Russia's new economic policy is still in an experimental stage, and it makes us realize that revolutionary schemes cannot entirely clear up economic difficulties. For this reason many Western scholars are opposing Russia's revolutionary plan and are advocating political action instead. As political action does not accomplish political and social reform in a day, this group is made up of the believers in slow progress, negotiation, and peaceable means. They do not think that the highly capitalistic states of the West should utilize Marx's method and attempt a precipitate solution of the social problem; they think that only peaceful methods will fully settle the problem.

These peaceful methods are the four which I described in my last lecture — social and economic reform, nationalization of transportation and communications, direct taxation or the income tax, and socialized distribution or coöperative societies. They are quite different from the methods which Marx proposed, and if we follow

them as the way to economic reconstruction we
will be in opposition to Marx's revolutionary
schemes.   Various Western nations are putting
one after another of these four plans into operation, and although the results so far are not all
that they hope for, yet they feel that the ultimate
solution of the social problem does lie in these four
plans, and many socialists are supporting them.
At the same time that they indorse these peaceful
methods, they resist Marx's revolutionary methods.

When Russia first started the Revolution, she
was hoping to settle the social question ; the
political question was secondary.   The Revolution resulted, however, in a solution of the political
question but no solution of the social question,
exactly opposite to that which was anticipated.
Such facts have led the anti-Marx faction to say
that Russia's experiment with Marx's methods has
been unsuccessful, a failure.   The members of
the Marxian Party, however, make the answer
that Russia has not been defeated in her use of
revolutionary methods for social reform, but that
Russia's industry and commerce are not so highly
developed as those in other European nations and
that Russia's economic organization is immature;
consequently she cannot successfully apply Marx's
methods.   But they certainly could be applied,
they say, in a highly industrialized and commercialized nation, where economic organization has

reached a mature stage. They would meet with sure success in other Western nations, and bring about fundamental social reconstruction. When we compare the two methods advocated, we find that Marx would " cut the tangled hemp with a sharp knife," while the opposite group would use gentle means.

In dealing with our social problems, shall we " cut the tangled hemp with a sharp knife " or shall we employ peaceful methods, such as the four policies we have already described ? Both the revolutionary method and the peaceful method are advocated within the Socialist Party and both are opposed by the capitalists. Western industry and commerce are now progressing very rapidly, capitalism is mounting to dizzy heights, the tyranny of capitalists has reached the limit, and people are finding conditions unbearable. The socialists, in their efforts to relieve the distress of the people under capitalistic domination and to reconstruct society, have, no matter whether they have chosen to use peaceful or radical methods, incurred the opposition of the capitalists. Which method the Western nations will finally employ in solving their social problems cannot now be foreseen or anticipated. But the champions of peaceful methods are meeting with all kinds of opposition and with fierce criticism from the capitalists; and they feel that while the pacific measures are very

advantageous to the people, yet they are working
no injury upon the capitalists and are not really
practicable. Consequently, many socialists are
gradually moving from their former position towards the advocacy of radical methods and the
use of revolutionary plans for social reconstruction. Marx's disciples say that if British workers
would really awaken, unite, and advance together
along the course proposed by Marx, they would
certainly attain success. Since American capitalism is as highly developed as in Great Britain, if
American workers would adopt Marxism they
would also reach their objectives. But now the
capitalists of Great Britain, the United States,
and other countries are absolute despots ; they are
forever thinking of ways to obstruct social progress
and to protect their own interests, as the old despotic kings tried to protect their thrones. The
old despots who feared the activity of an opposition party would use the terrible power of tyranny
and the cruelest measures to destroy it. Modern capitalists who want to protect their own
private gains also use all sorts of tyrannical
methods and subvert all principles of right in their
opposition to the socialist parties. The socialist
parties in the West may in the future be forced
by circumstances to adopt Marxian methods for
the solution of economic problems — who can
tell ?

The communistic system has already been
practiced in primitive times. When did it break
down ? From my own study of history, I think
it began to break down with the introduction of
money. When all the people acquired money
they could buy and sell at will ; they did not need
to exchange goods for goods, and buying and
selling took the place of bartering. Then it was
that the old communism was gradually wiped
out. The use of money made trade free and
easy, and then arose the great merchants who
were the capitalists before the day of industrialism.
When industry developed and production came
to depend upon machinery, then the owners of
machinery became the capitalists. The former
capitalists were those who possessed money; the
present capitalists are those who possess machinery. The ancient period of simple exchange,
when "in the noonday market they bartered
their goods, then went away each to his own
home," when there was no money or commercial
system but each supplied the wants of the other,
was a period of communism. Later when money
was introduced and was used as a medium of
exchange, it gave rise to the commercial system.
The moneyed merchants became the capitalists.
But since the invention of machinery in recent
times and the dependence of all production upon
machinery, the men who own machinery have

outstripped the men who own money. So the
coming of money broke down communism and
the coming of machinery broke down the merchant class. The capitalists now have their
machinery ; they depend upon the workers to
produce for them, but they deprive the workers of
their very sweat and blood. Thus they create
two radically different classes of society which
are in constant conflict, conflict that leads to
class war. A certain class of compassionate
moralists, who cannot beat to see the miseries of
the workers and who want to find some way to
avert class war as well as to reduce the sufferings
of the working class, propose that we revive the
ancient system of communism. For the happiest
period in human history was the period of communistic society which followed upon the age of
warfare with beasts. At that time man was
fighting only against nature or a few beasts ;
later, as industry developed and machinery was
invented, man began to fight against man. Soon
after man's conquest over nature and the wild
beasts came the introduction of money.

Now in modern times has come the invention
of machinery and the men with the keenest minds
have taken the world's most valuable materials
and have monopolized them for their own profit,
making other classes of men their slaves. This
has made our age one of fierce human struggle.

When can this struggle be settled? Only when
we initiate a new period of communism. What
is man struggling for, anyway? He is struggling
for bread, he is struggling for the rice bowl. In
the communistic age, when all have bread and rice
enough to eat, there will be no fighting between
men and the human struggle will be eliminated.
So communism is a very high ideal of social reconstruction. The Principle of Livelihood which
the Kuomintang advocates is not merely a high
ideal; it is also a driving force in society, it is
the center of all historical movements. Only
as this principle is applied can our social problems
be solved, and only as our social problems are
solved can mankind enjoy the greatest blessings.
I can put my distinction to-day between communism and the *Min-sheng* Principle in this
way; communism is an ideal of livelihood, while
the *Min-sheng* Principle is practical communism.
There is no real difference between the two principles — Communism and *Min-sheng* — the difference lies in the methods by which they are
applied.

What methods should our Kuomintang employ
for the solution of the livelihood problem, in
view of the position China occupies and the times
in which we are living? We must base our
methods not upon abstruse theories or upon
empty learning, but upon facts, and not facts

peculiar to foreign countries but facts observable in China. Only when we have facts as data can we settle upon methods of procedure. Method based simply upon theory will not be trustworthy, because theories may be true or false, and they must be verified by experiment. A newly proposed scientific theory must produce facts; it must work out in practice, before we can say it is true. Ninety-nine out of a hundred of the early scientific theories did not work; only about one per cent did work. If we mark out our course of action simply upon theory, we shall certainly fail. In working for a solution of our social problems, we must, therefore, ground ourselves upon facts and not trust to mere theories. What are these basic facts in China? All of us have a share in the distressing poverty of the Chinese people. There is no especially rich class, there is only a general poverty. The " inequalities between rich and poor " which the Chinese speak of are only differences within the poor class, differences in degree of poverty. As a matter of fact, the great capitalists of China, in comparison with the great foreign capitalists, are really poor; the rest of the poor people are extremely poor. Since China's largest capitalists are poor men out in the world, then all the Chinese people must be counted as poor. There are no great rich among us, only differences between the fairly poor and the extremely poor. How can we equalize this condition so that there will be no more extreme poverty ?

The process of social change and capitalistic development usually begins with the landowners, and from the landowners goes on to the merchant, and finally to the capitalist. Landowners arose out of the feudal system. Europe is not yet completely free from the feudal system, but China destroyed her feudal system as long ago as the Ch'in dynasty. When the feudal system was in existence, the nobles who owned land were the rich, and the people without land were the poor. Although China broke away from the feudal system two thousand years ago, yet because of the lack of industrial and commercial progress, social conditions now are just about what they were at that time. Although China has not had large landowners up to the present, yet she has had many small landowners. Most places in China have been quiet and content under this system and no trouble has arisen between the people and the landowners. In recent years, however, since the currents of Western economic life have begun to rush into China, all of our old systems have undergone a process of change. The land question has felt the first and most serious effects of the modern Western impact. Take, for example, land in Canton since the building of wide streets:

what a difference there is between land values on
the Bund now and twenty years ago ! Land on
the Shanghai Bund is about ten thousand times
as valuable now as it was eighty years ago.
Formerly, land ten feet square cost about a
dollar; now the same amount costs ten thousand
dollars. Land on the Shanghai Bund is now
worth hundreds of thousands of dollars a *mow;*
land on the Canton Bund is worth over a hundred thousand a *mow.* Chinese land has only to
come under Western economic influence to transform its owners into millionaires like the capitalists of the West. But this marked effect of
economic development upon land values is not
true only in China ; all other countries have
experienced the same thing. At first they did
not notice the fact or pay much attention to it.
Not until the disturbances in the economic order
became acute did they give their attention, and
then it was not easy to remedy the situation,
"to turn back with the accumulated burden."
The Kuomintang must, as a matter of foresight
and of precaution against future difficulties, find
a solution of this problem of fluctuation in land
values.

Western books on socialism are full of interesting stories about rise in land values. There was a
place in Australia, for instance, where land was
very cheap before the building up of a trade

center. The government once wanted to sell at auction a piece of land which at the time was simply waste ground, covered with trash piles and of no other use. Nobody was willing to pay a high price for the land. Suddenly a drunken fellow broke into the place where the auctioning was going on. The auctioneer was just then calling for bids on the land; there had been bids of one hundred, two hundred, two hundred and fifty dollars. As no one would bid higher, the auctioneer then called, " Who will bid three hundred ? " At that moment the drunken fellow, now completely befuddled, yelled out, "I will give three hundred ! " The auctioneer then took down his name and assigned him the land. Since the land was sold, the crowd left and the drunken man also walked away. The next day, the auctioneer sent the man a bill for the price of the land, but the man did not remember what he had done in his drunken condition the day before and would not acknowledge the bill against him. When he finally did call to mind what he had done, he was bitterly regretful; but since it was impossible to default to the government, he had to try all sorts of plans and exhaust all his resources in order to pay over the three hundred dollars to the auctioneer. For a long time after he acquired the land, he was not able to give it any attention. Over a decade passed; tall buildings and great

mansions had been erected all around that piece
of land, and the price of land had soared.   Some
people offered the owner of the empty tract
millions of dollars, but he refused to let it go.
He simply rented out his land and took the rent
money.   Finally, when the land was worth tens
of millions, the old drunkard became the wealthiest man in Australia. All this wealth came
from that first investment in a three-hundred-
dollar lot.   The owner of the land was of course
delighted when he became a millionaire, but
what about other people ?   After paying three
hundred dollars for the land, the man did not do
a bit of work to improve it; in fact he let it alone.
While he slept or sat with folded hands enjoying
his success, the millions poured into his lap.

   To whom did these millions really belong ?
In my opinion, they belonged to everybody.
For it was because the people in the community
chose this section as an industrial and commercial
center and made improvements upon it, that this
tract of land increased in value and gradually
reached such a high price.   In the same way it
is because we made Shanghai an industrial and
commercial center of central China that the land
values in this city have increased by the thousandfold ; and it is because we made Canton an
industrial and commercial center of southern
China that the land values in this city have also

increased by the thousandfold. Both Shanghai and Canton have only a little over a million people each; if the population of either city should suddenly move out of the city limits or some natural or artificial calamity should wipe out the population, do you think that land would still bring the same high price ? This proves that rise in land values should be credited to all the people and to their efforts; the landowner himself has nothing to do with the rise and the fall. So foreign scholars speak of the profits which the landowner gets out of the increased price of land as " unearned increment," a very different thing from the profits which industrial and commercial manufacturers get by dint of hard mental and physical labor, by buying cheap and selling dear, by all sorts of business schemes and methods. We have already felt that the profits which the industrial and commercial leaders make by monopolies over materials are not just profits. But these men at least work hard ; the landowner, however, simply holds what he has, does not use a bit of mental effort, and reaps huge profits. Yet, what is it that makes the value of his land rise ? The improvements which people make around his land and the competition which they carry on for possession of his land. When the price of land rises, every single commodity in the community also rises in price. So we may

truly say that the money which the people in
the community earn through their business is indirectly and imperceptibly robbed from them by
the landowner.

What is the present status of the social question
in China? Those who are studying social problems and advocating social reconstruction are
getting their ideas and theories entirely from
Europe and America. So when they talk about
methods of social reconstruction, they have no
new methods to propose beyond the pacific
methods or Marx's radical methods which are
advocated in various Western countries. At the
present time, the most fashionable speakers upon
socialism are the ones who indorse Marx's methods.
So as soon as social problems are mentioned, most
young men rise to champion communism and
want to apply Marx's theories in China. How
much careful thinking have these youthful zealots
done who are thus espousing Marxism? They
are a very thoughtful group; they are proposing
a radical solution; they feel that political and
social problems must be righted at the foundation and cleared at the source, and so radical
measures are necessary. Therefore they are
actively organizing a communist party and are
beginning to agitate in China.

This has given rise to many misgivings among
the older comrades in the Kuomintang, who

feel that communism is incompatible with the
San Min Principles of our party. They do not
realize that twenty years ago our comrades were
all favoring the merging of the Three Principles
into one. In the minds of most people before
the Revolution of 1911 there was only the idea
of nationalism. Every comrade who joined the
T'ung-meng Hui had as his sole aim the expulsion
of the Manchus. When they joined the society,
I wanted them to proclaim their adherence to
the Three Principles of the People, but most of
them were thinking only of nationalism and of
the overthrowing of the Manchus. If only the
Manchus were overthrown, they would still welcome a Chinese as emperor! When in their
manifesto they indorsed the application of the
Three Principles and at the same time approved
of a Chinese becoming emperor, were they not
contradicting the Principle of Democracy ? Even
the most thoughtful of our comrades, who supported the *San Min* Principles and understood
that they were three different things, and who
wanted to put them into force by revolution,
still thought that if the Manchus were only driven
out and the principle of Nationalism fully realized,
the principles of Democracy and Livelihood
would naturally follow, and no other contingencies
would arise. They did not make a thorough study
of the principles of Democracy and Livelihood

and so they naturally did not understand what
the People's Sovereignty meant, and they had no
conception at all of what the People's Livelihood
signified. When the 1911 Revolution had succeeded and the Republic was established and a
democratic system of government was selectéd,
no one thought of asking for an explanation.
Even now the comrades who willingly and sin-
cerely work for democracy and support the
Republic are few in number.

Why did everybody at the beginning support
a democratic form of government and not oppose
the Republic ? This is the main reason : after
the successful expulsion of the Manchus, the
revolutionary comrades in the various provinces,
the new military caste which developed out of
the Revolution, and the old Manchu militarists
who joined the Revolutionary Party, all moved
in a like direction — towards the formation of a
military system.   Each one wanted to be a small
king in his own place, and from his own little
domain as a base to expand his power.   The
militarists who seized Kwangtung wanted to
extend their domain.   The militarists who seized
Yünnan and Hunan wanted to widen their territory.   The militarists in Shantung and Chihli
wanted to enlarge their areas.   When they had
extended their domains far and wide, when they
were richly plumed and feathered, then they

would use their own power to unify China and would openly and boldly overthrow the Republic. The military caste who were created by the Revolution or who came over into the Republic from the Manchu régime all harbored such designs; they knew that their brief power could not unify China and yet they were unwilling for others to attempt unification. Each one resolved to be an opportunist, to keep an eye upon changes, to watch and to wait. This military caste, not understanding democracy and yet proclaiming adherence to democratic government, really thought only of imperial power. But they would make their pro-republican talk a door front until they could enlarge their domains sufficiently; then, when the proper moment arrived, they would oppose democratic government and solve all the national problems. This explains why a democracy was established in the beginning and yet why so many have tried to overthrow it these thirteen years. But the strength of these men has not been very great, so the name of the republic has been kept alive feebly until this day. This shows clearly the attitude which the members of the *T'ung-meng Hui* had toward democracy; many of them were ready to take either side of the issue, and none of them had any conception of what the Principle of Livelihood meant.

Let us analyze the situation more closely.
Since the Revolution of 1911 was accomplished
and the Republic of China took the place of the
old Chinese Empire, our Kuomintang has kept
alive its respect for democracy. But what has
been the attitude of our Revolutionary comrades
towards the *San Min* Principles? After thirteen
years of changes in our democratic government
and after thirteen years of experience, our comrades have all come to understand clearly the
principles of Nationalism and Democracy. But
their psychological reaction towards the Principle
of Livelihood is like that of the post-Revolution
militarists towards Democracy — it is not a live
issue and they don't comprehend it. Why do
I dare to say that our revolutionary comrades
have no clear idea of the *Min-sheng* Principle?
Because many of them, since our recent reorganization of the Kuomintang, have in their opposition
to the Communist Party declared offhand that
communism is different from the Three Principles;
the Three Principles are all that is necessary in
China and communism should under no conditions
be admitted. But what really is the Principle of
Livelihood? In my last lecture I revealed a little
of what it means; I said that *Min-sheng*, or Livelihood, has been the central force in the cultural
progress of society, in the improvement of economic
organization, and in moral evolution. Livelihood

is the driving power in all social movements; and if livelihood does not go right, social culture cannot advance, economic organization cannot improve, morals will decline, and many injustices such as class war, cruelty to workers, and other forms of oppression will spring up — all because of the failure to remedy the unfortunate conditions of livelihood. All social changes are effects ; the search for livelihood is the cause.

In view of this conclusion, what is the Principle of Livelihood ? It is communism and it is socialism. So not only should we not say that communism conflicts with the *Min-sheng* Principle, but we should even claim communism as a good friend. The supporters of the *Min-sheng* Principle should study communism thoughtfully. If communism is a good ally of the *Min-sheng* Principle, why do members of the Kuomintang oppose the Communist Party ? The reason may be that the members of the Communist Party themselves do not understand what communism is and have discoursed against the *San Min* Principles, thus arousing a reaction within the Kuomintang. But the blame for these ignorant and reckless communists should not be charged to the whole Communist Party or to the principles of the party. We can only say that they are acting as individuals; we cannot take the bad behavior of some individuals as representative and oppose the whole

Communist Party. Since we cannot use the actions of a few persons as an excuse for opposing the principles of a whole group, why has the question arisen among our Kuomintang comrades ? Because they have not understood what the *Min-sheng* Principle really is. They do not realize that our Principle of Livelihood is a form of communism. It is not a form that originated with Marx but a form that was practiced when primitive man appeared upon the earth. According to the biological evolutionists, man evolved from the animals. Gradually there developed the tribal system and living conditions of man were then very different from the living conditions of animals. The first society formed by man was a communistic society and the primitive age was a communistic age. What sort of life did these primitive men lead ? We can get some idea by studying the life of wild savages to-day in Africa or Malaysia, who have not been touched by civilized society. Their system of living is entirely communistic, which proves that the society of our primitive ancestors must have been communistic.

The first effect of the recent Western economic invasion of China has been upon land. Many people have taken land as something to gamble with and have gone into land speculation or "land squabbling," as the common saying puts it.

Much land which would not be worth a great deal until ten or twenty years later, and which would not naturally have been highly valued, has been raised in price ahead of time through the wire pulling of speculators. This makes the rise in land values all the more uneven.

Western nations have not yet found any satisfactory methods to deal with these evil practices arising out of the land question. If we want to solve the land question we must do it now; if we wait until industry and commerce are fully developed, we will have no way to solve it. Now that Western influences are coming in and our industry and commerce are undergoing such marked transformations, inequalities are arising not only between the rich and the poor, but also between common owners of land. For instance, A has a *mow* of land on the Shanghai Bund, while B has a *mow* of land in the country near Shanghai. If B cultivates his own piece of land, he may make a profit of ten or twenty dollars a year; if he rents it to some one else, he can get but from five to ten dollars at the most. But A can rent his *mow* of land in the city for ten thousand or more dollars. Land in Shanghai brings several thousandfold in return; land in the country but twofold. One *mow* of land in two different places produces such unequal results. The aim of our party's *Min-sheng* Principle is to equalize the financial resources in society. So we consider the Principle of Livelihood the same thing as socialism or communism. But each has its own methods of procedure. Our first step is to be the solution of the land problem.

The methods for the solution of the land problem are different in various countries, and each country has its own peculiar difficulties. The plan which we are following is simple and easy — the equalization of landownership. As soon as the landowners hear us talking about the land question and equalization of landownership, they are naturally alarmed, just as capitalists are alarmed when they hear people talking about socialism and want to rise up and fight it. If our landowners were like the great landowners of Europe and had developed tremendous power, it would be exceedingly difficult for us to solve the land question. But China does not have such big landowners, and the power of the small landowners is still rather weak. If we attack the problem now, we can solve it; but if we lose the present opportunity, we can never find a way out. The discussion of the land problem naturally causes a feeling of fear among the landowners, but if the Kuomintang policy is followed, present landowners can set their hearts at rest.

What is our policy ? We propose that the government shall buy back the land, if necessary, according to the amount of land tax and the price of the land. How, indeed, can the price of the land be determined ? I would advocate the landowner himself fixing the price. For instance, land on the Canton Bund would be reported at a hundred thousand dollars a *mow* or ten thousand dollars a *mow* by the owner himself. In almost every country the land tax is about one per cent of the land value : one dollar upon land worth a hundred dollars, a thousand dollars upon land worth one hundred thousand dollars. This is the usual tax rate. Our present plan is also based upon this tax rate. The landowner reports the value of his land to the government and the government levies a land tax accordingly. Many people think that if the landowners make their own assessment, they will undervalue the land and the government will lose out. For instance, the landowner might report a piece of land worth a hundred thousand dollars as worth only ten thousand. According to an assessment of a hundred thousand dollars the government would receive a thousand dollars in taxes, but according to an assessment of ten thousand, the government would get only one hundred dollars. The tax office would of course lose nine hundred dollars. But suppose the government makes two regulations: first, that it will collect taxes according to the declared value of the land; second, that it can also buy back the land at the same price. The land-owner who assesses his hundred-thousand-dollar land at ten thousand dollars fools the government out of nine hundred dollars and naturally gets the best of the bargain; but if the government buys back his land at the price of ten thousand dollars, he loses nine thousand dollars, a tremendous loss. According to my plan, if the land-owner makes a low assessment he will be afraid lest the government buy back his land at that value and make him lose his property; if he makes too high an assessment, he will be afraid of the government taxes according to this value and his loss through heavy taxes. Comparing these two serious possibilities, he will certainly not want to report the value of his land too high or too low; he will strike a mean and report the true market price to the government. As a result, neither landowner nor government will suffer.

After the land values have been fixed, we should have a regulation by law that from that year on, all increase in land values, which in other countries means heavier taxation, shall revert to the community. This is because the increase in land values is due to improvements made by society and to the progress of industry and commerce. China's industry and commerce have made little progress for thousands of years, so land values have scarcely changed through all these generations. But as soon as there is progress and improvement, as in the modern cities of China, land prices change every day, sometimes increasing a thousandfold or ten thousandfold. The credit for the improvement and progress belongs to the energy and business activity of all the people and not merely to a few private individuals. For example : if a landowner now assesses his land at ten thousand dollars and several decades later that land rises in value to a million dollars, this increase of nine hundred and ninety-nine thousand dollars would, in our plan, become a public fund as a reward to all those who had improved the community and who had advanced industry and commerce around the land. This proposal that all future increment shall be given to the community is the " equalization of land ownership " advocated by the Kuomintang; it is the *Min-sheng* Principle. This form of the *Min-sheng* Principle is communism, and since the members of the Kuomintang support the *San Min* Principles they should not oppose communism. The great aim of the Principle of Livelihood in our Three Principles is communism — a share in property by all. But the communism which we propose is a communism of the future, not of the present. This communism of the future is a very just proposal, and those

who have had property in the past will not suffer
at all by it. It is a very different thing from
what is called in the West "nationalization of
property," confiscation for the government's use
of private property which the people already
possess. When the landowners clearly understand
the principle involved in our plan for equalization
of landownership, they will not be apprehensive.
Our plan provides that land now fixed in value
shall still be privately owned. If the land problem can be solved, one half of the problem of
livelihood will be solved.

When modern, enlightened cities levy land
taxes, the burdens upon the common people are
lightened and many other advantages follow.
If Canton city should now collect land taxes
according to land values, the government would
have a large and steady income, and there would
be a definite source of funds for administration.
The whole place could be put in good order. All
miscellaneous taxes could be remitted. The
water and electric light systems used by the people
could be provided without charge by the government and would not have to be a burden upon
individuals. Funds for road repair and for upkeep
of the police system could also be appropriated
out of the land-tax receipts; extra road and police
taxes would not have to be levied upon the people.
But at present the rising land values in Canton

all go to the landowners themselves, — they do not belong to the community. The government has no regular income, and so to meet expenses it has to levy all sorts of miscellaneous taxes upon the common people. The burden of miscellaneous levies upon the common people is too heavy; they are always having to pay out taxes and so are terribly poor. And the number of poor people in China is enormous. The reasons for the heavy burdens upon the poor are the unjust system of taxation practiced by the government, the unequal distribution of land power, and the failure to solve the land problem. If we can put the land tax completely into effect, the land problem will be solved and the common people will not have to endure so much suffering. Although land values in foreign countries have risen very high and the landowners are consequently enjoying large incomes, yet the advance of science and the development of machinery, together with the heavy production on the part of machine-owning capitalists, have made the immense incomes which capitalists enjoy a far more serious matter than landowners' incomes. The capitalists in China with the largest incomes are still landowners, not machine owners. So it should be very easy for us now to equalize land-ownership, to regulate capital, and to find a way out of the land problem.

Speaking of taxing or buying back land acccrd-
ing to its value, we must make clear one important point.   Land value refers only to the value
of the bare land ; it does not include improvements
made by human labor or construction work upon
the surface.   For instance, if land valued at ten
thousand dollars has upon it buildings valued at
a million dollars, the land tax at the rate of one
per cent would be only one hundred dollars.   But
if the land were bought back by the government,
compensation would have to be made for the million dollars' worth of buildings upon the land.
Other land with artificial improvements such as
trees, embankments, drains, and such would have
to be paid for in the same way.

If we want to solve the livelihood problem in
China and " by one supreme effort win eternal
ease," it will not be enough to depend upon the
regulation of capital.   The income tax levied
in foreign countries is one method of regulating
capital.   But have these other countries solved
the livelihood problem ?   China cannot be compared to foreign countries ; it is not sufficient for
us to regulate capital.   Other countries are rich
while China is poor ; other countries have a surplus
of production while China is not producing enough.
So China must not only regulate private capital,
but she must also develop state capital.   But
our state now is split into pieces ; how are we ever

going to accumulate any capital for the state? It seems as if we could not find or even anticipate a way. But our present disunion is only a temporary state of affairs; in the future we shall certainly become united, and then to solve the livelihood problem we shall have to develop capital and promote industry. First, we must begin to build means of communication, railroads and waterways, on a large scale. Second, we must open up mines. China is rich in minerals, but alas, they are buried in the earth! Third, we must hasten to foster manufacturing. Although China has a multitude of workers, yet she has no machinery and so cannot compete with other nations. Goods used throughout China depend upon other countries for manufacture and transportation hither, and consequently our economic rights and interests are simply leaking away. If we want to recover these rights and interests, we must quickly employ state power to promote industry, use machinery in production, and give employment to the workers of the whole nation. When all the workers have employment and can use machinery in production, then China will have a great, new source of wealth. If we do not use state power to build up these enterprises but leave them in the hands of private Chinese or of foreign business men, the result will be simply the expansion of private capital and the emergence

of a great wealthy class with the consequent
inequalities in society. So in working out our
Principle of Livelihood, we cannot use or apply in
China the methods of Marx, although we have the
deepest respect for his teaching. The reason for
this is obvious. Russia has been trying to apply
Marx's methods since the Revolution until now,
yet she wants to change to a new economic
policy, because the economic life of her society
has not reached the standard of economic life in
Great Britain or the United States, and is not
ripe for the application of Marx's methods. If
Russia's economic standards are below those of
Great Britain or the United States, how could
China's economic standards possibly be high
enough for the application of Marx's methods ?
Even Marx's disciples say that we cannot use his
methods for the solution of all social problems in
China.

I remember, when I was a student in Canton
thirty years ago, how the sons of wealthy families
in Saikwan (West District) would put on their
fur-lined garments as soon as winter came.
The winters in Canton are not very cold and furs
are not really necessary. But these wealthy
young men had to wear their fur-lined garments
every winter to exhibit their wealth ; when the
first cold came, they wore the light furs, when
it became a little colder, their heavy furs.   In

the middle of the winter, no matter what the weather was, they always dressed in heavy furs. One day, when they went to a meeting with their heavy furs, and the weather suddenly turned warm, they complained, " Unless the wind changes to the north, the people's health will be impaired ! " They seemed to think that everybody in society wore furs, and so, unless the wind changed, everybody would get overheated and everybody's health would suffer. As a matter of fact, where do you ever see all the people wearing furs ? The Canton people in winter wear cotton-wadded garments or double-lined garments; many people wear only single garments. When do you ever find them afraid that the north winds will not blow ? The youthful scholars to-day who are pinning their faith on Marxism, and who, as soon as socialism is mentioned, advocate Marx's way for the solution of China's social and economic problems are no different from young Cantonese in furs who cried, "Unless the wind shifts to the north, the people's health will be impaired ! " They do not take it in that China now is suffering from poverty, not from unequal distribution of wealth. Where there are inequalities of wealth, Marx's methods can of course be applied; a class war can be started to destroy the inequalities. But in China, where industry is not yet developed, class war and the dictatorship of the proletariat

are unnecessary. So to-day we can take Marx's
ideas as a guide, but we cannot make use of his
methods. In seeking a solution for our livelihood
problem, we are not going to propose some
impracticable and radical method and then wait
until industry is developed. We want a plan
which will anticipate dangers and forearm us
against emergencies, which will check the growth
of large private capital and prevent the social
disease of extreme inequality between the rich
and the poor. Such a plan will rightly solve our
immediate social problems and will not be like
first wearing furs and then hoping for the north
winds.

As I said a little while ago, the regulations of
capital to-day in China will not be enough to
solve our livelihood problem. It will also be
necessary to build up state capital. What does
this mean ? Simply the development of state
industries. The details of this scheme can be
found in the second volume of my "Plans for
National Reconstruction," [1] under the heading
"Material Reconstruction or Industrial Measures "
In this volume I have given the outline of the plan
for building up state capital. As I said before,
money was capital in the commercial age, but
machinery is capital in the industrial age. The

[1] Written in 1918. In three parts: *Psychological Reconstruction,
Material Reconstruction, Social Reconstruction.*

state should lead in business enterprises and set up all kinds of productive machinery which will be the property of the state. During the European War, it was the policy of each country to nationalize its great industries and its factories. But this policy was abandoned soon afterwards. China has never had any great capitalists; if the state can control and develop capital and give the benefits to all the people, it will be easy to avoid the conflicts with capitalists. The United States has developed capital in three ways : through railroads, through manufacturing, and through mining. We shall not be able to promote one of these three great industries by our own knowledge and experience with our own capital; we cannot but depend upon the already created capital of other countries. If we use existing foreign capital to build up a future communist society in China, "half the work will bring double the results." If we wait until we ourselves have enough capital before we start to promote industry, the process of development will be exceedingly slow. China now has no machinery to speak of. We have only six or seven thousand miles of railroad. To meet our needs, we should have a mileage ten times as great. At least sixty or seventy thousand miles are necessary. So we shall certainly have to borrow foreign capital to develop our communication and transportation facilities, and foreign brains and experience to manage them.

As for our mines, we have not even begun to
open them. China exceeds the United States
in population and in size of territory, yet the
United States produces 600,000,000 tons of coal
and 90,000,000 tons of steel every year, while
China does not produce a thousandth of that
amount. If we want to open up our mines quickly,
again we must borrow foreign capital. To construct steamships, to develop a merchant marine,
and to build up all kinds of manufacturing
industries on a large scale, it will be absolutely
necessary for us to borrow foreign capital. If
these three great industries — communications,
mining, and manufacturing—should all begin to
thrive in China, our annual income from them
would be very great. If the industries are carried
on by the state, the rights and privileges which they
bring will be enjoyed by all the people. The
people of the whole nation will then have a share
in the profits of capital and will not be injured by
capital, as in foreign countries, where large capital
is in private hands. This concentration of capital
among a few private individuals means that a
large number of people suffer; class war then
breaks out as an attempt to eliminate the suffering.
In the solution of the social problem, we have the
same object in view as that in foreign countries:
to make everybody contented and happy, free

from the suffering caused by the unequal distribution of wealth and property. When we try to get away from such suffering, we have communism.

We cannot say, then, that the theory of communism is different from our *Min-sheng* Principle. Our Three Principles of the People mean government "of the people, by the people, and for the people" — that is, a state belonging to all the people, a government controlled by all the people, and rights and benefits for the enjoyment of all the people. If this is true, the people will not only have a communistic share in state production, but they will have a share in everything. When the people share everything in the state, then will we truly reach the goal of the *Min-sheng* Principle, which is Confucius' hope of a "great commonwealth."

August 10, 1924.

LECTURE 3

The food problem in China — Vital importance of adequate
food supply, as during the European War — Food supply of
various nations : the United States, Germany, France — Food
shortage in China — China's loss of necessary food through
exports — Necessary elements of food : air, water, meat,
vegetables — Abundance of the first two elements — China
an agricultural nation, yet her peasants suffer — Liberation
of the peasants — Methods of increasing agricultural production — Use of machinery — Use of fertilizers — Native and
imported fertilizers — How China could manufacture fertilizers inexpensively through water power in her rivers — Crop
rotation — Eradication of pests — Food manufacture, can-
ning — Food transportation and exchange of products —
Waste of goods through lack of transportation facilities —
Waterways and the Grand Canal, railroads, motor roads, and
coolie transport as means of transportation — Prevention of
natural disasters, floods, and droughts — Regulative measures ; deepening of streams, irrigation, etc.— Radical and
preventive measures : reforestation on national scale — Agricultural development in the United States; state interest
in farm problems — But agriculture still under capitalistic
system and aiming for profits — *Min-sheng* Principle makes
support of the people the aim of agriculture — Food distribution — Four necessities of life : food, clothing, shelter, means
of travel — Duties of the state and of the people.

My topic to-day is the "food problem." When
you hear this, you will say that eating food is
a daily and familiar habit. People often remark
that nothing in the world is easier than eating.

It is true that eating is a very simple and customary activity; why, then, should there be any problem connected with it? We do not realize that food is a most vital problem of livelihood which, if not solved, will cause the whole problem of livelihood to fail of solution. The chief problem in the *Min-sheng* Principle is the food problem. The saying of the ancients, " The nation looks upon the people as its foundation; the people look upon food as their heaven," is revealing as to the importance of the food question. Before the European War, statesmen in the various nations did not concern themselves about the food problem. But we observers of the European War in this past decade have begun to study into the reasons for Germany's defeat. When the European War raged most fiercely, Germany was victorious. Whatever opposing forces met — infantry, artillery, or cavalry on land, torpedo destroyers, submarines, and all kinds of battleships on the sea, airships or aëroplanes in the sky — Germany always triumphed. From first to last, Germany never lost a battle. Yet the European War resulted in severe defeat for Germany. Why? Because of the food difficulty. Germany's ports were blockaded by the Allies, the food supply in Germany gradually decreased, and finally both citizens and soldiers were unable to get food and nearly starved. They could not hold out

forever so were in the end defeated. This shows
that the food problem bears a vital relation to
the life and existence of a state.

The United States now leads the world in food
supply. Each year the United States sends
consignments of food to the relief of Europe.
Next to the United States comes Russia, which,
with its wide territory and comparatively sparse
population, is able to produce a great deal of
food. Other countries, like Australia, Canada,
and Argentina in South America, depend upon
food as a great source of national wealth, exporting large quantities of it every year to supply the
shortage in other countries. But during the
European War many ships which were ordinarily
used to carry grain were taken over by the government and converted into military transports.
There was a great scarcity of commercial ships;
Australia, Canada, Argentina, and such countries
were unable to export their surplus food to
Europe and the European nations consequently
suffered for food. China fortunately experienced
no serious floods or droughts at the time of
the European War; the farmers reaped good
harvests, and so China did not suffer from
famine. If China then had met with a flood
like the one this year and the farmers' crops
had failed, she, too, would certainly have been
foodless. That China during the war should

have escaped such disasters and should not have been without food supply was a stroke of natural good fortune.

Some countries in the world produce enough food for themselves, but many do not. The British Isles, for example, only raise food sufficient for three months' consumption out of the whole year; food for the other nine months has to be imported from other countries. In the fiercest days of the European War, when the German submarines were blockading British ports, Great Britain almost starved. The Japanese Isles of the East also do not produce enough food for their own use during the year; but Japan's shortage is not so grievous as Great Britain's. Japan can supply her own people with food for eleven months out of the year; one month's supply is lacking. Germany's food supply is sufficient for ten months' use; two months' supply of food is lacking. Among the smaller nations of Europe are many which do not produce sufficient food. Germany's food supply is inadequate in ordinary times; during the war, when great numbers of farmers became soldiers and when production was reduced, the food supply was all the more inadequate. And so the great four-year war resulted in defeat for Germany. You can see why the food problem of an entire nation is of such serious consequence.

It is easy to solve the difficulty when one person or one family lacks food, but when a whole nation, such as China with her four hundred millions, does not have any adequate supply of food, the problem becomes very grave and difficult of solution.   Is China's food supply really sufficient or not ?   Do the Chinese people have enough to eat ?   Kwangtung Province imports $70,000,000 worth of food annually.   If no rice were imported for one month, Kwangtung would at once be disturbed by a food famine, which proves that Kwangtung does not have an adequate food supply.   We are speaking only of Kwangtung, yet many other provinces are faced with similar conditions.   China has a much larger area than the United States and three or four times the population of the United States, yet our food supply cannot of course compete with that of the United States.   Let us draw a comparison with European nations.   Germany's food supply is inadequate and consequently a famine developed within the country two or three years after the outbreak of the war.   France has an adequate food supply ; in peace times she has enough to eat without depending upon food imports.   Compare China and France : the population of France is forty millions, of China four hundred millions ; the area of France is about one twentieth the area of China.   Thus China's population is ten

times that of France and her territory twenty
times that of France; yet the forty million French
people with one twentieth of China's land can,
by improved methods of agriculture, produce a
sufficient supply of food for themselves.   If China,
twenty times the size of France, would follow
France's example, develop intensive agriculture
and multiply production, we would certainly
produce at least twenty times as much food as
France.   France can now support forty million
people; China would be able to support at least
eight hundred million people.   Not only would
all the people of the country be free from the
dread of famine, but there would exist a food
surplus which we might contribute to the use of
other countries.

To-day, however, China's populace is poverty-
stricken and her wealth is being squandered.
What is the true status of the food problem?
Nowhere in China is there enough food for the
people.   Every year tens of thousands die of
starvation.   This is an estimate of ordinary years;
when floods and famines come, a far greater number perish with hunger.   According to reliable
foreign investigations, China at present does not
really have more than 310,000,000 people.   Several
decades ago we had a population of 400,000,000
which means that we have lost 90,000,000.   This
is a frightful fact and raises a serious problem

for our consideration. The reason why the
population of China has decreased ninety millions
in a few decades is, to put it very briefly, food
shortage. There are many reasons why China
does not have an adequate food supply; the main
reason is the lack of progress in agricultural
science and the next reason is foreign economic
domination.

When I was lecturing upon Nationalism, I
described the economic forces with which foreign
countries are oppressing China. Every year they
rob China of rights and privileges worth $1,200,-
000,000. Because of foreign economic domination, China is losing this amount every year.
How is it paid over to foreign countries? Is the
loss all in money? No, part of the loss is in
food. Why, when she does have food sufficient
for her own people, does China yet send food
to other countries? How do we know that this
is being done? Foreign trade reports issued a
few days ago placed the number of eggs alone
exported annually to the United States at one
billion. This simply includes eggs in shells and
not those used in manufacturing albumin. Great
quantities of eggs are also shipped to Japan and
to England. Those of you who have visited
Nanking have noticed a gigantic structure as
soon as you reached Hsiakwan. This structure
is a foreign-owned meat-canning factory where

Chinese pigs, chickens, geese, ducks, and other domestic fowls and animals are used in the manufacture of canned meat for shipment abroad. Again, think of the barley, rye, and soy beans of North China, a considerable percentage of which is shipped out of Chinese ports. Three years ago there was a severe drought in North China; along the Peking-Hankow and Peking-Mukden railways people were dying by the thousands. Yet at the same time huge quantities of wheat and beans were being shipped out of Newchwang and Dairen. Why? Because of foreign economic domination; China had no money to send abroad, so had to starve herself and send her grain. No wonder China's food problem is unsolved!

When we speak of the Principle of Livelihood we mean that we want our four hundred millions all to have food and very cheap food; only when there is abundant, cheap food can we say that the livelihood problem is solved. How shall we begin our investigation of the food problem? Eating is a very simple act; you all eat and sleep and you don't see any difficulty involved. The poor people of China, however, have a common proverb, "Seven things to worry about when you throw open your door each morning — fuel, rice, oil, salt, soy, vinegar, tea." Food, then, is a serious problem and we must study it minutely if we want to find a solution.

What does mankind need to eat in order to live?
There are several important elements in our
food which we are constantly in danger of forgetting. As a matter of fact, we daily depend upon
four most important kinds of food to nourish our
life. The first of these is air. In plain talk, we
must "eat wind." When I say this, you will
think I am joking, for the common expression,
"Go and eat wind," is generally used in a
disparaging sense. But you do not realize that
eating air is really more important than eating
food. The second kind of food we need is water.
The third is animal food, that is, meat. The
fourth is plant food, the five cereals, fruits, and
vegetables. Air, water, meat, and vegetables are
the four vital elements of our food. Let us take
them up separately.

First, air! Do not think that I am making fun;
if you do not believe that eating air is important,
stop doing it for one minute by stopping up your
nose and mouth and see how you feel. Can you
stand the lack of air? We eat air sixteen times
a minute; that is, we take sixteen meals of air
every minute. You do not eat more than three
meals of food in one day. Canton people never
eat more than four meals a day, counting even
their midnight revels. The poor usually eat two
meals a day and the poorest can keep alive on
one meal a day. But as for air, we eat twenty

thousand and forty meals of it a day and if we
miss one meal we are uncomfortable. If we do not
eat it for a few minutes, we are sure to die. Air,
then, is the first important means of subsistence
for the human race. The second is water. We
cannot live by food alone, without water. A man
can do without food and hold out five or six days
without dying, but he will die in five days without water.

The third and most important means of subsistence is plant food. Only after man had made
great progress in seeking a living did he know how
to eat plant food. China is an ancient, civilized
nation, so the Chinese people all eat plant food.
Savage people all eat animal food; and it, too, is
an important means of subsistence for the human
race. Air and water are found everywhere. If
people live on the banks of streams, they can
use running water, otherwise they use water from
springs and wells or rain water. Water is to
be found everywhere. Air, too, is all around us.
So, although air and water are indispensable
elements in human subsistence, yet because
they are limitless and inexhaustible, because they
are bestowed by nature and do not require
man's effort, we shall call them "natural gifts."
Consequently, they do not constitute problems
for us. But animal and plant food are serious
problems. Primitive man, like the present-day

savages, lived by hunting and fishing; he caught animals in the water and upon land for his food. As civilization advanced, man came to the agricultural stage and learned how to plant the five cereals. He then depended upon plant life for his nourishment. China has had four thousand years of civilization, so we have progressed further in the civilized use of food than Western nations. We depend chiefly upon plants for food. Although plants grow out of the ground, yet much labor must be expended and many various methods must be used before they can be of service to us. If we want to solve the problem of plant food, we must first study the question of production.

Since olden times China has been a farming nation. Agriculture has been the great industry for the production of food. By what methods can we increase plant production? Chinese agriculture has always depended entirely upon human labor, yet cultivation has developed to a very high point and all the various products are of a superior and beautiful quality. Foreign scientists have been led to give high praise to Chinese farming. Since the production of food in China depends upon the peasants, and since the peasants have to toil so bitterly, we must have the government make regulations by law for the protection of peasants if we want to increase the production of food. A large majority of the people in China are peasants, at least nine out of every ten, yet the food which they raise with such wearisome labor is mostly taken away by the landowners. What they themselves can keep is barely sufficient to keep them alive. This is a most unjust situation. If we are to increase the production of food, we must make laws regarding the rights and interests of the farmers; we must give them encouragement and protection and allow them to keep more of the fruit of their land. The protection of the farmers' rights and the giving to them of a larger share in their harvests are questions related to the equalization of land ownership. A few days ago our Kuomintang invited the farmers to a celebration in this Higher Normal School in order to launch a farmers' movement and to make a start toward the solution of agrarian problems. Later, when the *Min-sheng* Principle is fully realized and the problems of the farmer are all solved, each tiller of the soil will possess his own fields — that is to be the final fruit of our efforts.

What are the real conditions among Chinese farmers ? Although China does not have great landowners, yet nine out of ten farmers do not own their fields. Most of the farming land is in the possession of landlords who do not do the cultivating themselves. It seems only right that the farmer should till his farm for himself and claim its products, yet farmers to-day are tilling for others and over half of the agricultural products from the farms are taken by the landlords. We must immediately use government and law to remedy this grave situation. Unless we can solve the agrarian problem, there will be no solution for the livelihood problem. Of the food produced in the fields, sixty per cent, according to our latest rural surveys, goes to the landlord, while only forty per cent goes to the farmer. If this unjust state of affairs continues, when the farmers become intelligent, who will still be willing to toil and suffer in the fields ? But if the food raised in the fields all goes to the farmers, the farmers will be more eager to farm and production will increase. But as it is now, the produce of the farms goes largely to the landowners. Only four tenths is kept by the farmers ; most of the fruit of a year's unremitting toil goes finally to the landowner. As a result, great numbers of farmers are abandoning their farms and many fields are becoming waste and unproductive.

In dealing with agricultural production, we should study not only this question of liberating the peasants but also the seven methods of increasing production. These methods are: use of machinery, use of fertilizers, rotation of crops, eradication of pests, manufacturing, transportation, and prevention of natural disasters. The first method is the use of machinery. For these thousands of years China has farmed entirely with man power and has never used machinery. If we should introduce farming machinery, we could at least double China's agricultural production and we could reduce the cost of production to one tenth or one hundredth of what it is now. If China with human labor can support four hundred millions, she should with machine power produce enough for eight hundred millions. If machinery were substituted for human labor in the production of food, then much waste land, which cannot now be cultivated because it is too elevated, might be irrigated with pumps and pipes and opened up to cultivation. Good land already under cultivation could be irrigated by machinery and freed from the danger of drought, thus increasing its productivity. If the old, uncultivated waste lands can be opened up, then China naturally will produce more food. The cultivating and pumping machines in use now are all shipped in from other countries, but if the farmers all begin to use machinery and the demand for it increases, then we ought to manufacture our own and recover the profits which are flowing abroad.

The second method of increasing production is the use of fertilizers. In the past China has

used night soil and manures, and various kinds
of decayed vegetable matter but never chemical
fertilizers. Only recently has Chile saltpeter
begun to be used for fertilizing in China. Many
places in Kwangtung and Honan are now using
this in the cultivation of sugar cane. When
sugar cane is fertilized with Chile saltpeter, it
grows twice as fast and the stalks are several
times as large. If Chile saltpeter is not put on
the land, the sugar cane not only grows much
more slowly but its stalks are much shorter. Chile
saltpeter, however, is shipped in from Chile in
South America; it requires a heavy outlay of
capital and is very expensive; so only cane growers have been able to buy and use it. Ordinary
cultivators cannot afford it. Besides Chile
saltpeter, the phosphorus from all kinds of Crus-
tacea and the potassium from mineral mountains
and cliffs make very good fertilizers. If com-
pounds of nitrogen, phosphorus, and potassium
are combined, an excellent fertilizer is formed,
which makes the cultivation of any plant easy
and greatly stimulates production. For example,
an unfertilized mow of land will produce five
baskets of corn, but if the same mow be fertilized,
the crop will be two or three times as large. So
to increase production we must apply fertilizers
to the land, and in order to apply fertilizers we
must study science and manufacture fertilizers by

scientific methods. China has the raw materials for fertilizers everywhere. The material in Chile saltpeter was long ago used by Chinese in the manufacture of gunpowder. Formerly all fertilizers which the world used were produced in Chile, but with the advance of science, scientists have discovered a new method of manufacturing nitrates by use of electricity. So now the different countries do not have to depend upon natural sodium nitrate shipped from Chile, but are manufacturing artificial nitrates by means of electricity. The artificial nitrates are just as effective as natural nitrates and require very little initial expenditure ; consequently people in every country gladly use them.

How is electricity generated ? The ordinary, expensive electricity is generated by steam power but the newer and cheaper kind of electricity is all generated by water power. Recently foreign countries have begun to use their waterfalls and rapids for driving their dynamos. Enormous electric power can be generated in this way, and the power can be used to manufacture artificial nitrates. The natural power of waterfalls and rapids does not cost anything and consequently the price of the electricity generated is very low. With cheap electric power, the manufactured, artificial nitrates are inexpensive. There are many waterfalls and rapids in China. On the

Sikiang[1] above Wuchow are numerous rapids ; near Nanning there are the Fu-po Rapids, which are very strong and which interfere dangerously with vessels going up and down the river. If the water power in this undercurrent could be harnessed and used to generate electricity, and if another waterway could be built for boats and junks, would there not be a double advantage ? Some have estimated that the water power in these rapids could generate one million horse power of electricity. On the Fo and Hung rivers in Kwangsi are also many rapids which could be used to generate electric power. The Weng River in northern Kwangtung could generate, according to the calculations of engineers, between twenty and one hundred thousand electrical horse power. This would supply the city of Canton with electric light and every factory with electric power, and would even be sufficient to electrify the Canton-Hankow Railway according to the most modern foreign plan.

Or consider the tremendous water power in the Kuei Gorges of the upper Yangtze. Some who have studied the stretch of river between Ichang and Wanshien estimate that the water power there could generate over thirty million electrical horse power. Such an immense power

West River, Kwangtung.

is much greater than that produced at present in any country. It would not only supply all the railways, electric lines, and factories in the country with power, but it could be used to manufacture staple fertilizers. Consider again the Yellow River which at Lungmên Waterfalls could also generate many million electrical horse power. You see how great are China's natural resources! If the water power in the Yangtze and Yellow rivers could be utilized by the newest methods to generate electric power, about one hundred million horse power might be obtained. Since one horse power is equivalent to the power of eight strong men, one hundred million horse power would be equivalent to eight hundred million man power. A man works eight hours a day, according to the law in most countries; a longer working-day is injurious to the worker's health and lessens production. I have already given the reasons for this in my last lecture. Man power can be used only eight hours a day, but mechanical horse power can be used all twenty-four hours. This means that one horse power for a day and night accomplishes as much work as twenty-four men. If we could utilize the water power in the Yangtze and Yellow rivers to generate one hundred million horse power of electrical energy, we would be putting twenty-four hundred million men to work! When that time comes, we shall have enough power to supply railways, motor cars, fertilizer factories, and all kinds of manufacturing establishments. Han Yü [1] says, "One household makes implements while six households use them." How many out of our four hundred millions are really at work ? Young children and old people of course cannot work. Many strong men, like the landowners who receive farm rents, are also depending on the work of others for their support. A large number of Chinese are not working ; they are sharing, not creating wealth. And as a result China is getting very poor. If we could make use of the Yangtze and the Yellow River water power to generate a hundred million horse power, or twenty-four hundred million man power, and let this great electrical energy work for us, China would produce a great deal, and would certainly turn her poverty into riches. So in the matter of agricultural production, if we can improve upon human labor and use machinery, if, moreover, we can use electric power to manufacture fertilizers, we can certainly greatly increase the yield of our fields.

The third method of increasing production is crop rotation. This means planting different things or different brands of seed on the same piece of land in successive years. For example,

---

[1] Chinese essayist, of the T'ang dynasty.

Kwangtung seed might be planted this year; Hunan seed, next year; and Szechwan seed, year after next. What advantage is there in such rotation ? It means change and rest for the various soils and increase in crop yield. When the seeds fall into new soil and spring up in a fresh atmosphere, the plants are stronger and the harvest is more abundant. Thus crop rotation increases production.

The fourth method is eradication of pests. On the farm there are both plants and animals which are injurious. For example, rice is to be planted in the fields, but at the time of planting all sorts of malformed grain stalks and weeds spring up very fast and hinder the growth of the rice as well as suck the fertility of the soil. They are very harmful to the rice. The farmer should use scientific principles and study how to get rid of these noxious darnel and weeds and so prevent their injuring the crop; at the same time he should find out if there is any way to use them to increase the yield. What animals are pests ? There are numerous species. One of the most common is the locust. If the locust or any other of the injurious insects attacks a ripening plant, it gnaws and destroys the plant so that there is no crop. The Kwangtung litchi trees this year, just as they were ready to bear fruit, were attacked by caterpillars which ate away the litchi flower. As a result, this year's litchi crop is very small. There are many other kinds of injurious insects, and the state should employ specialists to make a careful study of them and to find ways to eradicate them. The United States now is much concerned over these problems and is spending a great deal of money every year in a study of methods for destroying pests. Consequently, the income from agriculture is showing an annual increase of hundreds of millions. Although an entomological bureau has been established in Nanking for the study of pest eradication, yet its sphere is too limited and its work is not very effective. We must use the great power of the state and imitate the United States' methods of destroying injurious insects, then agricultural pests throughout the country will diminish and production will increase.

The fifth method of increasing production is by manufacture. If food is to be preserved for a long time and to be sent to distant places, it must pass through a preserving process. In our country the most common methods of preserving foods are by drying and salting : we have dried vegetables, dried fish, dried meat, salted vegetables, salted fish, salted meat, and so on. Recently a new method has been introduced in the West : the food is first thoroughly cooked by boiling or baking, then put into cans and the cans sealed.

No matter how long the food is kept, it has a fresh flavor when taken from the cans. This is the best method of preserving food; any kind of fish, meat, fruit, vegetable, or biscuit can be canned and distributed throughout the country or sold abroad.

The sixth method of increasing production is by means of transportation. When there is a surplus of food, we must begin to exchange ; we must take the surplus here and make it supply the deficiency there. For example, the Three Eastern Provinces of Manchuria and North China have beans and wheat but no rice, while all the southern provinces have rice but no beans and wheat. We ought to take the surplus beans and wheat from Manchuria and North China and send them to South China and use the surplus rice in South China to supply North China and Manchuria. But such an exchange of goods depends upon means of transportation. The greatest problem now in China is that of transportation. A great deal of waste results from unsuitable methods. In many parts of China, transportation of goods depends entirely upon coolie carriers. The strongest coolie cannot carry more than a hundred catties or travel more than a hundred li in one day, and he has to be paid at least a dollar for this labor. This is a waste not only of money but also of time, and thus much of China's resources have been used imperceptibly in moving goods.

Now if we can make the five improvements which I have just described and increase our agricultural production but still have no easy and convenient means of transportation, what will be the situation ?   A few years ago I met a chieftain of a Yünnan tribe who owned large tracts of farm land and took in great quantities of rent grain every year.   He told me that yearly he had to burn several thousand piculs of grain. I said, " When grain is such an important food, why do you burn it ? "   He replied: " I get too much grain every year.   I cannot eat it all myself and the near-by people all have enough to eat. No dealer comes to buy the grain and with methods of transportation as they are, the grain can only be carried a few score li away.   There is no way to transport it for sale in distant places. Each year the new grain piles on top of the old grain.   As I do not have many granaries in which to store my grain and as people in the market prefer new grain to old grain, the old grain is useless.   So, at harvest time, I can only burn the old grain and clean out my granaries to receive the new grain."   The reasons for the burning of the grain were the surplus supply of grain and the poor means of transportation.   China's greatest waste has been in the use of coolie transportation.   Here in Canton we used to have a great number of carriers, but since the building of large streets and the introduction of wheelbarrows, we do not have to depend upon carriers for everything. One wheelbarrow can carry several coolie loads and save several coolie fares, while a motor car can carry ten or more coolie loads and save ten or more coolie fares. The use of wheelbarrows and motor cars in transportation not only reduces the expense but also saves time. In Saikwan (West District), where there are no modern streets, coolies are still employed for moving goods. In the country, if we want to transport a load of a hundred catties for a distance of a few score li, we are obliged to use coolies. When wealthy people travel, they ride in sedan chairs and use chair coolies. Because of our imperfect means of transportation in the past, the most valuable and necessary food has not been able to circulate freely, and the food problem has remained unsolved.

China's best means of transportation have been natural waterways and canals. The Grand Canal is a very long stream ; it commences at Hangchow, passes through Soochow, Chinkiang, Yangchow, Shantung, and Tientsin and comes to an end finally at Tungchow, not far from Peking, after traversing a total distance of three thousand li. It is indeed the world's longest canal. Such a waterway is extremely convenient, and if the number of modern steamboats and motor boats upon it were increased, it would be yet more serviceable. Little attention, however, has been paid of late to the Grand Canal. If we want to solve the food problem of the future and be able to transport food easily, we must restore the old canal system. The present Grand Canal should be repaired and the canal system should be extended to where no waterways at present exist. In transportation upon the sea we need large steamships, for the world's most inexpensive way of carrying freight is by water.

Next in cheapness comes railway transportation. If railroads could be built in the eighteen provinces of China, in Sinkiang, Manchuria, Chinghai (Kokonor), Tibet, Inner and Outer Mongolia, and all these railroads could be linked together in one system, China's food supply could circulate in all directions, and people in every part of the country would have cheap food to eat. So railways are one good means of solving the food problem. Railroads, however, can be built only through busy and prosperous sections of the country where they can make money. If they are built through poor country and obscure sections, there will not be much produce to transport nor many passengers to carry. The railways would not only make no profits but would lose money. So we cannot construct railroads through poor and remote country; in such sections we should build only motor roads upon which motor cars can travel. The large cities would then have railroads and the small towns and villages motor roads and all these roads could be connected in a complete system of transportation. The large cities could use the big trains and the small towns and villages motor cars for food transportation.

For example, on both sides of the Canton-Hankow Railway, from Wongsha to Shiukwan, are numerous villages; if these villages should all build motor roads to connect with the railway, not only would the railway make a great deal of moey, but each village would have a convenient means of communication. If many branch railroads were built out to these villages and trains instead of motor cars were used for transmission of goods, there would certainly be financial loss. In many rural sections of foreign countries railroads have been built and trains can run, but because the railways' business is poor, motor cars are being used instead. Every time a train is run, a great deal of coal is consumed; the capital expenditure is large and profits are hard to make. But a motor car can be run with very little capital and can bring in very large profits. These are facts which all modern directors of transportation must be familiar with.

Again, travel between Canton and Macao has always depended upon steamers, but now some people are proposing a Canton-Macao Railway. The distance from Canton to Macao, however, is not more than two hundred li. If a railroad were built and three trains run in both directions every day, the railway would not make money, while if only two trains were run there would be a loss on the investment. If, for the sake of reducing expenses, fewer trains were run, travel would not be any more convenient than at present. So the best plan would be to construct a motor road and run motor cars between Canton and Macao. The capital expenditure for a motor road is much less; moreover, a train has to pull seven or eight cars on each run in order to clear expenses, the consumption of labor and of coal is very heavy, and if the passengers are too few there is no chance to make any profit. It would be much better to run motor buses on a motor road. A large or small number of people can start at any time. When there are many passengers, a large bus can be used, when there are still more passengers, two or three more large buses can be added; when only a few are traveling a small car can be used. A motor car can start whenever passengers arrive; it does not have to run by a regular schedule as the trains do because of the danger of collision with another train. So we find that the construction of a motor road between Canton and Macao would be much cheaper than the construction of a railroad. When the motor road is built, only the poor and remote communities which the road does not traverse will have to use coolie transportation. From this we see that four means are essential if we are to solve the question of food transportation: first, canals; second, railroads; third, motor roads; and fourth, coolie transportation. If we develop these four means of transportation in the best way, our four hundred millions will have cheap food to eat.

The seventh method of increasing agricultural production is prevention of natural disasters. Look at this flood to-day in Kwangtung! The first crop of rice should be harvested within this half month, but just as the first crop was ripening, it was immersed in water and ruined. The rice from one mow of land is worth at least ten dollars, so one flooded mow means a loss of ten dollars? In all Kwangtung Province how many mow do you think have suffered from flood? Certainly several million mow. A loss of tens of millions of dollars! So if we want to find a complete solution for the food problem, the prevention of natural disasters is a very important matter. How shall we go about preventing a flood like this one in Kwangtung? At present this method is used: conservancy bureaus have been established, and at the low places along the banks of the streams many high embankments have been built up. These embankments are very solid, so that they can resist any heavy flow of water and not give way before a flood that would inundate the fields on both sides. Last year when I was fighting along the Tung Kiang, I saw some of those high dikes. They are all strongly built and can help to prevent flood disaster yet not be broken down by the rush of the waters. This dike-building method is regulative and puts a check upon the waters. But it is only half of the method for flood prevention and cannot entirely control the waters. Besides building dikes, we must also deepen the rivers and harbors and dredge all the silt and sand along the bottoms. If there is no silt in the harbors to hinder the flow of the rivers and the river beds are deep, then it will be easy for the waters to pass out to sea, the rivers will not overflow everything, and flood calamities will be reduced. So the deepening of waterways and the building of high dikes are two kinds of engineering which must be carried out simultaneously if we want to keep the rivers in complete control.

But what about fundamental methods of flood prevention? Why is it that flood disasters are becoming more common every year now? Why were floods very rare in olden times? Because in the old days there were extensive forests; but too much timber has been cut off by the people and the land has not been reforested. As a result there are now very few forests, while numerous mountains and ranges are completely bare. When a heavy rain falls, the mountain sides have no forests to absorb the rain or to check the flow of rain water, and so the water off the mountains flows immediately into the rivers, the rivers immediately swell, and a devastating flood follows. Hence, forestation has an important bearing upon the prevention of floods. The planting of more forests is the fundamental method of flood prevention. Then, when the heavy rains come, the branches and leaves of the trees will absorb the water in the air, and the roots will absorb the water on the ground. Very thick forests can absorb a tremendous amount of water. The water thus collected by the trees flows gradually down to the rivers, rather than directly and suddenly, and does not cause floods. The radical method of flood prevention, then, is forestation. So if, n order to solve the food problem, we want to prevent floods, we must first create forests. Then we can avert the flood evil throughout the country. Reforestation of the whole country, in the final analysis, must be carried out by the state. Only under state direction can such an enterprise easily succeed. This year the provinces of China, north and south, are all afflicted with heavy floods. The loss from these floods must be hundreds of millions of dollars. Already the people are poor and the nation is bankrupt. Continue to add such losses and it will be exceedingly difficult to solve the food problem that stares us in the face.

Then there are also drought disasters. How are we to deal with the problem of drought? Russia, since her great revolution, has had two or three years of drought, which have caused great numbers of people to die of hunger and have almost caused the failure of the revolution. Drought is, like flood, a serious calamity. People used to think that droughts were fixed by fate and could not be prevented. But as science advances ways are being found to avert all kinds of natural disasters. The prevention of droughts requires also the strength of the whole nation and a broad, unified plan. The fundamental method in this plan is, again, forestation. Where forests grow, there is a more suitable proportion of moisture in the air, rains are frequent, and droughts are much less common. For high land and places without springs, we can arrange to pump water by machinery, thus relieving their drought. This irrigation method of preventing droughts may be compared to the dike method of preventing floods — both are only regulative. The regulative methods make it possible to save the situation when floods or droughts come suddenly. The radical method of preventing floods or droughts is forestation — forestation on a national scale. The regulative methods depend upon the use of pumping machinery, upon the building of high dikes, and the deepening of waterways. If we can fully carry out both the regulative and the radical measures, we can avert flood and drought, and then the food produce of our land will not be lost.

If China can liberate the farmers and put into effect the seven methods of increasing agricultural production which I have described, will our food problem then be completely solved ? Even if we succeed beautifully in dealing with these questions of production, we will not have completely solved our food problem. You all know that the European and American nations have all been founded upon industry and commerce, but you may not know that their industrialized and commercialized governments devote a great deal of time also to the study of agricultural problems. The United States, for example, omits nothing of the smallest significance in the study of rural problems for the improvement of rural life. The government not only makes detailed investigations of agricultural conditions in the home country, but constantly sends specialists to the interior of China, to Manchuria, Mongolia, and other places, in order to learn about conditions there. They take Chinese methods of farming and all

kinds of Chinese seeds back to the United States
to test and to use. The United States of late has
been placing great emphasis upon agriculture ;
railway facilities for transporting food, means of
preventing natural disasters, all kinds of scientific
equipment, are complete and up to date.

Yet has the United States really solved her food
problem ? I do not think that she has. Every
year the United States ships vast quantities of
food for sale in other countries and her food
supply is abundant — why, then, do I say that
her food problem is unsolved ? Because agriculture in the United States is still controlled by
capitalists. Under the system of private capital
which still exists, methods of production are overdeveloped, while no attention at all is paid to
proper methods of distribution. So the problem
of livelihood cannot be solved. In order to reach
a solution, we must not only deal with questions
of production but must also lay emphasis upon
the questions of distribution. Equitable methods
of distribution are impossible under a system of
private capital, for under such a system all production heads towards one goal — profit. Since
the production of food aims at profit, when food
prices are low in the native country, the food
will be shipped for sale and greater profits abroad.
Just because private individuals want to make
more money ! Even when there is a native

famine, when the people are short of food and many are starving, these private capitalists are not concerned. With such methods of distribution, which aim wholly at profit, the problem of livelihood can never be well solved. If we want to carry out the *Min-sheng* Principle we must give thought to methods of distribution — methods which will aim not at profit, but at supplying the people with food. China's food supply is now insufficient, yet each year we ship billions of eggs as well as rice and soy beans to Japan and the nations of Europe and America. This is like the situation in India: India not only has an insufficient food supply but experiences yearly famines, yet she holds third place every year among the nations which ship food to Europe. What is the explanation of this fact? — Europe economic domination of India. India still lives in a capitalistic period when the aim of agricultural production is profit. Hence, although India has famines every year, the capitalists behind production know that giving food to the hungry millions will bring them no profit, so they ship the food to the various nations of Europe and sell it at a high profit. They would rather let the hungry multitudes in their native country starve than not sell the food to the countries of Europe. Our *Min-sheng* Principle aims at the destruction of the capitalistic system. China already has an inadequate food supply, yet every year we still ship a lot of food to other countries to be sold because a group of capitalists want to make money.

If we apply the *Min-sheng* Principle we must make the aim of food production not profit but the provision of sustenance for all the people. To do this we must store up the surplus in production every year. Not only must we wait to see if this year's food supply is sufficient, we must wait until the supply next year and the year after is abundant before we ship any food for sale abroad. If after three years the food supply is still short, we will not make any shipments abroad. If we can apply the *Min-sheng* Principle in this way and make the support of the people rather than profit the aim of production, then there will be hope for an abundant food supply in China. The fundamental difference, then, between the Principle of Livelihood and capitalism is this: capitalism makes profit its sole aim, while the Principle of Livelihood makes the nurture of the people its aim. With such a noble principle we can destroy the old, evil capitalistic system.

But in applying the *Min-sheng* Principle for the solution of China's food problems, we can only make gradual changes in the capitalistio system; we must not try to overthrow it immediately. Our first aim is to give China an abundant food supply; when this is realized, it will be easy to go the next step and greatly reduce the price of food. At the present time in China "rice is as precious as pearls and fuel as rare as cassia," and the reason is because other countries are taking a part of China's food supply. Our imports and exports do not offset each other. Being under foreign economic domination, we have no other goods to give in payment, so we can only offer the food which our people sorely need as a settlement. For this reason, millions in China are without food, our living generation is in danger of perishing, our unborn generation will be reduced in number, the population of the whole country is gradually diminishing, and we have dropped from four hundred millions to three hundred and ten millions — all because we have not solved the food problem and have not applied the Principle of Livelihood.

What shall be our plan for the distribution of food ? Food is the greatest need of the people as they seek for their livelihood. Economists have always spoken of three necessities of life — food, clothing, and shelter. My study leads me to add a fourth necessity, an extremely important one — means of travel. In order to solve the livelihood problem we must not only greatly reduce the cost of these four necessities, but we must make them available for all the people of the nation. If the *San Min* Principles are to become effective and a new world is to be built up, then no one must lack any of these four necessities of life. It is essential that the state undertake the responsibility for providing these necessities ; anyone should be able to call the state to task if it does not provide enough of each. The state must shoulder the burden of meeting the people's living needs. What of the people's responsibility to the state ? The people have very definite obligations : the farmer must produce food, the industrial worker must manufacture tools, the business man must connect supply and demand, the scholar must devote his intelligence and ability — every man must fulfill his duty. Then all will be supplied with the four necessities of life.

We are studying the *Min-sheng* Principle in order to solve the problems involved in these four necessities. To-day I have begun by discussing the food problem. The first step in dealing with the food problem is to solve the problem of production ; then comes the problem of distribution. In order to have a fair and equitable distribution of food, we must save food every year. Only when we have saved enough for three years' food supply will we ship any surplus for sale abroad. Such a plan of saving grain is like the old system of public granaries.[1] In recent times,

1 The public granaries distributed grain to the poor in time of need

however, the public granary system has broken
down, and this, together with foreign economic
domination, has resulted in widespread poverty
and national bankruptcy. So now is the critical
time to solve our livelihood problem. If we fail
to take advantage of the present time and wait
till some future day, we will find the task harder
than ever. Our Kuomintang sets forth the Three
Principles of the People as the basis upon which
to build our new nation. As we work out the
Principle of Livelihood, let us not merely empha-
size the theories connected with it, let us also pay
serious attention to its practical application.
The first practical problem which we have to deal
with is the food problem. The solution of this
problem depends first upon abundant production
and next upon equitable distribution. But after
production has been increased and distribution
has been regulated, the people must still fulfill
their obligations. It the people will all do their
part, then they can certainly enjoy peace and
plenty and the food problem will be solved. With
the food problem out of the way, the other problems of livelihood can easily be solved.

August 17, 1924.

LECTURE 4

The "problem of clothing"— A problem that comes with civilization — Development of living standards : necessities, comforts, luxuries — The necessary clothing for China's population our problem — Sources of clothing material : silk, hemp, cotton, and wool — China's ancient silk industry now outstripped by silk industry in other countries — Modern scientific methods of sericulture — Contribution of Pasteur — Sericultural improvements needed in China — China's silk chiefly for export — Hemp cultivation and the development of a linen industry in China — China's large cotton production exported and brought back to China in cotton goods — Effect of foreign economic and political domination upon cotton industry in China — Reasons for failure of Chinese cotton mills after European War — Native yarn and fabrics unable to compete with foreign cotton goods on account of low tariff — China's need of protective tariff for her cotton industry — Agitation for use of native goods and boycott of foreign goods ineffective unless tariff is raised — The function of clothing — State-directed clothing factories which would provide adequate supply of clothing for all the people — Coöperation of government and citizens essential — All must have a share in production.

The subject of my lecture to-day is the problem of clothing. The first important problem in the Principle of Livelihood is food, the next problem is clothing, and that is what I shall discuss now. As we take an evolutionary view of life in the universe, we see that all living things — plants and animals — have depended upon food, upon some form of sustenance for their existence. Without some form of sustenance life perishes. So food is a vital problem, in the vegetable world as well as in the animal world. But man is the only form of life in the universe that faces the problem of clothing. Only man, only civilized man in fact, wears clothing. Other animals and the plants do not have clothes to wear, nor do savages wear clothes. Food, then, is the chief problem of livelihood and clothing is the second. The uncivilized races of Africa and Malaysia go without clothes, and so our primitive ancestors must also have lived naked. The wearing of clothes has come with the progress of civilization; the more civilization advances, the more complex becomes the problem of clothing. Primitive man had natural clothing to protect his body just as birds and animals have their fur and feathers provided by Nature. His body was covered with hair. Later, as human civilization advanced to the pastoral age, man learned how to fish and to hunt. He began to make clothes out of the skins of animals, and as he continued this practice, the hair upon his body lost its function and gradually disappeared. The more civilization advanced, the more complete clothing became and the less hair grew. So races far advanced in civilization

have very little hair upon the body, while savage
races and races which have only recently begun
to progress are very hairy. Compare Chinese
and Europeans : all European people are more
hairy than the Chinese and the reason is that
they have not developed so far in the process
of evolution as the Chinese. We see, then, that
clothing originated with the bodily hair provided
by Nature; as man progressed, he began to slay
the wild beasts, and he used their flesh for food
and their skins for clothing. Animal skins formed
the clothing of early man. There is a very old
saying, " Eating flesh and sleeping upon skins,"
which has been used in an abusive way to describe
a person as an animal, but which proves that
ancient man, when he had killed an animal, used
its flesh for food and its skin for clothing. Then,
as men increased and animals decreased, there
were not enough animal skins to supply the need,
and men had to look for other material with which
to make clothes. Where did they discover such
material ? In my last lecture, I said that the
common food materials are the meat of animals
and the fruits and seeds of plants. Clothing
materials like food materials depend upon animals
and plants ; there is no other important source.

How far have we got towards a solution of
the clothing problem ? Clothing is one of the
necessities of life. In the progress of human

civilization, living standards evolve through three
stages. The first stage is that of necessities.
Without these necessities human life of course
cannot exist, and without a sufficient amount of
them life is incomplete, half dead and half alive.
The necessities of the first stage man could not
do without. Then man advanced to the second
stage, the stage of comforts. When man reached
this standard of living, he began to seek not only
the necessary things of life but also joy and comfort. Then he went a step further and looked for
luxuries. Take clothing, for example. In ancient
times " grass cloth in summer and fur in winter "
were considered ample. But when man reached
the standard of comfort, he was not content with
clothing that should simply meet his physical
needs ; he wanted his clothing also to fit his body
and to be comfortable. Later man advanced another step and began to seek beauty and refinement
in his clothing — light raw silks and delicate
lustering in place of grass cloth in the summer;
otter and sable furs in place of ordinary animal
furs in the winter. Thus the wearing of clothing
has developed from the wearing of plain, necessary
clothing to the wearing of comfortable clothing,
and from the wearing of comfortable clothing to
the wearing of beautiful and luxurious clothing.
In the same way the eating of food has evolved.
At first man simply sought to fill his stomach

with "green vegetables and coarse rice." Then
he began to desire the sweet and juicy flavors
of wine and cooked meat. Further on, he began
to comb the mountains and the seas for delicacies
and dainties. So now in our Canton feasts, the
meat of all kinds of game, birds' nests and sharks'
fins, everything strange and tasty, is brought to
the table ; luxuries are exhausted and every want
is indulged ; this is the stage of luxury in eating.

But in seeking a solution for the problem of
livelihood we are not dealing with comforts or with
luxuries: we are simply trying to solve the problem
of necessities. We want the four hundred millions throughout the nation to have the necessary
food and clothing, enough to eat and to wear.
As I said before, China's population has dwindled
from four hundred millions to three hundred and
ten millions. Now we must lay a comprehensive
plan that shall include both production and manufacture in order to clothe these three hundred and
ten millions. We must find a way to solve the
clothing problem, otherwise in two or three years
the population will probably decrease several
million more. If this year's surveys show a population of three hundred and ten millions, after a
few years the number will be still less ; let us say
three hundred millions. We must begin to plan
comprehensively on a large scale how to clothe
this number of people. The first step towards a

solution of the problem is a study of how materials for clothing are produced. Clothing materials come from animals and plants — two kinds from animals and two kinds from plants. These four materials are silk, hemp or flax, cotton, and wool. Cotton and hemp are secured from plants, silk and wool from animals. Silk is spun by the *ch'an*, or silkworm; wool grows upon the backs of camels and other animals. These four products are the essential materials for man's clothing.

Let us first consider silk. Silk is a fine material for clothes and was first discovered in China. The Chinese in very ancient times wore silks. Although the civilization of the Western Powers has now far outstripped ours, yet at the time when China discovered silk their peoples were still in the age of savagery and were still " eating raw meat and drinking blood." They not only did not wear silks; they wore no clothes whatsoever and their bodies were covered with hair. They were wild men, wearing the clothing of Nature. Not until two or three centuries ago did their civilization begin to advance beyond ours and did they learn to use silk as the material for beautiful clothes. Now Westerners use silk to make some necessities but chiefly to make articles of luxury.

Although China discovered silk several thousand years ago, yet the key to the clothing problem of our three hundred millions is not silk. Our

necessary articles of clothing are not made of silk,
and a large proportion of the people cannot afford
to wear silk. The silk which we produce every
year is for the most part shipped to foreign
countries to be made into articles of luxury.
When China first opened trade with other countries, our chief export was silk. China exported
great quantities of silk while importing only a
small quantity of foreign goods. China's exports
not only offset her imports but exceeded them.
Next to silk, China's most important export is
tea. Silk and tea were leading exports from China
as long as the West did not produce them. Before
they used tea foreigners all drank wines ; later,
when Chinese tea was introduced, they began to
drink it in place of wine, and tea drinking became
a habit and finally a necessity. Because formerly
China was the only country which produced silk
and tea and other countries were without these
things, and because the Chinese were not in great
need of foreign goods and foreign countries were
not as yet manufacturing goods in very large
quantities, our exports of silk and tea for several
decades were able to pay for our imports ; that
is, our exports and our imports balanced. But in
recent years foreign imports have been increasing every day, while our exports of silk and tea
have been constantly decreasing. Our exports no
longer pay for our imports. Foreign countries have

now learned the Chinese secret of producing silk. France and Italy in Europe now produce great quantities of silk; they have also made a careful study of sericulture and silk-reeling methods and have made many new discoveries and improvements. The Japanese silk industry has not only followed Chinese methods but has selected the newest European discoveries. Japanese silk has improved much in quality, Japan's silk output exceeds China's, and Japanese silk goods have become superior to Chinese goods. Due to these reasons Chinese silk and tea do not have many buyers now in the international market; silk and tea of other countries have taken our trade from us. Now the amount of silk and tea which we export is constantly diminishing, yet we have no other commodities to market in return for our imports; so each year we are paying in international trade a tribute of five hundred million dollars to other countries. This is what foreign economic domination means to us. As this domination becomes more and more serious, the problem of livelihood becomes more and more difficult of solution. Chinese silk has been entirely driven out of the international market by foreign silk: Chinese silk goods are inferior in quality to foreign silk goods. But because we want foreign cotton goods and yarn to make our necessary articles, we cannot use this silk ourselves, but must send it abroad in exchange for still cheaper cotton cloth and gauze.

Our silk industry, the methods of producing silk and of making silk goods which we discovered, was once all very fine. But we were satisfied with our first accomplishment; we did not know how to make improvements; and later when foreigners copied our industry, applied modern science to it and introduced improvements in it, they were able to make silk superior to Chinese silk and to supplant the Chinese silk industry. Investigation will show that the decline of the Chinese silk industry is due to poor methods of production. A great many Chinese silkworms are diseased; in fact, half the silkworms in every crop turn out badly and die before maturity. If by chance they live, the raw silk from the cocoons of diseased silkworms does not make goods of fine quality or color. Our methods of silk reeling are also imperfect; the threads have too many breaks in them and are not suited to the use of foreign silk looms. Consequently Chinese silk has gradually lost out in competition with foreign silk. Several decades ago the foreign methods of sericulture were just like the Chinese methods. When the Chinese farmer raises silk-worms, the results are sometimes good; at other times, there is a complete loss of the crop. The farmer has no other way to explain such different outcomes but to attribute them to fate. This was also the case with foreign farmers. Then scientists began to discover the principles of biology and to study minutely all forms of life, not only those visible to the naked eye, but also, by means of microscopes which magnified thousands of times, those too small for the naked eye.

In the course of such investigations, a French scientist named Pasteur made the discovery that all diseases of animals, whether of human beings or of silkworms, are caused by minute organisms, or microbes. Unless these miscrobes can be destroyed, the diseased animal will surely die. After spending much time and making extended researches, Pasteur understood thoroughly the nature of these microörganisms and was able to discover methods to eradicate them and so to rid the silkworms of disease. When these methods were communicated to the silk growers of France and Italy, the diseased silkworms were greatly reduced in number and the cocoon spinning turned out very well. The silk industry was then able to make great progress. Later on, Japan began to study these methods and her silk industry began to advance. China's farmers, however, have always been conservative and unwilling to learn new methods, so our silk industry has steadily declined. The silk merchants of Shanghai have now established a

station for testing raw silk and for studying the
quality of silk ; they hope to apply methods which
will improve the silk. Lingnam University in
Canton is using scientific methods to improve
silkworm eggs ; the use of the improved egg
results in fine silk and silk products. But these
scientific methods of improving sericulture are
still known only to a few ; the majority of silk
growers are not familiar with them.

If China is to reform her silk industry and to
increase silk production, her silk growers must
learn foreign scientific methods and must improve
the silkworm egg and the mulberry leaves; they
must also study the best methods of reeling the
silk from the cocoons and of sorting and improving
the various grades, qualities, and colors of raw
silk. Then China's silk industry will gradually
progress and will be able to compete in the world's
silk market. If Chinese do not improve their
mulberry leaves and silkworm eggs and the quality
of the raw silk, but stick to the old methods,
China's silk industry will not only fail but will
probably, in the course of natural selection,
be utterly wiped out. Most of the people now in
China do not wear silk, but our raw silk is shipped
abroad in exchange for cotton fabrics and yarn.
If Chinese silk is poor in quality, other countries
will not want it and the silk will have no market.
China then will not only lose one of her chief

sources of wealth, but she will also have no material for making clothing, since she cannot export her silk in exchange for cotton goods and yarn. So if China wants her people to have the material necessary for clothing in order to solve their clothing problem, she must preserve her ancient industry, improve her silkworm eggs and mulberry leaves and reform her methods of silk reeling. China's gauzes and satins used to be very fine, unexcelled in any foreign country. But now the silk goods which come from foreign machine looms are much superior to Chinese goods. The exquisite silk goods which are now being used by wealthy Chinese families all come from abroad, which shows how our splendid native industry has been ruined. To solve the silk problem, we must not only improve silkworm eggs and mulberry leaves, and reform methods of sericulture and of silk reeling in order to produce better silk, but we must also learn foreign methods of weaving silks and satins by machinery. Then we can make beautiful silk goods for the use of our people; when the home demand is met, we can ship the surplus abroad in exchange for other goods.

The second material of which clothes are made is hemp. Hemp also owes its first discovery to China. In ancient times Chinese found the method for making cloth from hemp, and this old method is still followed by all to-day. But Chinese agriculture never progresses, so the linen industry has recently been taken from us by other countries. Now foreign machinery makes linen thread with a luster almost like that of silk and also uses linen and silk thread together to make all kinds of fabrics. These fabrics are very popular in the West and are also much liked in China, where they have recently been introduced. But they are driving out our linen industry. All the provinces of China raise hemp to a great extent, but the goods made from hemp are suitable only for summer clothing and do not last more than one season. If we want to better the linen industry, we must make a detailed and radical study of its agricultural side — how to cultivate hemp and flax and how to apply fertilizers; and also of its manufacturing side — how to produce fine linen thread. Then the linen industry will develop and manufactured linen goods will be inexpensive. In the past the linen industry has depended solely upon hand labor; no machinery has been used. Hand manufacture not only consumes time and produces poor linen fabrics but also requires expensive capital. If we want to improve the linen industry and manufacture linen fabrics, we must have a broad plan. All along the line, from the fields, where the hemp or flax is grown, to the factories, where the linen fabrics are woven, we must apply the most modern scientific methods. If we can effect such a reform, then we shall get good linens and inexpensive material for clothing.

Silk and hemp as raw material for clothing were first discovered in China. But clothes nowadays are made not only of silk and hemp or flax; most clothes are made of cotton, while wool is being used to an increasing extent. Cotton and wool are now necessary material for everyone's clothing. Cotton is not native to China; the Ceiba tree cotton[1] was introduced from India. After China obtained cotton seeds from India and began to plant them in various sections of the country, and after she learned how to spin and to weave cotton, a cotton industry was built up. Lately, however, foreign cotton cloth of a better quality than the native cloth, and quite inexpensive, has been imported into China. Chinese have preferred the foreign to the native cloth, and so our native industry has been driven to the wall. This means that Chinese have to depend upon foreign countries for the necessary clothing material. Small native industries still in existence use foreign yarn in the weaving. You can see from this how the bottom has been knocked out of our cloth industry by other countries.

After the introduction of cotton seed from India, China began to plant cotton everywhere.

1 Referring to what is commercially known as "Indian cottons."

and now produces a large crop every year. Among
the cotton-growing countries of the world,
the United States comes first, India second, and
China third. Although China produces a great
deal of cotton of good natural quality, yet, because
her industries are undeveloped, she cannot herself
use the raw cotton in the manufacture of good
fabrics and yarn ; she can only ship it for sale
abroad, mostly to Japan and Western countries.
Japan and the Western countries buy Chinese
cotton and mix it with their native cotton in order
to produce good fabrics. More than one half of
the raw material used in the spinning and weaving
mills of Osaka, Japan, comes from China. After
they have used Chinese cotton in the manufacture,
they send the finished cotton fabrics back to China
to be sold at a profit. China has great numbers
of workingmen, and wages here are lower than in
other countries. With native cotton and cheap
labor, why does China still export cotton to Japan
to be manufactured into cloth there ? Why does
China not weave her own cloth ? Japan does not
have a great many workers, and wages are high;
how, then, can she buy Chinese cotton, weave
it into foreign piece goods, send these back to
China, and sell them at a profit ? The reason is
simply the backwardness of Chinese industry.
We cannot manufacture cheap cloth. Japanese
industry is highly developed and can manufacture

inexpensive cloth. Therefore, in order to solve the clothing problem, we must first solve the agricultural and industrial problems. Unless these two other problems are solved, we cannot increase agricultural production or manufacture cheap clothing. As long as China herself cannot manufacture cheap clothing, she will have to depend upon foreign imports of cloth. But foreign countries are not exporting their cloth to China as a service or in payment of tribute! They are exporting their goods in order to make profits, in order to get two dollars of Chinese money for every dollar's worth of goods. China's money goes into foreign profits. This is the foreign economic domination from which we are suffering. And if we ask why we are under this domination, we find again that the reason is our poor industrial development. China sends her cotton abroad, then buys the coarse cotton goods manufactured abroad. The clothes we wear every day are made of imported material for which we have to pay a high price. The high price we pay is the sending of our valuable money and food abroad in settlement. China is like the black sheep in a decadent family who himself could not produce anything or contrive to earn clothing and food, so took the rare and precious heirlooms of the family and exchanged them for something to eat and to wear. Such is the present condition of China under foreign economic domination.

In my lectures upon Nationalism I have explained how China, because of foreign economic domination, is losing from twelve to fifteen hundred million dollars a year. The greater part of this billion and a half dollars' loss is due to our balance of trade ; our imports do not match our exports. According to the customs reports of the last two or three years, the value of our imports is three hundred million taels below the value of our exports. These taels are Haikwan or customs' taels which would amount to five hundred million silver dollars in Shanghai currency, or six hundred million dollars in Canton small currency. This is the value of our balance of trade. What goods do we import ? Our chief imports are foreign yarn and cotton goods. So China's main loss through imports comes from cotton. According to the customs reports, the value of cotton imports is two hundred million Haikwan taels annually, which would amount to three hundred million Shanghai dollars. This is the cost of the foreign cloth which we use. It means that every person in China, if we take the most recent census as the basis of estimate, wears one dollar's worth of foreign cotton cloth every year. Thus the second great necessity of life is supplied for us by foreign material. China has cotton and numerous low-waged workers, yet because we do not know how to stimulate our industries and to recover our rights, we have to wear foreign cloth and send a great deal of our money away to foreigners. As long as we send our money abroad, we cannot remove the difficulty of a foreign economic domination, nor can we solve the immediate problem of clothing.

If we want to recover our lost rights, we must first solve the problem of clothing and reduce the amount of imports of foreign cotton goods. How shall we solve the problem ? During the European War, Western countries had no cotton goods to export to China and China's cotton goods all came from Japan. But Japan at that time was making much more money by supplying the Allies with military materials than by exporting cotton goods to China, so the large factories in Japan were all working to supply the Allies and only the small factories were manufacturing yarn and cotton cloth for export to China. There was a shortage of cotton fabrics in the Chinese market and prices soared. Then some Chinese business men who were willing to speculate promoted the organization of several spinning and textile factories which would spin yarn from native raw cotton and weave cloth from native yarn. Later, scores of such factories were built in Shanghai and all made huge profits. One dollar

of capital investment brought dividends of three
or four dollars ; profits of several hundred per
cent were declared. When the owners of capital
saw these great profits being made, they all
wanted to win fortunes, and more capital than
ever was invested in the spinning and textile
factories. There was a boom in the cotton
industry and many of the newly rich capitalists
were termed cotton kings. But what is the
situation now ? Former millionaires have lost
heavily and become poor; most of the factories
which were built have failed and are closed. If
they had not closed, they would have run into
worse debt and have become bankrupt.

What is the reason for such conditions ? There
were those who thought that foreign countries
could ship their textiles and yarns to China
because they spun and wove by machinery.
Since machine-made textiles and yarns were
better in quality than the handmade and required
less financial capital, therefore foreign countries
could buy Chinese raw cotton, carry it back to
their own factories, send it again to China as yarn
and piece goods, and, in spite of this zigzagging
to and fro, make a good profit. The reason that
they could make these profits, it was argued, was
because they owned machinery. So a number
of Chinese capitalists copied after foreign
countries ; they bought spinning and weaving

machinery and built numerous modern-style spinning and weaving factories. The investments
of capital ranged from millions up to tens of
millions. During the European War the factories
made a great deal of money; but now they
are all losing money, most of them are closed,
and the one-time cotton kings have become
" poor fellows." But our modern spinning and
textile factories employ machinery just like that
in foreign countries. Why, then, do foreign
factories make profits while our factories fail ?
Again, how can foreign countries afford to buy
Chinese raw cotton, pay the freight to have it
transported to their own factories, and then pay
a second freight bill to have it sent back to China
in cotton goods ? Finally, Chinese wages are
much lower than foreign wages, and it seems
reasonable to expect that, with cheap native labor,
native cotton, and machinery like foreign machinery, Chinese factories would make profits
while foreign factories would lose by sending
goods to China. Yet why are the actual results
just the opposite ?

This is the reason : China's cotton industry
is suffering from foreign political domination.
Foreign nations do not oppress China with economic power alone; economic power is a natural
force, what we have called in China *Wang-tao*, or
the royal way. When foreign nations at times

find their economic strength weak and cannot
attain their objectives in other ways, they add
political force. This political force is what we
have called *pa-tao*, or the way of might. In
former days China's handwork competed against
foreign machinery and lost out, but that was
purely an economic problem. The failure after
the European War of Chinese spinning and textile
factories, which were competing against foreign
nations with machinery modeled after theirs, was
not an economic but a political problem. What
methods do foreign nations use in their political
domination over China? After the Manchu government of China and carried on wars with foreign
nations and had been defeated, China was forced
to sign many unequal treaties. Foreign nations
are still using these treaties to bind China, and as
a result China fails at whatever she attempts. If
China stood on an equal political basis with other
nations, she could compete freely with them in
the economic field and be able to hold her own
without failure. But as soon as foreign nations
use political power as a shield for their economic
designs, then China is at a loss how to resist or
to compete successfully with them.

What is the connection between these binding
treaties and the cotton problem? When foreign
countries send cotton yarn into our ports, the
Maritime Customs collects five per cent duty;

when the yarn circulates in the interior of China,
two and a half per cent more of likin is charged.
Altogether, foreign yarn and textiles pay only seven
and a half per cent duty and enjoy an unlimited
market throughout China. But what about the
yarn and piece goods from our own factories?
During the Manchu dynasty, the Chinese people
were simply dreaming; they listened stupidly to
foreign proposals and imposed a five per cent duty
upon cloth manufactured upon Chinese soil, the
same as upon imported cloth. But when Chinese-
manufactured cloth goes into the interior, it does
not like foreign cloth pay only one likin tax; it
has to pay a likin tax at every station. When
native cloth is compelled to pay customs duty
just like foreign cloth and in addition pays more
likin taxes than foreign cloth, its price naturally
rises very high. And when native cloth is too
expensive, it cannot circulate through the provinces, so our own machine-manufactured cloth
still cannot compete with imported cloth. Foreign
nations use the treaties to bind China's customs
and likin taxes; neither the customs nor the
likin stations are free to raise the tariff rate on
foreign goods, but they can increase duties at will
upon Chinese goods. For example, the Canton
Maritime Customs is not under the control of
Chinese but of foreigners: we are not free to increase the tariff on foreign goods, but foreigners

can levy duties freely upon Chinese goods passing through the customs. Moreover, after passing through the customs barriers, Chinese goods still have to pay likin taxes several times, while foreign goods pay duty once and then pass without hindrance through the country. Because the tariff rates on foreign and Chinese goods are not equal, Chinese native cloth goes to the ground.

The equal and independent states of Europe and America all levy tariffs freely upon each other's exports ; none are bound by treaties. Each government can increase its tariff rate at will. Changes in the tariff are determined by economic conditions existing between the home country and foreign countries. If a country has a large quantity of goods to export which would displace native goods, the home government can immediately levy a high tariff to stop the foreign goods from coming in and to protect its own goods. This is called a protective tariff system. For example, if China ships goods to Japan, they are charged with at least thirty per cent duty, while Japanese goods circulate duty free. Japanese goods which cost one hundred yen wholesale and have no duty imposed upon them are sold for one hundred and twenty yen, and make a clear profit of twenty yen; but if Chinese goods worth a hundred yen should be shipped to Japan and sold for one hundred and twenty yen, there would be a loss of ten yen on the capital investment. Japan can thus resist Chinese goods and protect her native goods. Such a method of protecting the development of native industries and of resisting the invasion of foreign goods is a general economic policy of the nations.

If we want to solve our livelihood problem and protect our native industries so that they cannot be attacked by foreign industries, we must first have the political power to protect them. But China to-day in the grip of the treaties has not only lost her sovereign rights and the power to protect her own industries, but is actually giving protection to foreign industries. This comes of the capitalistic expansion, mechanical progress, and economic superiority of foreign countries; but foreign economic power is backed up by political power. So only during the European War, when she did not have to compete with Western yarn and textiles, was China able to make profits in her industries. After the European War, foreign goods again poured into China and competed with ours, and we suffered great financial loss. The most important factor in the clothing problem is cotton. At present we have no solution of the cotton problem in sight. China's cotton industry is still an infant industry. Our machinery is not so adequate and effective as foreign machinery, and the discipline and